Macromedia® FLASH 5

ACTIONSCRIPT™
FOR FUN & GAMES

Gary Rosenzweig

201 West 103rd Street,
Indianapolis, Indiana 46290

Macromedia® Flash 5 ActionScript™ for Fun & Games

Copyright © 2001 by Que

International Standard Book Number: 0-7897-2524-X

Library of Congress Catalog Card Number: 2001087265

Printed in the United States of America

First Printing: April 2001

04   03   02   01   4 3 2

Trademarks

Warning and Disclaimer

EXECUTIVE EDITOR
Beth Millett

DEVELOPMENT EDITOR
Sarah Robbins

MANAGING EDITOR
Thomas F. Hayes

SENIOR EDITOR
Susan Ross Moore

COPY EDITOR
Julie McNamee

INDEXERS
Sheila Schroeder
Rebecca Hornyak

PROOFREADER
Harvey Stanbrough

TECHNICAL EDITOR
Kevin Darbro

TEAM COORDINATOR
Julie Otto

MEDIA DEVELOPER
Michael Hunter

INTERIOR DESIGNER
Trina Wurst

COVER DESIGNER
Anne Jones

PAGE LAYOUT
Gloria Schurick

ILLUSTRATOR
William Follett

Overview

Introduction

Appendixes

Contents

About the Author

Gary Rosenzweig is a game designer, programmer, entrepreneur, and the author of six books on Macromedia Director and Flash. He owns and operates CleverMedia, a Shockwave game development company that runs four game sites on the Internet: http://clevermedia.com, http://gamescene.com, http://gamespark.com, and http://flasharcade.com.

Since founding CleverMedia in 1996, the company has produced more than 150 games. The games on the four sites that make up the "CleverMedia Network" are all free for Web surfers to play. Many of the games have also been licensed to other Web sites.

Rosenzweig started in the multimedia business by obtaining a bachelor's degree in computer science from Drexel University in Philadelphia. His interest in newspapers took him to the University of North Carolina in Chapel Hill where he earned a master's degree in journalism and mass communication.

Rosenzweig wrote his first book in 1995 on Macromedia Director Lingo and distributed it free on the Internet. In 1996, *The Comprehensive Guide to Lingo* was published by Ventana, followed the next year by *The Director 6 Book*. In 1999, *Special Edition Using Director 7* was published by Macmillan Computer Publishing and *Special Edition Using Director 8* followed in 2000. Gary has also spoken at many Macromedia User Conferences and the Game Developers Conference.

Gary reads a lot of classic science fiction books, likes to go to the movies, and enjoys travel. He lives in Denver, Colorado, with his wife, Debby; cat, Lucy; and dog, Natasha.

Dedication

This book is dedicated to my Aunt Barbara and Uncle Rick, who helped foster my love for games.

Acknowledgments

Thanks to my wife, Debby, who enjoys challenging me to board games on our front porch and likes to test out the latest games at CleverMedia.

Thanks to my mom and dad, Jacqueline and Jerry, who always had a closet full of games while I was growing up and never complained that I was playing the Atari too much.

Thanks to my brother, Larry, who played games with me while we were growing up, even though he was several years younger and I always won.

Thanks to my grandmom, Rebecca Jacob, who bought me my first computer. A week later I had written my first game.

Thanks to my aunt and uncle, Barbara and Richard Shifrin, who collected chess sets and taught me how to win at Risk™.

Thanks to William Follett and Jay Shaffer, my friends and co-workers at CleverMedia. When you work with these guys, you realize that the only thing more fun than playing games is making them.

Thanks to my in-laws, Tage and Anne Thomsen, and Andrea Thomsen for their support while writing this book.

Thanks to all of the people at Que who helped put this book together: Beth Millett, Sarah Robbins, Julie McNamee, Kevin Darbro, Mandie Frank, Julie Otto, Brandon Penticuff, and Aaron Price.

Tell Us What You Think!

As the reader of this book, *you* are our most important critic and commentator. We value your opinion and want to know what we're doing right, what we could do better, what areas you'd like to see us publish in, and any other words of wisdom you're willing to pass our way.

As an executive editor for Que, I welcome your comments. You can fax, e-mail, or write me directly to let me know what you did or didn't like about this book—as well as what we can do to make our books stronger.

Please note that I cannot help you with technical problems related to the topic of this book, and that due to the high volume of mail I receive, I might not be able to reply to every message.

When you write, please be sure to include this book's title and author as well as your name and phone or fax number. I will carefully review your comments and share them with the author and editors who worked on the book.

Fax: 317-581-4666

E-mail: feedback@quepublishing.com

Mail: Beth Millett
           Executive Editor
           Que
           201 West 103rd Street
           Indianapolis, IN 46290 USA

Introduction

After writing five books on Macromedia Director, this is my first book on Macromedia Flash. What made me cross over from Director to Flash?

Well, first of all, I haven't "crossed over" at all. I'm merely using both tools to build my creations. My passion for Director's programming language, Lingo, now exists side-by-side with my passion for Flash's ActionScript.

I've watched Flash develop over a short time from a simple vector-animation tool to a complex programming environment. Although Flash 3 could be used to make simple games by exploiting odd features and using tricks, Flash 4 included some of the basics of programming, such as loops and conditional statements.

Flash 5, however, is a huge leap forward. ActionScript is a complex programming language that can be used to create toys, gadgets, games, and applications. ActionScript is so deep that no one book could possibly delve into all of its complexities and possibilities.

This book, therefore, looks at ActionScript by presenting many complete programs. Each program contains a lot of ActionScript code that you can look at, learn from, and alter. Better still, these programs are toys, gadgets, and games

What Is in This Book?

Although Flash is just now coming of age as a programming environment, it has already established itself as an entertainment medium. Flash is used for everything from Web site window dressing to long-playing animated features.

With ActionScript, there is another side to Flash that still deals with entertainment: games. The contents of this book deal primarily with teaching you how to make games with Flash.

I start off by reviewing some Flash basics in Chapter 1, "Flash Elements Used to Make Games and Toys," by focusing on how different elements of Flash can be used to make interactive applications. Chapter 2, "An Introduction to ActionScript," will come in handy for someone who has used Flash a lot, but hasn't done much programming before. It will also help people who have programmed in other languages, but never before in Flash.

Chapter 3, "ActionScript Elements Used to Make Games and Toys," looks at different ActionScript elements and techniques and shows you how they can be used to create games and other things. This chapter gives you the background you need for the rest of the book. In Chapter 4, "The Game-Creation Process," you learn about game planning and programming.

The rest of the book, except for the last chapter, contains many example programs with all the source code. Chapter 5, "ActionScript Design Effects," Chapter 6, "Toys and Gadgets," and Chapter 7, "Construction Toys," describe toys and gadgets that are fun, but not necessarily games. Then, starting with Chapter 8, "Hunt and Click Games," all the way through to Chapter 16, "Arcade Games," the rest are all about games.

Each section in Chapters 5 to 16 starts by describing the game to be built. Then, it describes my approach to building the game. Next, the elements needed to make the game are reviewed. Finally, the code for each game is revealed, with descriptions about what each part of the code does. Each section ends with some comments about how the game can be taken even further.

The book ends with Chapter 17, "Advanced Techniques," in which you learn some special techniques, such as high score boards and preloading screens. Finally, don't miss the comprehensive list of Web resources in Appendix A, "Internet Resources for the Flash Developer."

The bottom line is that this book contains lots of ActionScript code! There are far more lines of code in this book than in any other I've ever seen on Flash. There are about 25 games here, with all the source code printed in the book and available to you on the Web site: `http://www.garyrosenzweig.com/flash5funandgames`.

Who Is This Book For?

This is a hands-on guide to learning ActionScript; it's not a book for dummies or idiots. What this means is that I don't hold the reader's hand through every step of every project in every chapter. If a technique is covered in an earlier chapter, I might not explain it all over again. Instead, I will take that project deeper and explain a new technique so that you can continue to learn new things.

This book requires you to learn and think. If you don't understand something the first time, read over the text again, try the example on the Web site, and play with the technique in Flash before moving on. You'll benefit in the long run with a deeper understanding of how ActionScript works and how to use it in projects beyond the scope of this book.

This book can be used by a variety of people. If this book has caught your eye in a bookstore, an online bookseller, or you are looking at a friend's copy, then chances are you fall into one of these groups.

Animators

As an animator, you already use Flash to create linear animation. Perhaps you know how to make a button or two as well. This book takes you beyond that into the wonders of ActionScripting. You'll learn how to put your animated characters and scenes inside toys and games.

Illustrators

If you are a graphic designer, chances are that you have worked in Flash or another vector-drawing program. By using the tutorials that come with Flash 5, you can learn how to draw in Flash. Then, you can use this book to make your drawings interact with the users in toys and games.

Programmers

Perhaps you are a programmer who has worked in another language such as Java, C++, or Lingo. This book teaches you how to use your programming skills in Flash. You can get a good overview of ActionScript in Chapters 1 to 3, or just dive right into source code starting with Chapter 5.

Flash 3 and Flash 4 Programmers

This book is also good for Flash 3 or Flash 4 programmers looking for a guide to help them take the leap to Flash 5. The difference between programming Flash 5 and earlier versions is quite large. The environment and commands are almost completely different. To really use the power of Flash 5, you'll have to forget about many techniques used in earlier versions and start learning again from scratch.

Web Home Page Owners

Maybe you are not a computer professional, but just someone who has a home page and some spare time to improve your skills. Flash 5 is a fairly inexpensive development program for you to use to improve your site. With this book, you can immediately grab a game that you like, maybe alter the graphics a bit, and post your own game. Don't expect miracles without putting in the time to learn Flash basics and the material in Chapters 1 through 4, but a smart, hands-on learner should be able to get going quickly.

Professional Web Site Developers

If you are a professional Web site developer, you might be expected to have many skills under your belt. You'll need to know HTML, style sheets, JavaScript, Perl, and several programs such as PhotoShop or Fireworks, Dreamweaver, and so on. Flash is also quickly gaining status as one of the tools that every Web site developer should know.

But knowing the basics probably isn't enough. You'll eventually need to use it to create something. Although other books teach you the basics and leave it up to you to figure out how to put the pieces together to create full programs, this book shows you how to create these programs. You can learn from this to create your own programs from scratch, or use one of the games here as a jump-start to quickly create your own version.

Students

Flash is being taught in many colleges and universities today. This trend will continue as Flash continues to gain popularity. This book could be used as a hands-on text for students wanting to learn ActionScript. Some classes might only teach Flash basics, and you can use this book to place you ahead of everyone else. Other classes might be more advanced and use this book as a text for hands-on learning.

What Should You Already Know?

This book is obviously not meant to be a general reference book for Flash 5. Instead, it is a hands-on learning resource for Flash 5 ActionScript. The book already assumes that you are somewhat familiar with Flash's interface and operation.

This does not mean that you need to be an expert graphic artist. I'm not. Many people associate Flash only with graphic talent. This was true when graphics were all that early versions of Flash could do, but now it is a programming environment as well. This book can be used by expert illustrators and programmers alike.

What you should know is how to use the basics of Flash. You should be familiar with all the ideas in the tutorials that come with Flash 5. You should know how to work with the main timeline to add frames and label them. You should know how to create movie clips, buttons, and graphics. They don't have to look great; you just need to know the procedure for creating them in Flash.

On the other hand, some people will be able to use this book even if they have never used Flash before. If you are a patient, hands-on learner, willing to spend the time to immerse yourself into a new subject until you learn it, you can use this book to jump right past beginner Flash techniques and into expert ActionScript programming.

What Can You Do with This Book?

So now that you've determined that you are one of the types of people who can use this book, the next question is, "What can this book do for you?"

Learn ActionScript

There are several ways to use this book—the first is to use it to learn ActionScript. This book goes way beyond a simple beginner's guide, teaching you how to use ActionScript for complex things.

You'll learn about a wide variety of commands, functions, and techniques used in games and other applications. You'll not only learn what these things do, but see them inside real programs so that you can better understand how they work.

Learn How to Create Games in Flash

All the programs in this book can be considered some type of game or something that can be used as part of a game. Even if you already know ActionScript, this book can teach you how to use that knowledge to create games. In Chapter 4, I will go into detail about how games are made. The rest of the book is packed with examples.

Steal Games

Of course, you can buy this book, take the source code, and make your own games. You can take the source code as it is and post the games on your Web site; however, you will probably want to give them your own graphic style first.

Keep in mind, however, that the book and source code are written for those interested in learning about ActionScript. Don't expect to be able to jump right to Chapter 16 and start tinkering with code. Although some people might be able to do this, others will have difficulty without the information in Chapters 1 to 15.

Chapter 4 will go into some detail about how to take the games in this book and customize them to make your own. Then, each section of each chapter after that gives suggestions on what you might do to the games to make them your own.

The Web Site

A book like this would not be very useful if you had to type in every source code listing yourself. The way Flash movies are put together makes this even harder, because so many different elements, such as movie clips, buttons and graphics, need to be placed in just the right spot.

To make the process of understanding the programs easier, you should always refer to the source code files on the Web site: `http://www.garyrosenzweig.com/flash5funandgames/`.

Username: "reader", password: "iownthebook"

While you go through each project, always remember to open the example movie from the Web site to see the real program in action. Then use this source file to make modifications or test out new code.

You'll see a symbol like this to tell you which file to use:

Example file: Example.fla

Although typing in the source code and trying to recreate the examples is probably a good exercise, even the most precise developer will find it hard to recreate complete, complex programs from the pages in a book.

Conventions

There are several conventions in this book to help you understand what you are reading. Any words that you see in *italics* are real commands, functions, or other syntax that are part of ActionScript. You can look up any of these in the Flash 5 documentation. For instance, *gotoAndPlay()*, *stop()*, and *_x*.

On the other hand, if you see something in quotes, such as "myVariable", then it is a user-defined piece of syntax. These are usually variable names or user-defined function names.

While you are looking through the code, you will see two slashes together like this: "//". This is Flash's way of saying that the text after the slashes is a comment. This often happens at the beginning of lines, so that the entire line is a comment. If you typed in the code without any of my comments at all, it would still work in the same way. The comments are just my way of letting you know what is happening in the code. You should adopt the practice of commenting your code as well.

Sometimes, a code line was broken to fit on the printed page. You'll see this symbol, ➥, at the beginning of such a line. Type the two lines as one, ignoring the symbol.

Updates and Communication

While writing producing this book, a lot of care has been taken to make sure no errors or omissions exist. I write as carefully as I can, and several editors look over the text before publication. However, there is only a limited about of time to produce a book like this. If I took all the time I needed to make sure the book was perfect, it would be obsolete by the time it was published.

It is inevitable that the readers will discover minor issues with some of the code. It is also probable that future versions or bug fixes of Flash will produce some changes in ActionScript that will require some changes in the code here. When this happens, I will post updates and corrections on a special subsite located here:

```
http://garyrosenzweig.com/flash5book/
```

This address will contain information about the book for those who have not bought it yet, updates, links to resources, and a way for you to send feedback to me about the book.

Have Fun

I hope you can learn something from this book that helps your career, your company, or your Web site. But most of all, I hope you enjoy it.

Although many people are buying this book for professional or education reasons, remember that this is a book about games. Games are a form of entertainment. I hope you find that making games is even more fun than playing them.

Flash Elements Used to Make Games and Toys

- The Flash Interface
- Creating Buttons
- Creating Text
- Organizing Your Movie
- Finishing Your Movie

Before learning how to make games in Flash, let's look at the basics of Flash from the viewpoint of the ActionScript programmer. Because this is not a beginner's book, it won't try to teach you the basics, as that is a job better left to the tutorials that come with Flash 5. Instead, this book reviews many of the elements in Flash 5 and shows you how they will be useful in building toys, gadgets, and games with ActionScript.

The purpose of the first four chapters of this book is to prepare you for the rest of the chapters that will present specific examples. These first four chapters will help you build your skills so you are ready to take on these examples.

The Flash Interface

To create complex programs with ActionScript in Flash, you should first become an expert at using the Flash interface. The interface is the collection of windows, panels, and menus that make up the application called Flash 5.

The Main Flash Window

The Flash interface is centered around the main window. Its main feature is the Stage, which can be seen in Figure 1.1 with a large tree and a fox holding a basket.

Figure 1.1
Flash's main window is the centerpiece of the Flash interface.

Some features of the main window are more useful than others for the ActionScript programmer. The timeline is at the top of the window. You can see frames going across, with the numbers 1, 5, 10, and 15 marking some of the frames. Down the side of the timeline are layers. There are two layers in this case: "Background" and "Fox".

You might notice that the frames in the timeline seem a lot wider than what you might be used to seeing. This is because the Frame view has been expanded. You can do this by using the Frame view pop-up menu, indicated in Figure 1.1. There are several other options, such as shortening the height of each layer, which you can investigate as well.

The Stage area in the main window can show a lot more than just the Stage. In fact, it will show you whatever element in your movie you want: the Stage, a graphic, a button, or even a movie clip.

The image shown on the Stage portion of the main window can be enlarged and shrunk. The Scale pop-up menu at the lower left corner of the main window is hardly worth noting, although the shortcut keys to control the scale are much more useful. You can use Command+3 on the Mac and Ctrl+3 in Windows to scale an item in the main window to fit the space available. Likewise, Command+1 on the Mac and Ctrl+1 in Windows quickly return the Stage to 100%. Using the Mac Command key or the Windows Ctrl key and the + or - keys will zoom in and zoom out as well. After you master these keys, you'll never need to use the pop-up menu.

The last things to point out in the main window are the Show/Hide and Lock/Unlock dots. These are incredibly useful for allowing you to see layers by themselves or with only a few other layers visible. Locking layers allows you to select items without items in other layers getting in the way of your cursor. Of course, it also prevents you from making changes on the Stage to the elements in that layer.

Panels

Although the Flash main window is your canvas, it actually shows you very little precise information about your movie and its elements. The details are all in the small panel windows that originally appear to the right of the main window, but can be moved anywhere.

These panels can be customized in all sorts of ways. Panel windows house the panels, and can hold several panels at once. For instance, Figure 1.2 shows a panel window that contains the Info, Transform, Stroke, and Fill panels.

Figure 1.2
This panel window contains four panels. The title of the window is "Info" only because it is the name of the currently selected panel.

Panels can be rearranged in panel windows, and new panel windows can be created as well. This is all done by clicking and dragging the tabs at the top of each panel. It takes some practice to get used to moving the panels about, but you can always reset them by choosing Window, Panel Sets, Default Layout.

TIP

Just because you can move panels from panel window to panel window doesn't mean you should. I find the default layout to be the best and I stick to it. This will also help you work on other computers if you need to, because you won't have become used to some nonstandard arrangement.

The Info panel, shown previously in Figure 1.2 is useful for the precise placement of items on the Stage. If you select an item, you can type in values for the position of the item (X and Y) and the width and height of the item (W and H).

The Transform panel is found in the same panel window as the Info window. This panel, shown in Figure 1.3, allows you to scale and rotate an item that you have selected.

Figure 1.3
The Transform panel allows you to scale and rotate items.

Another panel that the ActionScript programmer will use all the time is the Instance panel. This panel shows information about the currently selected item if the item is a graphic, button, or movie clip. In Figure 1.4, this panel has been used to name a movie clip "myMovieClip". You'll need to name all your movie clips so that your code can refer to them.

Figure 1.4

The Instance panel lets you name movie clips.

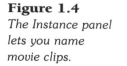

The Frame panel lets you name frames. The funny thing about naming frames is that you can do it in any layer you want. So you can name the first frame by selecting the first frame in the top layer, and then name the second frame by selecting the second frame in another layer. Sound confusing? It is. I recommend always using just one layer to label all the frames.

Perhaps the most important window besides the Stage for both the ActionScript programmer and the graphic artist is the Library palette. Figure 1.5 shows this panel with a bitmap, a button, a graphic, a movie clip, and a sound.

Figure 1.5

The Library palette window shows you what elements are in your movie.

The Library palette shows you a list of all the different types of elements in your movie. What is listed and what is not might seem arbitrary at first. For instance, graphics drawn directly on the screen, even after they have been grouped together, are not shown. Make them into a graphic symbol, and they are shown.

Think of it this way: The library stores reusable items for you. Any symbol, whether it is a movie clip, graphic, or button, can be used in one or more places throughout your movie. However, a series of lines and fills drawn directly on the Stage can only be used in the frame or series of frames where it is located in the timeline.

Just because a symbol is in the library doesn't mean that it will be exported with the movie. For instance, you can import a bitmap or sound and then never place it on the Stage or in the timeline. Or, you could create a movie clip and then never use it. In that case, Flash is smart enough not to include the item in the final compressed Flash file. This will make the file smaller for users to download.

What if the library element never appears on the Stage but your code uses the library element? Flash won't know about this, and it won't be included in the final file. To tell

Flash to include a library element, even if it doesn't seem to need it, you must set the linkage of the item using the Symbol Linkage Properties dialog box, shown in Figure 1.6. This dialog box is opened by selecting the Options pop-up menu that you can see at the upper-right corner of Figure 1.5, shown previously.

Figure 1.6
The Symbol Linkage
Properties dialog
box lets you force
Flash to include
items in the library
for export.

Menu Items

Like panels, the menu item choices in Flash are plentiful. However, only a handful of them are used on a regular basis. For the common menu choices, the ActionScript programmer should know where to find them, as well as their keyboard shortcuts.

File Menu

The File menu contains the standard set of commands that all Macintosh and Windows programmers should be familiar with. Along with Open, Save, and Save As, there is also the Import command, which will let you import bitmap and vector graphics and sounds.

The most important command in the File menu is the simple Save command, with the keyboard shortcut Command+S on the Mac and Ctrl+S in Windows. Use this often. If you work on a file for hours without saving, and then Flash or your computer crashes, you'll be sorry if you didn't remember to hit the Save keyboard shortcut every five minutes or so.

> **TIP**
> Flash 5 can occasionally crash and you will lose all your work since your last save. This is an unfortunate fact. Macromedia is under a lot of pressure to deliver timely new releases of Flash with new features demanded by developers. The downside of the rapid growth of Flash is that it is not the most stable program. However, if you remember to save often, these crashes will be only a minor annoyance.

The File menu is also where you will find the Publish, and Publish Settings command. You'll learn more about those commands at the end of this chapter.

Edit Menu

The Edit menu contains the usual commands: Copy, Cut, and Paste. The Undo command is particularly useful in Flash because you can undo 100 actions. This allows you to back up quite a bit. You can set the number of undo levels by choosing Edit, Preferences.

The Preferences command brings up the dialog box shown in Figure 1.7. In addition to setting the number of undo levels, you can also set a number of preferences arranged in three different tabs. I prefer to stick with the defaults, but it is good to know that the options are there. However, I change the default Expert to Normal in the Actions Panel Mode, so I can type ActionScript directly into the script window.

Figure 1.7
Choose Edit, Preferences to reach the Preferences dialog box.

View Menu

In the View menu, you can change the magnification of the Stage, choose how much graphic detail you want shown on the Stage while working with your movie in Flash, and work with the grid and guides.

The grid is useful to quickly line up elements on the Stage when you are more interested in ActionScripting than in tweaking the positions of various graphics. Figure 1.8 shows the Grid dialog box that you get by choosing View, Grid, Edit Grid. You can set the size of the grid as well as its color, whether it is visible, and whether items snap to it. If you use the Grid dialog box rather than the Show Grid and Snap To Grid commands, you can turn both of those options on and off at the same time more quickly.

Figure 1.8
The Grid dialog box lets you set the color and level of activity of the grid.

The View menu also contains an item called Hide Panels, which can be reached much more easily by using the Tab key. This will quickly hide and show all the panels, including the Tools palette. This is handy when some of the panels are covering the Stage and you need to get to them, but don't want to lose the positions of your panels on the screen.

Insert Menu

The Insert menu has two useful functions for ActionScript programmers. The first is the Convert to Symbol command. This will take whatever elements you have selected on the Stage, and quickly convert them to a graphic, movie clip, or button. The new symbol is placed in the library, but it also remains on the Stage in exactly the same position as the original elements.

When you use this command, you are immediately presented with a simple Symbol Properties dialog box that forces you to choose the type of symbol and name it (see Figure 1.9).

Figure 1.9
The Symbol Properties dialog box appears when you choose Insert, Convert to Symbol. It is the same dialog box that appears if you want to change the symbol properties later on.

The Convert to Symbol command allows you to create all your graphics, movie clips, and buttons directly on the Stage, and then add them to the library afterward. You can also nest this command to create symbols inside symbols. For instance, you could create a button-looking item, use Convert to Symbol to turn it into a button, and then use Convert to Symbol again to place the button inside a movie clip.

The other important functionality of the Insert menu is the series of commands that allows you to insert frames in the main timeline. You can use Insert, Frame to insert a new frame, stretching the current keyframe. Or you could use Insert, Keyframe or Insert, Blank Keyframe to insert a new keyframe into the timeline. Using Insert, Keyframe will make a copy of the current keyframe, whereas Insert, Blank Keyframe will create a new keyframe with no items on the Stage in that layer. You can also use Insert, Remove Frames to delete the frames selected in a layer, or Insert, Clear Keyframe to remove a keyframe without deleting actual frames in the layer.

TIP

The difference between a frame and a keyframe is that a keyframe defines a point in the timeline where all the items in that layer are set to exact positions on the Stage. Until the next keyframe, they won't move. However, animators can choose to tween movement between keyframes so that the items on the Stage move gradually from the position specified in one keyframe to the position specified in another keyframe. Try the animation lesson that comes with Flash 5 to learn more about keyframes.

These commands might seem a bit confusing to someone who has not done any animation work in Flash before. The best way to learn them is to use them. Create a movie and try to insert and remove frames and keyframes. You'll begin to understand the way these commands work.

Modify Menu

The Modify menu gives you a few other ways to quickly access panels. The Instance and Frame commands bring up the Instance and Frame panels. You can use the shortcut keys Command+I and Command+F to do this on the Mac, and Ctrl+I and Ctrl+F to do this in Windows.

The Modify, Movie command opens the dialog box shown in Figure 1.10. The Movie Properties dialog box allows you to change the dimensions of your movie, the speed at which the move runs, and its background color.

Figure 1.10
The Movie Properties dialog allows you to set some of the most important properties of your movie.

Movie Properties	
Frame Rate: 12 fps	OK
Width Height	Cancel
Dimensions: 550 px X 400 px	Save Default
Match: Printer Contents	
Background Color:	
Ruler Units: Pixels ▼	Help

The set of commands under the Transform menu item should be mentioned as well. These commands allow you to scale, rotate, and flip graphics on the Stage. You'll be learning how to do these sorts of things in ActionScript throughout the book, but these commands can be used on items that are not controlled by ActionScript to modify graphics and symbols.

The Group command should also be mentioned. When graphics are drawn on the Stage, they are drawn on top of each other and remove previous lines and fills under them. For instance, if you draw a big blue circle, then draw a small red circle in the middle of it, and then remove the red circle, you'll get a hole in the middle of the blue circle where the red one used to be. However, if you group the blue circle before drawing the red one, then the blue circle will not be partially erased by the red one. Instead, the blue circle exists as it originally was drawn, under the red circle. Grouping is covered in detail in the "Drawing" lesson that comes with Flash 5.

Text Menu

These commands give you quick access to properties in the Text panels. You'll learn more about working with text in the "Creating Text" section later in this chapter.

Control Menu

The Control menu contains a command that you will be using constantly as an ActionScript programmer: Test Movie. This command, which has the keyboard shortcut of Command+Return on the Macintosh and Ctrl+Enter in Windows, will take your current movie, make a final compressed Flash file from it, and then run that movie in a preview window.

When this movie runs, it is running just as it would be in the Flash player, or in the user's Web browser. This is different from the Play command in the Control menu, which will *not* use any complex ActionScript code at all. Play is completely useless for the ActionScript programmer, whereas Test Movie is invaluable.

Window Menu

The Window menu is where you have access to open all your panels as well as assorted other windows. It is important that you master some of the keyboard shortcuts here so you can have quick access to your most useful tools:

To Access ...	Press ...
Instance Panel	Command+I on Mac; Ctrl+I in Windows
Info Panel	Command+Option+I on Mac; Ctrl+Alt+I in Windows
Frame Panel	Command+F on Mac; Ctrl+F in Windows
Text Panel	Command+T on Mac; Ctrl+F in Windows
Library	Command+L on Mac; Ctrl+L in Windows
Actions	Command+Option+A on Mac; Ctrl+Alt+A in Windows

Help Menu

The Help menu gives you access to Flash's ActionScript Dictionary. Even the best ActionScript programmer won't know all the parameters, uses, and idiosyncrasies of all the Flash syntax. This instant help, shown through your Web browser, can quickly get you the information you need on a particular command or function.

Creating Buttons

There are three types of symbols in Flash: graphics, buttons, and move clips. Both buttons and movie clips can have scripts attached to them. Graphics, on the other hand, cannot. Because the ActionScript programmer will need to create and use a lot of buttons and movie clips, let's look at each, starting with buttons, and see how they are made.

The Button Timeline

You can create a button by either choosing Insert, New Symbol, or selecting a set of items on the Stage and choosing Insert, Convert to Symbol. You can also open the Library window and use the pop-up menu at the top and choose New Symbol.

After you have a button, you can double-click it on the Stage to edit it while still seeing it in the context of the Stage. Or you can double-click its name in the Library window to edit it by itself in the Flash main window.

Either way, you will see a special type of timeline at the top of the Flash main window. As shown in Figure 1.11, this special timeline defines the four images needed to define a button: Up, Down, Over, and Hit.

Figure 1.11
The timeline above a button presents a predefined set of four frames.

Although you can add as many layers as you want to a button, only the first four frames shown in Figure 1.11 are used. Here is what they are used for:

- **Up**—The image of the button that is normally shown.
- **Over**—The image of the button shown when the user moves the cursor over it.
- **Down**—The image of the button shown when the user has pressed the button, but not yet released it.
- **Hit**—The shape of the area that is used to determine when the cursor is over the button or when the button is clicked.

Typically, you would focus your button-creation efforts on the Up frame. Then, you would create variations of that frame for the Over and Down frames. The Over frame might highlight the button in some way, whereas the Down frame might show the button depressed or highlighted in some other way. In the next section, you'll see some examples of button design.

TIP

You can create a button that only has an Up frame. If you leave the other three frames blank, without even a keyframe there, then the Up frame is used for all four states of the button.

The Hit frame is special in that it is never seen. It also doesn't care about the color or type of graphics in it. You can choose not to create a Hit frame, as well as an Over or Down frame. In that case, the Up frame will be used for each of these.

Think of the Hit frame as an invisible shape under the button that defines the clickable area of the button. You can therefore create a clickable area that is larger or smaller than the visible graphic of the button.

TIP

You can actually create an invisible button by placing nothing in the Up, Over, or Down frames, but something in the Hit frame. When you do this, the button is shown on the Flash main window as a light blue shape. However, when you run the movie, it will not be visible at all. The button, however, can be clicked and the script in it will be executed.

Button Example
⊕▷⊰Example file: Samplebuttons.fla

Let's take a look at an example of a button. Figure 1.12 shows a labeled button with a rectangular shape. It was drawn directly on the Stage with a rectangle tool, and then converted to a button by choosing Insert, Convert to Symbol. You can see this button in the file Samplebuttons.fla on the Web site in the folder for this chapter.

Figure 1.12
This simple button was created with one rectangle and some text.

This button was created by first selecting the Rectangle tool. If you double-click that tool, you get to set the corner radius for the curved corner of the rectangle. The corner radius for this example button is two. The color for the stroke of the rectangle was set to black and the fill color to blue. After drawing the rectangle, I selected the Text tool, and typed "PRESS ME!". After centering the text, the result is the image you see in Figure 1.12.

When I used Convert to Symbol, I named the button "My Button". This new symbol appears in the library, and remains on the Stage at the location of the original elements.

If you double-click the symbol in the library, you can edit the button by itself on the Stage. The four prelabeled frames appear at the top of the Flash main window. However, only the Up frame contains anything. The Over, Down, and Hit frames are all blank. The Press Me! button will work just fine, but it will use the same image for the Up, Over, and Down states, and the shape of that image for the Hit state.

To continue to develop this button, the first thing to do is create a keyframe for each of the four preset frames. You do this by selecting the frame in the timeline and using the F6 key. Then, go back to the Over and Down states and alter them in some way. In the case of this sample button, I changed the color of the fill on each of these frames. For the Hit frame, there is no need for the text, because only the shape of the image in the Hit frame matters.

Creating Text

There are three different types of text boxes in Flash 5. The first, static text, is little more than text-shaped graphics as far as the ActionScript programmer is concerned. The other two, dynamic text and input text, can be accessed and changed by ActionScript.

Text Properties

There are three types of text panels in Flash 5: the Character panel, the Paragraph panel, and the Text Options panel. The first two panels control the appearance of the text.

The Character panel's primary purpose is for you to be able to change the font, size, style, and color of the font used to display the text (see Figure 1.13).

Figure 1.13

The Character panel allows you to change the font properties of text.

Like the Character panel, the Paragraph panel doesn't contain much that is useful to the ActionScript programmer. You can see it in Figure 1.14. However, because you will be using text boxes to display information to the user, you should be familiar with how to change font properties.

Figure 1.14
The Paragraph panel allows you to set the alignment of text and change the margins, indentations, and line spacing.

The third panel, Text Options, can look completely different depending on how you set its primary property, seen as a pop-up menu at the top. In Figure 1.15, this unnamed pop-up menu is set to Static Text. In this case, there is no ActionScript interaction with the text, and the only options shown are Use Device Fonts and Selectable, two properties that have nothing to do with ActionScript.

Figure 1.15
The Text Options panel shows that the selected text box is Static Text.

You can change the Text Options panel to make the text box dynamic text or input text, the two options you'll look at next.

Dynamic Text

If you change the Text Options pop-up menu to Dynamic Text, you get a very different-looking Text Options panel. Figure 1.16 shows this version of the panel.

Figure 1.16
The Text Options panel now shows the properties for a dynamic text box.

Another pop-up menu will let you choose whether you want the text to be Single Line or Multiline. If you choose Multiline, the Word Wrap option (not shown in Figure 1.16) appears on the right.

The other three options that you can see are HTML, Border/Bg, and Selectable. The HTML option lets you use some basic HTML tags such as <B> in your text. The Border/Bg option places a thin border around the text and makes its box opaque. The Selectable option allows users to highlight portions of the text as they would in a word processor.

The most important option in this panel for the ActionScript programmer is the Variable text box. You can enter a name of a variable here. When the movie runs, the variable and this dynamic text box will be linked. When the value of one changes, so does the other. This enables you to set a variable with code, and have the user see it on the screen.

At the bottom of this panel is a set of buttons and a field for you to specify which character shapes you want Flash to save in the final Flash file so they can be used in the text box. For instance, if the text box will only contain numbers, you might want to specify that rather than making Flash save a complete character set with the movie. On the other hand, you could choose to not save any character shapes at all, which will force the text area to be drawn with the fonts installed on the user's machine.

TIP

Flash is smart enough so that it never includes more than one copy of each character shape with the final compressed Flash movie. So if you specify two dynamic text areas that use all the characters in the font Arial, then this font will be saved only once and shared with both text areas. It's useful, therefore, to choose a primary font for each movie and specify that this font be used with every dynamic text area you create.

Input Text

The third option for a text box is Input Text. Figure 1.17 shows the Text Options panel when this option is chosen. You can see that it is similar to the panel when it is set for Dynamic Text.

Figure 1.17

The Text Options panel for an Input Text text box is shown here.

With input text boxes, there is a third option in addition to Single Line and Multiline. This third option is for a Password text box. As you might guess, this type of text box will not show the characters typed, but dots instead.

There is also the addition of a Max Chars setting that limits the number of characters typed. Setting this to 0 allows unlimited characters to be typed in.

TIP

Flash has a great feature associated with single-line input text. When the user types beyond the size of the text box, the text automatically scrolls to the right. The user can still use the arrow keys to move the cursor back. This allows for large piece of text to be entered without you having to worry about creating large text areas for the user to type.

Importing Media into Flash

Although Flash has a vector drawing tool at its heart, it can also use a variety of other media, such as bitmap graphics and sounds. However, it isn't capable of editing these forms of media, just displaying them.

To create bitmaps and sounds, you'll need to use other programs. For instance, you might use Adobe Photoshop to create bitmaps and Sound Forge to create sounds. Let's take a brief look at these two types of media and how ActionScript can use them.

Bitmaps

To get bitmaps into Flash, choose File, Import. You can import a wide variety of image file formats, including JPEG, GIF, PICT, and BMP formats. Figure 1.18 shows the Import dialog box with a variety of files in the left list. To import any one of them, select the file, use the Add button to move it to the list on the right, and then click the Import button. The media will be added to your library.

Figure 1.18

The Import dialog box allows you to import bitmaps, vector graphics, and sounds.

After you have a bitmap image in the library, there's not much you can do with it using ActionScript. You can certainly place this bitmap inside a movie clip or button and use it that way, however.

You can only do a few things with a bitmap after it is in Flash. Figure 1.19 shows the Bitmap Properties dialog box that you get when you double-click the bitmap in the library.

Figure 1.19

The Bitmap Properties dialog box allows you to set the compression level for the bitmap, turn smoothing on and off, and re-import the bitmap with the Update button.

You can also convert bitmaps to vector graphics by selecting the bitmap on the Stage and then choosing Modify, Trace Bitmap. The dialog box that appears is shown in Figure 1.20.

Figure 1.20
The Trace Bitmap dialog box allows you to convert a bitmap to a vector drawing.

Trace Bitmap

Color Threshold: 100   OK

Minimum Area: 3   pixels   Cancel

Curve Fit: Very Tight

Corner Threshold: Normal   Help

The Trace Bitmap function replaces the bitmap on the Stage with a set of filled vector areas. In many cases, this will result in a drawing that looks worse than the original bitmap, but at least it can be scaled like vector graphics can.

TIP

Many graphic artists convert bitmaps to vector graphics at some point during production. For instance, the artist might draw something on paper, scan it in, and then trace the resulting bitmap to create a vector graphic. However, many of these artists use another program, such as Abode Streamline, to do the conversion, not Flash. Then, the graphic is imported into Flash. The graphic artist also does a lot of work on the vector graphic afterward to get it to look the way they originally intended.

Sounds

Importing sounds into Flash is done the same way that you import bitmaps. In fact, Figure 1.18 (shown previously) shows some sounds listed, waiting to be imported. Flash can import standard sound formats such as AIFF, MP3, Sun AU, and Wave.

After a sound is in Flash, you can double-click its entry in the library to get the Sound Properties dialog box shown in Figure 1.21.

Figure 1.21
The Sound Properties dialog box allows you to set the compression rate used when the sound is included in the final Flash movie.

Sound Properties

My Sound   OK

..:Sounds:beep.aif   Cancel

    Update

Monday, September 11, 2000 12:44 AM

22 kHz Mono 16 Bit 0.1 s 4.4 kB   Import...

    Test

    Stop

Export Settings   Help

Compression: MP3

Preprocessing: ☒ Convert Stereo to Mono

Bit Rate: 16 kbps

Quality: Fast

16 kbps Mono 0.2 kB, 4.5% of original

> **TIP**
>
> The sound compression settings in the Sound Properties dialog box are important if you value the quality of the sound in your final movie. For instance, using MP3 compression at 16KBps (kilobytes per second) will yield a sound of moderate quality good for special effects and such. However, if you are using some nice music, you might want to go with 32KBps or even 64KBps. Experiment with different settings to find one that fits the sound, while keeping it as low as possible to save file space. You'll also be able to set a default setting for all the sounds in the movie when you publish.

The typical use of sound elements is to drag them to the timeline and place them in a keyframe. This will mean that the sound will be triggered when this keyframe is reached. You can dictate how the sound will play by selecting the keyframe with the sound attached, and then opening the Sound panel.

Shown in Figure 1.22, the Sound panel lets you set the way the sound is triggered, decide whether it loops or not, and even apply an effect such as a fade. However, this is not how you will be using sound in this book, so I won't go into detail about how to control this type of sound usage.

Figure 1.22

The Sound Panel allows you to control a sound that appears in the timeline.

Instead, you will use sound triggered by ActionScript commands. You can control when and how any sound plays with ActionScript.

However, if the sound is not used in the timeline at all, Flash will not include it when the final Flash file is made. Then, when your ActionScript attempts to use the sound, it won't be there.

To make sure a sound is included with the final movie, you'll need to set its linkage properties (refer to Figure 1.6). The name you give a sound in the Linkage Properties dialog box will be the name you use to refer to that sound in ActionScript.

Organizing Your Movie

Organization is even more important to ActionScript programmers than it is to Flash animators. Symbols in the library should be thoughtfully named. They should be organized in folders if needed. The layers in the timeline should make it easy for the programmer to access different elements on the Stage.

The Library

Organizing the library can be done by creating folders inside the library palette. Folders work just like folders or directories in your operating system. You can create folders and store various library elements in them. For instance, if you have 52 graphics to represent the 52 cards of a deck, you could place them all in a folder called "cards". This will mean that all 52 cards will be shown as one item in the library. That item can then be expanded to show the 52 graphics inside it.

To create a folder, open the Library palette and choose New Folder from the pop-up menu at the upper right. When something is in a folder, it can be used just as easily as if it were not. You don't have to refer to the folder's name in either the animation tools or your ActionScript code.

The Library palette also includes several other tools that help you organize. For instance, you can sort by any of the criteria listed at the top as column headings. Figure 1.23 shows a full-expanded Library palette. If you want to sort by the Date Modified column, just click the column title. The little button with a pyramid-shaped icon on it just to the right of the column headings allows you to switch from ascending to descending order and back again.

Figure 1.23
This Library palette includes a folder that has been expanded to show its contents.

With this view, you can see what items are used and how often. Of course, this does not take into account usage by your ActionScript code.

Frames

Labeling keyframes in your movie should not be an option for ActionScript programmers. In your code, you will be able to tell the movie to jump from one frame to another in a nonlinear fashion. To do that, you'll need to name the frames. You can do this by using the Frame panel, seen in Figure 1.24.

Figure 1.24
The Frames panel lets you name a keyframe.

Although you can reference frames by their number in ActionScript, you shouldn't. Why? Well, suppose you write code that jumps from frame 7 to frame 13 to frame 8. Then, you decide to insert a frame before frame 1. Now, what used to be frames 7, 13, and 8 are frames 8, 14, and 9. You'll have to change your code in all three places.

If you name frames, you can refer to them by name in your code. No matter how many frames you insert or delete, you can always rely on a keyframe to keep the same name.

Layers

Although layers don't actually come into play for most ActionScripting, they are valuable organizational tools. You can and should have layers for labels, timeline-based ActionScript code, and graphics. Figure 1.25 shows a layer setup that organizes things well.

Figure 1.25
This timeline setup includes a layer just for labels, one for ActionScript, and then others for graphics.

You can also double-click the little icon to the left of each layer name to bring up the Layer properties dialog box shown in Figure 1.26. You can choose to show the layer as an outline, or use it as a guide layer. This means that the layer appears to you in Flash, but is not used in the final movie.

Figure 1.26
The Layer Properties dialog box lets you define what type a layer is.

Remember to not only use layer organization in your main timeline, but also in movie clips, graphics, and buttons. For instance, the border and text shown in Figure 1.12 could have been placed in a keyframe of the second layer that ran from frames one to three of Figure 1.11. Then, the fill, which is different for each frame, could have been included in each of the four keyframes in the first layer. This way, if you want to change the border you only have to do that in the one and only keyframe of layer 2, rather than each and every frame of layer 1.

Scenes

A higher level of organization in Flash involves scenes. Each Flash movie is made up of one or more scenes. Many of the examples in this book only use one scene and you could easily forget that scenes even exist.

However, scenes can also be great organizational tools. Think of them as combining movies, one after the other, in a single movie. Each scene has its own main timeline. Figure 1.27 shows the Scene panel with three scenes. They are played in the exact order shown, although ActionScript can override this and play the scenes in any order, or even jump from one frame in one scene to one frame in another scene.

Figure 1.27
The Scene panel
allows you to create
and rearrange scenes
in your movie.

Off-Stage Area

One part of Flash that is very useful for ActionScript programmers, but is rarely mentioned in texts like this, is the off-Stage area. If you look back at Figure 1.1, you can see that the Stage is in the middle of the window, but there is a gray area outside of the Stage rectangle as well. You can place elements in this off-Stage area. When the movie is played back in the user's browser or in the Flash player, they will not see this area.

CAUTION

Actually, there is a way that the user can see the off-Stage area. If the Flash movie is scaled in the Flash player, the Flash preview window, or in a browser, the Flash movie usually tries to hold its proportions. This means that some area at the top or bottom might show. However, if the movie is placed in a Web page with the proper tags, this will not happen.

One example of how you will use the off-Stage area in this book is to place a small movie clip that will have some ActionScript attached to it. Although ActionScript in the main timeline will execute once, you can make ActionScript attached to movie clips execute once every frame. So, by placing a small movie clip off the Stage where it will not be visible, you can write ActionScript that will perform repetitive actions such as animation and user-controlled movement.

Finishing Your Movie

When you are done with your movie, whether it is a simple animation or a complex application, you'll need to export it as a compressed Flash file, also known as a .swf file. You can do this with the File, Publish command.

However, before you do that, you'll need to check your movie over for a few things, and then use File, Publish Settings to make sure the .swf is exactly how you want it.

Final Checklist

Before publishing your movie, here's a handy checklist of things to look over to avoid easy-to-solve problems:

- **Movie Clip Instance Names**—Make sure all the movie clips you placed on the Stage are named what your code expects them to be named.
- **Linkage Properties**—If you have movie clips that are not used on the Stage, but your code needs them, make sure to set the linkage properties of these movie clips in the library so that export with the movie. Also be sure to set the linkage name so it matches your code. The same is true for sounds in the library.
- **Dynamic Text Names**—If you are using any dynamic text on the Stage that links to an ActionScript variable, be sure its name is the same as what your code expects.
- **Fonts**—In any dynamic text or input text, make sure you have set the text box to include any characters you might need from the font. Otherwise, the movie might look very different on a machine that does not have the same fonts as yours.
- **Stops**—The basic ActionScript command *stop()* needs to be placed on any frame that has some interaction with the user. Without *stop()*, the frame is no more than a single frame in an animation. This is also true for movie clips in your movie. If they are controlled by ActionScript, they need a *stop()* on the first frame. You'll learn more about *stop()* in Chapter 2, "An Introduction to ActionScript."

Publishing

Before using the File, Publish command, you'll want to check the Publish Settings dialog box by choosing File, Publish Settings (see Figure 1.28). This large dialog box has three panels. The Formats panel allows you to select the different formats that can be exported. However, formats such as GIF, JPEG, and PNG are just still images. Formats such as QuickTime Movie and RealPlayer will not support Flash 5 ActionScript. This leaves the .swf format, as well as Projectors, as your only real options. You can also choose to export an HTML page that can be used with the .swf file.

Figure 1.28
The Publish Settings dialog box allows you to export Flash movies as one of several formats.

The Flash panel allows you to control several settings of the final .swf file (see Figure 1.29). The Generate Size Report option places a rundown of the contents of the .swf file in the Flash Output window for you to see. This allows you to track down file-size hogs, such as large sounds that can be trimmed.

Figure 1.29
The Flash panel of the Publish Settings dialog box allows you to change some important settings for making a .swf file.

The Omit Trace Actions option allows you to turn off the messages sent by ActionScript *trace* commands. These aren't used in .swf files shown in browsers anyway, however.

The Protect from Import option should stop anyone, including yourself, from importing the .swf file back into Flash.

The Debugging Permitted option allows you to debug your movie when it is running. There will be more about debugging in Chapter 4, "The Game-Creation Process."

The next set of settings allows you to set the default compression for images and sounds. You can even check the Override Sound Settings option to force all sounds to be compressed by these defaults, even if one or more is set to some custom compression level.

The Version setting at the bottom of the window seems like it could work miracles. It claims that you can save the movie as a Flash 1, 2, 3, 4, or 5 movie. So you can make movies with complex ActionScripting that will work with Flash 3 players? Wrong. If you have any ActionScripting at all, chances are that the movie needs to be exported as Flash 5. That's your only option.

The last panel of the Publish Settings dialog box, seen in Figure 1.30, allows you to determine what the HTML file exported with the .swf file will be like.

Figure 1.30

The HTML panel of the Publish Settings dialog box allows you to control the HTML file that gets exported with the .swf file.

All the properties shown in Figure 1.30 seem to control the .swf file, right? Nope. They actually only set the tags of the HTML page. The next section looks at these tags.

Putting Flash on the Web

To put your movies on the Web, they should be embedded into an HTML page. Sure, you can place them on the Web as just raw .swf files, but then they will attempt to scale to the size of the browser window, which is probably not what you want.

Instead, by using two tags, you can place the .swf into a Web page for both Internet Explorer and Netscape browsers. Better yet, you can specify a lot of custom settings for how the movie appears. Most of this can be done automatically by Flash when you publish. You can use the Publish Settings dialog box shown in Figure 1.30 to set most of the options. However, it might be useful for you to know what the tags are really like. If you are like me, you would rather build your own HTML than use a template generated by a program like Flash.

The following object tag embeds a 550×400 Flash movie named Sample.swf. The movie starts by playing immediately, the quality level is high, it uses device fonts, and the background color of the movie is white.

```
<OBJECT classid="clsid:D27CDB6E-AE6D-11cf-96B8-444553540000"
codebase="http://download.macromedia.com/pub/shockwave/
cabs/flash/swflash.cab#version=5,0,0,0"
WIDTH=550 HEIGHT=400>
<PARAM NAME=movie VALUE="sample.swf">
<PARAM NAME=play VALUE=true>
<PARAM NAME=quality VALUE=high>
<PARAM NAME=devicefont VALUE=true>
<PARAM NAME=bgcolor VALUE=#FFFFFF>
</OBJECT>
```

The long string of characters starting with "classid" is the designation for Flash that Internet Explorer understands. The part that starts with "codebase" tells Internet Explorer to go and get Flash if the user doesn't already have it.

Netscape doesn't understand the OBJECT tag. This is because OBJECT tags are used to designate ActiveX controls. ActiveX is a technology used to embed media into Internet Explorer. Flash is an ActiveX control as far as Internet Explorer is concerned. For Netscape, you'll need an EMBED tag which will tell the browser to use the Flash plug-in to run the Flash movie.

```
<EMBED src="sample.swf"
play=false
quality=high
devicefont=true
bgcolor=#FFFFFF
WIDTH=550 HEIGHT=400
TYPE="application/x-shockwave-flash" PLUGINSPAGE="http://www.macromedia.com/shockwave/
download/index.cgi?P1_Prod_Version=ShockwaveFlash">
</EMBED>
```

You can see that these tags are pretty similar. The TYPE parameter tells Netscape that this is a Flash movie, and the PLUGINSPAGE tells Netscape where to send the user if it turns out they don't have Flash.

CAUTION

Although the OBJECT tag includes the number of the version of Flash needed to play your movie, the EMBED tag does not. That means that if someone has Flash 4 in Netscape, and he plays your Flash 5 movie, the browser will attempt to do it, even though his version of Flash can't understand your Flash 5 ActionScript commands. The result is that your movie will appear not to work properly. You can include a message, such as "Requires Flash 5", on the Web page to warn users. Also check with the sites listed in Appendix A, "Internet Resources for the Flash Developer," for the latest JavaScript techniques for determining which version of Flash the user has.

So you need to include both the OBJECT and EMBED tags, right? Yes. But it's more complex than that. You see, Internet Explorer can also use the EMBED tag to show media with plug-ins. So it is possible that someone with Internet Explorer could have both the Flash ActiveX control and the Flash plug-in. In that case, they would see your Flash movie twice on the same page.

There is an easy way to prevent this, fortunately. If you place the EMBED tag inside the OBJECT tag, Internet Explorer will ignore it. So the final version looks like this:

```
<OBJECT classid="clsid:D27CDB6E-AE6D-11cf-96B8-444553540000"
codebase="http://download.macromedia.com/pub/shockwave/cabs/
flash/swflash.cab#version=5,0,0,0"
WIDTH=550 HEIGHT=400>
<PARAM NAME=movie VALUE="sample.swf">
<PARAM NAME=play VALUE=true>
<PARAM NAME=quality VALUE=high>
<PARAM NAME=devicefont VALUE=true>
<PARAM NAME=bgcolor VALUE=#FFFFFF>
<EMBED src="sample.swf"
play=false
quality=high
devicefont=true
bgcolor=#FFFFFF
WIDTH=550 HEIGHT=400
TYPE="application/x-shockwave-flash" PLUGINSPAGE="http://www.macromedia.com/shockwave/
download/index.cgi?P1_Prod_Version=ShockwaveFlash">
</EMBED>
</OBJECT>
```

This code works well, but it poses one problem: Almost every parameter is repeated twice, once for the OBJECT tag and once for the EMBED tag. If you make a change, you need to remember to make it in both places.

Now that you know how the basics of Flash relate to ActionScript programming, you're ready to learn how to be an ActionScript programmer. The next chapter gets you started using ActionScript.

An Introduction to ActionScript

Programming in ActionScript can be done by people experienced in other programming languages, or by people who have no programming experience but know how to use Flash to create graphics and animation. You can learn ActionScript by approaching it from either direction.

This chapter starts by defining the basic elements of ActionScript, and then moves on to some hands-on examples. You'll learn how to program in ActionScript in 24 easy lessons. This chapter contains the first 14 lessons, which show you the most basic ActionScript commands. Chapter 3, "ActionScript Elements Used to Make Games and Toys," continues with the final 10 lessons.

Lesson 1: What Is ActionScript and Where Does It Go?

ActionScript is the programming language inside Flash 5. It allows you to provide more than just linear animation instructions like you can do with the main timeline. With ActionScript, your Flash movie can react to events, such as user choices or random chances. ActionScript can take control of what the user sees, so that instead of plain animation, you can show nonlinear presentations, interactive applications, or games.

> **NOTE**
>
> ActionScript in Flash 5 is derived from two sources. The first is the set of macro commands that existed in all the previous versions of Flash, particularly Flash 4, where a similar, but very basic programming language was used. The other influence on Flash 5 ActionScript is JavaScript. This is the language used to write short programs that appear in HTML pages for Internet Explorer and Netscape browsers. It has become popular with Web developers who are the primary audience for Flash 5. To make it easier for Web developers to learn ActionScript, many of the new commands, functions, and other syntax have been made to look like JavaScript.

ActionScript programs are lists of instructions for Flash to follow. They can be put in several places in your Flash movie. Knowing where to put a script is half the battle. Let's look at some of the places where scripts go and when Flash will use these scripts.

Frame Scripts

You can place scripts on keyframes in the main timeline of your movie. To do this, just double-click the keyframe in the main timeline. The Actions window appears, with Frame Actions in the title bar at the top of the window. (You'll be examining the Actions window in the next section.) You can also bring up the Actions window by selecting the keyframe and using the keyboard shortcut (Command+Option+A on the Mac, and Ctrl+Alt+A in Windows).

Frame scripts can contain two different script elements. The first is a list of commands that will be executed as soon as the keyframe is reached while the movie is playing. These commands will be followed, one after the other, until the script is done.

The second type of script element that can be included in frame scripts are called functions. Functions are reusable pieces of code that can be used by commands in the frame script as well as by other scripts throughout the movie.

Button Scripts

You can also attach scripts to buttons that appear on the Stage. First, you have to create the button as a library element. Then, drag it to the Stage if there is not already a copy of the button there. With the button selected on the Stage, choose Window, Actions, or use the keyboard shortcut (Command+Option+A on the Mac, and Ctrl+Alt+A in Windows) to bring up the Actions window. If the Actions window is already on the screen, just selecting the button will focus the Actions window on the script attached to the button.

The Actions window is now titled Object Actions. Any script you enter here is used by the button. However, you can't just enter a series of commands. Instead, you must tell the button how it should react to different button events, such as being pressed, having the cursor roll over it, and so on. The code that handles these events are called handlers. Button scripts are a series of one or more handlers.

Movie Clip Scripts

You can also attach a script to a movie clip. To do this, first create a movie clip so that it appears in the library. Then, place an instance of the movie clip on the Stage. Now you can open the Actions window, with the movie clip instance selected, just like you can with buttons.

The Actions window is titled Object Actions, just as it was with the button script. Like buttons, you can't enter a series of commands like you would with frame scripts. Instead, you must place your commands inside handlers that react to events that occur to movie clips. However, movie clips react to a whole different set of events than buttons do.

In the next few sections, you'll be looking at examples of frame scripts, button scripts, and movie clip scripts.

Lesson 2: Using the Actions Window

To program in ActionScript, you'll need to use the ActionScript window. This window has two modes: normal and expert. In normal mode, the window acts like the Flash 4 Actions window. You can select commands, functions, operators, and other syntax from the list to the left, and the item is automatically placed in the ActionScript program to the right.

Figure 2.1 shows the Actions window in normal mode. A one-line program containing the command *gotoAndPlay* was placed there by finding the command in the list on the left and double-clicking it to place it in the program to the right. When this command is selected in the program to the right, information about it appears at the bottom of the Actions window. You can change this information by using the pop-up menus and text fields there. For instance, Frame Label has been selected as the type and My Frame Name as the frame. The command in the window will change to reflect these choices.

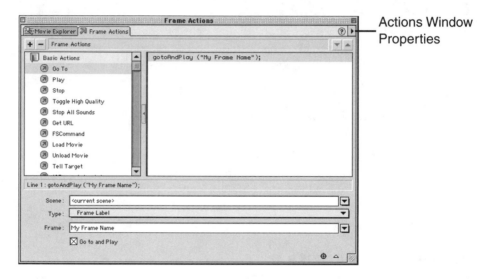

Actions Window
Properties

Figure 2.1   *The Actions window in normal mode allows you to select commands and customize them.*

All the programming I do uses the Actions window expert mode. This name is a little misleading, as it implies that the Actions window will be harder to use. In fact, the opposite is true. Expert mode makes the Actions window little more than a simple text editor where you actually type in the code instead of selecting it from a list. It becomes easier to use, but also easier to create code that won't work.

To switch between normal and expert mode, you can use the Actions window properties pop-up menu that is brought up by the little arrow button at the upper-left corner of the Actions window (refer to Figure 2.1). You can also use the keyboard shortcuts, Command+N and Command+E on the Mac and Ctrl+N and Ctrl+E in Windows. However, make sure that the Actions window is in focus when you use these shortcuts, because when it isn't, these commands perform other tasks entirely.

Figure 2.2 shows the Actions window in expert mode. The editable properties of the *gotoAndPlay* command are no longer at the bottom of the screen. The list of commands on the left is still there, however, and you can double-click them to add commands to the program on the right. However, you can also just type the commands straight in, something you cannot do when the Actions window is in normal mode.

Figure 2.2
*The Actions win-
dow in expert mode
allows you to type
directly into the
program listing.*

Deciding which mode of the ActionScript window to use is not hard. To write anything but basic programs, you'll need to use the expert mode. The normal mode does not let you easily enter the types of syntax needed for real programming.

On the other hand, the normal mode of the Actions window can be a great learning tool. Instead of having to guess at the syntax of each command, or use the documentation to look each one up, the normal mode spells it out for you. This can help you quickly learn your way around commands such as *gotoAndPlay*.

TIP

You can also switch between expert and normal mode easily with the keyboard short-cuts mentioned previously. This will allow you to type in your code in expert mode, but also will give you quick access to the properties of commands that the normal mode gives you. However, you cannot switch from expert mode to normal mode if your code has even a single error in it. Because fixing an error might be the very reason you want to switch to normal mode temporarily, this is unfortunate.

Lesson 3: Your First ActionScript Program

The first ActionScript command you should learn is called *trace*. *trace* writes some information to the Flash Output window. The Output window is a little text window that can appear when you preview your movie in Flash. It is typically used to send debugging messages while you develop your program.

Although this example will not be anything you can use in a real Flash movie, it is the quickest way to show that you can write ActionScript that can actually make Flash do something.

To create this example, open a new Flash movie. The timeline will automatically contain a single layer with a single keyframe in it. Double-click this keyframe to bring up the Actions window. Then, switch the Actions window to expert mode by using the pop-up menu at the upper-right corner of the window.

Now, you can click in the empty program listing area on the right side of the Actions window. Type this single line of code:

```
trace("Hello World!");
```

> **NOTE**
> A semicolon is used at the end of each complete Flash command that appears on a single line, as is the case at the end of the *trace* example.

The *trace* command is a built-in Flash function. Functions use parentheses to enclose parameters. Parameters are bits of information that are given to the function so it can complete its task. The *trace* command requires exactly one parameter: the text to be placed in the Output window. Some functions require more than one parameter, whereas others require none.

Your screen should now look something like Figure 2.3. Here you can see the single layer and keyframe in the timeline. The Actions window is titled Frame Actions to indicate that it is holding ActionScript that pertains to the currently selected keyframe. The *trace* command is the only thing in the program listing.

Figure 2.3
The "Hello World" program is attached to the first and only keyframe.

Try to create this movie yourself from scratch. However, if you need it, the movie is also included as Helloworld.fla on the Web site in the folder for this chapter.

To run this program, choose Control, Test Movie. Flash might take a second to create the .swf file, and then the file opens in the preview window. This window remains blank because there are no graphics in the movie. However, the Output window also opens, showing the words "Hello World!" (see Figure 2.4).

Figure 2.4
The Flash Output window contains the results of the simple trace program.

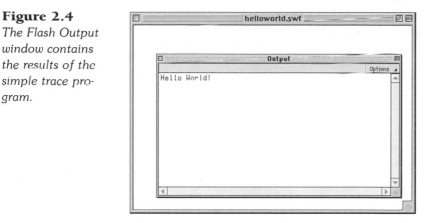

This is a significant step in becoming an ActionScript programmer. You have given Flash a command. In return, Flash has indicated that it understands you and will obey!

NOTE

The "Hello World" program is a tradition that dates back to the earliest programming languages. It is seen as the most basic program there is, and is thus usually the first lesson taught, whether the language is assembly language on an ancient hulking mainframe computer, BASIC, Pascal, C, Java, or ActionScript. You have just followed in the footsteps of millions of computer programmers when they started to learn their trade.

Lesson 4: Controlling Flash Playback

In "Lesson 2: Using the Actions Window," you caught a glimpse of the ActionScript command *gotoAndPlay*. This command tells Flash to forget about playing the next frame in the timeline, but instead jump to a completely different frame. By using *gotoAndPlay*, you can control the playback of a Flash movie.

Create a new Flash movie. This time, you'll add several keyframes to it. Create a series of four keyframes and name them "part1" to "part4". These keyframes represent four parts of an animation. In addition to naming these four keyframes, also place a piece of static text on each so that the user can tell which part they are seeing on the screen.

In the example movie Gotoandplay.fla, static text "PART 1" to "PART 4" has been placed on each of the keyframes. So the text "PART 1" appears on the keyframe "part1", the text "PART 2" appears on the keyframe "part2", and so on.

The keyframes have also been separated by several frames so that the labels can be read in the main timeline. Figure 2.5 shows the main timeline, where you can see the four labels. The second keyframe is selected and you can see the text "PART 2" on the Stage.

Figure 2.5

This movie contains four keyframes and script placed in the second key-frame. The second keyframe is selected and the Actions window shows the script in it.

Open the Actions window with the second keyframe selected. Now, type this command in the Actions window:

```
gotoAndPlay("part4");
```

Notice that after you add some ActionScript to a keyframe, it contains a little "a" in the timeline.

This is the only ActionScript in the movie. When you test this movie, here's what should happen: The Move starts off at the keyframe "part1" and shows the text "PART 1" on the screen. It then advances along the timeline until it hits the keyframe "part2". This is where the ActionScript is located. Flash then follows the command and jumps to keyframe "part4". It will do this before it even has a chance to display the "TEXT 2" text on the "part2" keyframe. The movie is now at "part4", and the text "PART 4" is displayed. The movie then continues to move down the timeline until it hits the end. At this point, the movie loops back to the first frame and displays "PART 1" again. The whole process repeats endlessly.

You have used ActionScript to make Flash do something other than play a straight animation. The movie could have proceeded from "part1" to "part2" to "part3" to "part4", but because of your script, it skipped "part2" and "part3" altogether. You can learned how to control the movement of a Flash movie with ActionScript.

Example file: Nonlinear.fla

Let's look at another example. Using the same basic movie setup, you'll create little keyframes at the end of each part of the movie. You'll be placing scripts that run after a part is over, rather than when one begins.

Figure 2.6 shows this setup. There are four labeled keyframes just like in the previous example, but also four other keyframes that come after each part of the movie. It is these unlabeled keyframes that contain the code.

Figure 2.6

This movie has four parts. Each part starts with a labeled keyframe and ends with an unlabeled keyframe that contains a small script.

The keyframe that comes after "part1" contains this code:

```
gotoAndPlay("part3");
```

The keyframe that comes after "part2" contains this code:

```
gotoAndPlay("part4");
```

The keyframe that comes after "part3" contains this code:

```
gotoAndPlay("part2");
```

The keyframe that comes after "part4" contains this code:

```
gotoAndPlay("part1");
```

When you run this movie, found on the Web site as Nonlinear.fla, the movie starts by showing "PART 1". Then, instead of continuing to the frame "part2", it is forced by the ActionScript to jump to "part3". So, the movie goes from "PART 1" to "PART 3". Then, at the end of "part3", the movie is told to jump back to "part2". At the end of "part2", the movie is told to jump ahead to "part4". The sequence, therefore, is "PART 1", "PART 3", "PART 2", and then "PART 4". It then repeats.

By using ActionScript, you've completely circumvented the normal animation sequence of the movie and replaced it with your own.

Although these two examples create predictable results, you can use the *gotoAndPlay* command in other ways, in conjunction with buttons and such, to give the user control over which part of the Flash movie gets played next.

Lesson 5: Creating Buttons to Give the User Control

⬤▷ Example file: Stop.fla

In the previous example, ActionScript controlled the playback of the movie without any user interaction. Let's add some buttons that will allow the user to tell the Flash movie what part to play next.

The first step in giving the user some control over the playback of the movie is to take away some of the control from Flash. Flash wants to animate. It starts with frame 1 and pushes forward to the next frame and the next. You can tell Flash to cut that out by using the *stop()* command. This halts the animation and leaves the Flash movie sitting on a single frame.

Figure 2.7 shows the example movie Stop.fla. There are four keyframes, each with a label in the timeline and some text on the Stage. The first keyframe includes a short script with the *stop()* command. When you run this movie, the movie stops at frame 1, and never advances past it.

Figure 2.7

This movie contains a sequence of keyframes, but the stop() command in the first frame halts the movie there.

Now that you have taken control of the movie away from Flash, you can give the user some control. Create a simple button symbol and place it on the Stage. It doesn't have to be anything fancy. In the example movie, a small circle is used as a button.

Next, I created a new layer with only one keyframe, so that the same items appear throughout the movie. I placed four different instances of the same button from the library in this layer. You can see the result in Figure 2.8.

You'll use the same *stop()* command placed on the first keyframe of this movie. This halts the movie as soon at it begins. The four buttons are visible at the bottom of the screen. You'll attach a script to each one of these buttons.

The first script can be seen in Figure 2.8. The first button is selected so the Actions window displays its script. Here it is again:

```
on (press) {
    gotoAndStop("part1");
}
```

This is what a typical button script looks like. It uses handlers to define what should be done during different button actions. In this case, the action is *press*. The syntax *on* is used to define the beginning of a handler like this. Then, the bracket symbols { and } are used to contain the commands that should be executed when the event occurs.

Figure 2.8

This movie has two layers. The first is divided into four parts with four keyframes, although the second contains a single keyframe that stretches across the whole movie.

In this case, a *gotoAndStop* command is issued. This is the sibling of *gotoAndPlay*. The difference is that the first command jumps to a new frame and halts, whereas the second command jumps to a new frame and immediately begins animating through to the next frame.

In addition to this script attached to this button, also attach three similar scripts to the other three buttons. The only difference should be that the other buttons should jump to frames "part2", "part3", and "part4".

Example file: Navigation.fla

When you run this movie, it begins with the movie stopped at the first frame. From there, the user can press any one of the four buttons to jump to any one of the other four frames. Try the example movie, Navigation.fla, to see how it works.

This is your first usable Flash movie. Instead of the simple "PART 1" to "PART 4" text shown on each keyframe, you can place a presentation similar to one seen in PowerPoint or other presentation software. This creates a whole other use for Flash beyond simple animation.

Lesson 6: Animating with ActionScript
⊕▷Example file: Animate.fla

Next, you need to learn how to move items around the Stage with ActionScript. To do this, you'll place a script on a movie clip in the same way you placed a script on a button in the previous lesson.

Start by creating a new movie. Then, place a movie clip on the Stage. A movie clip that contains the image of a fox was placed on the Stage for the Animate.fla example movie. You can do something simpler if you want, such as make a simple circle.

After you have the movie clip in the library, you can place an instance of it on the Stage. At this point, you should have a movie with a single layer and single frame in it, with this movie clip on the Stage. You can see this in Figure 2.9.

Figure 2.9

This movie contains just one movie clip with a script attached to it.

The script attached to the movie clip uses a handler just like the button script in the previous lesson. Instead of using an *on* to define the handler, you need to use *onClipEvent* to define events that affect movie clips. In this case the event is *enterFrame*. This is an event that happens automatically, several times a second. If the movie is set to run at 12 fps, then the *enterFrame* event should be sent to the handler 12 times per second.

Just like with the *on(press)* handler in the button script, the *onClipEvent(enterFrame)* handler uses { and } brackets to contain the commands that will be executed when the event occurs.

There will only be one command here, which moves the movie clip 1 pixel to the left. Let's look at the script, and then the explanation of how it moves the movie clip to the left will follow.

```
onClipEvent(enterFrame) {
    this._x--;
}
```

The command *this._x--* probably seems like Greek to anyone not familiar with programming languages, so I'll break it down, piece by piece.

The *this* means it's used when code in a movie clip refers to itself. So, in this case, *this* is a way to refer to the movie clip to which the script is attached.

After *this* is a period, usually called a dot. A dot after an object like *this* means that you want to access a property of the object. The property in this case is _x, which refers to the horizontal position of the movie clip.

So *this._x* refers to the horizontal position of the movie clip. The -- is a decrement command. It takes the value of what is before it and reduces it by exactly 1. The command *this._x--* then takes the horizontal position of the movie clip and subtracts 1, thus moving the movie clip to the left.

If you wanted to move the move clip to the right, you could use ++, called the increment command. Likewise, if you wanted to move the movie clip several pixels at a time, you could have used += or -= like this:

```
onClipEvent(enterFrame) {
    this._x -= 5;
}
```

The previous code would move the movie clip 5 pixels at a time.

Lesson 7: Letting the User Control Movie Clips

⊕▷⊰**Example file: Usercontrol.fla**

Instead of moving the movie clip to the left or right like in the last example, let's make it follow the user's cursor.

The last lesson showed you how you can access the horizontal position of a movie clip. You can access the vertical position just as easily with the _y property. Now all you need to learn is how to set this to the cursor location.

The cursor location is stored in two properties, _xmouse and _ymouse. These are the horizontal and vertical positions of the cursor. The question is, what are these properties *of*?

Well, they can be properties of any movie clip, or the movie itself. For instance, *this._xmouse* would return the horizontal location of the mouse as it relates to the center of the current movie clip.

What you need is the position of the movie clip in relation to the Stage. To get the properties of the Stage, you need to use the _root object instead of *this*. So _root._xmouse is the horizontal location of the mouse relative to the upper-left corner of the Stage.

To set the movie clip's position to the position of the cursor, you need to set both the _x and _y properties of the movie clip to the _xmouse and _ymouse properties of the Stage. Here is how the code will look:

```
onClipEvent(enterFrame) {
    this._x = _root._xmouse;
    this._y = _root._ymouse;
}
```

Figure 2.10 shows how the example movie Usercontrol.fla is put together. There is a single frame with a *stop()* command place on it. The movie clip has the script from the previous code placed on it. That is all that is required. When you run this movie, the movie clip with the fox will follow the cursor.

Figure 2.10
The script attached to this movie clip causes it to follow the cursor.

Now that you know how to control both the movie playback and the placement of movie clips, let's look into some of the basic elements of programming.

Lesson 8: Using Variables

Variables are little storage units in which you can put numbers and strings of characters. For instance, you can create a variable and place the number 5 in it. You can then add 2 to that variable and it will then hold the number 7. Here's how that would look in ActionScript:

```
myVariable = 5;
myVariable += 2;
```

The term "myVariable" above refers to a variable that you, the programmer, created. To create variables in Flash, all you need to do is to use them for the first time. Flash automatically creates a variable of that name. In this case, it did that, and placed the value 5 in it.

The next line uses this variable, adding 2 to it. The variable "myVariable" now contains the number 7.

TIP

Deciding what to name your variables is important. A variable's name should reflect its purpose. For instance, if a variable is to store the user's name, it should be something like "userName". When you look at your code later, there will be no confusion as to what that variable is for.

You can also place strings into variables. A string is a sequence of characters such as "Hello World". You can store strings in variables by just using the = symbol as you would if you were assigning a number to the variable.

```
myVariable = "Hello World";
```

Variables in Flash are not typed. Variable typing is a restriction used in other programming languages that would only allow a variable to be set to one type of data. So if a variable is created to store a number, it could only be used to store numbers, never a string. However, because Flash ActionScript does not have this restriction, you can store either numbers of strings in any variable.

Variables can also hold other things besides numbers and strings. You can hold a pointer to a movie clip for instance. Remember how you used *this* in the previous two lessons to refer to the current movie clip? You can assign *this* to a variable and then refer to the movie clip through this variable.

Although this might not be that useful when all you need to do to refer to the current movie clip is *this*; it comes in handy when there is more than one move clip that needs to be controlled. You'll be dealing with situations like that often in the games in the book. For now, it is enough to know that variables can hold numbers, strings, and references to movie clips.

Lesson 9: Performing Operations

After you have variables storing information, you might want to change that information in some way. You've already seen that you can use ++ or += to change the value of a variable. You can also use a wide array of other operations on variables.

Let's start by looking at variables that contain numbers. You can perform a wide variety of mathematical operations on numerical variables with +, -, /, and * symbols. Here are some examples.

If you create the variables "a" and "b", you can add them together and place the result in "c".

```
a = 7;
b = 5;
c = a + b;
```

In the previous example, "c" would end up holding the number 12. Here are some similar examples:

```
c = a - b;
c = a * b;
c = a / b;
```

The variable "c" will hold the value 2 after the first line, 35 after the second line, and 1.4 after the third line.

You can also perform more complex math operations by using a set of mathematical functions built into Flash. All these functions are prefaced with the term "Math" followed by a dot, and then the function name. For instance, you can get the square root of a number by using the *Math.sqrt* function:

```
a = 9;
b = Math.sqrt(a);
```

The value of "b" is 3, which is the square root of 9.

One of the most crucial elements of a computer language that allows programmers to make games with it is a random number generator. Without random numbers, games would be completely predictable and unchallenging.

Flash can create random numbers by using the *Math.random()* function. This will produce a random decimal value between 0.0 and 1.0. You can produce more useful numbers by multiplying this by a larger integer, and then using the *int* function to convert it to an integer. For instance, the following will give you a random number from 0 to 9:

```
myRandomNumber = int(Math.random()*10);
```

You'll be seeing other mathematical functions throughout this book as they are needed by the examples.

Strings can also have functions performed on them. For instance, to combine two strings, you can use the + symbol:

```
a = "Hello";
b = "World";
c = a + b;
```

The value of "c" after this will be "HelloWorld". Notice that there is no space between the two words. You have to tell Flash to put a space there. The following code will do that to give you "Hello World" as a result:

```
a = "Hello";
b = "World";
c = a + " " + b;
```

An easier way to concatenate one string on to the end of another is to can use the += syntax:

```
a = "Hello";
a += "World";
```

Now that you know a little more about variables and how to use them, look at how ActionScript can be used to make decisions.

Lesson 10: Conditional Statements

In "Lesson 5: Creating Buttons to Give the User Control," you learned how to use buttons to allow the user to jump from one frame to the other. The user decides what part of the movie he wants to see next, presses a button, and the script attached to the button moves the movie to that frame.

ActionScript can also make decisions. To do this, it needs to base these decisions on the comparison of values. This is done with the *if* statement. For instance, two values could be compared. If both values are equal, then the program will do something in reaction to that fact.

Here is a program that compares a variable against a value. If this condition is met, then the code inside the { and } brackets is executed. Otherwise, it is skipped.

```
if (a == 7) {
    gotoAndPlay("special frame");
}
```

The == symbol is used to compare two values to see whether they are equal. If they are, then the condition is true. If not, then the condition is false. The job of the *if* statement is to examine the condition and test to see whether it's true. If it is, the code in the brackets is used.

You can extend the *if* statement to also perform actions if the condition is not met. By using an *else* after the *if* statement, you can include another set of brackets that will tell Flash what to do if the condition is not met:

```
if (a == 7) {
    gotoAndPlay("special frame");
} else {
    gotoAndPlay("another frame");
}
```

You can also have a longer *if* statement that makes several conditional tests. The code that comes after the first condition that is true is used. If none of the conditions are true, then the code in the *else* portion of the statement is used instead.

```
if (a == 7) {
    gotoAndPlay("special frame");
} else if (a == 12) {
    gotoAndPlay("very special frame");
} else if (a == 15) {
    gotoAndPlay("extremely special frame");
} else {
    gotoAndPlay("a not so special frame");
}
```

You can also use the == symbol to compare two strings. For instance, to see whether the variable "username" contains the string "Gary", you could use this line of code:

```
if (username == "Gary") {
```

In addition to ==, you can use < to determine whether a number is less than another number, > to determine whether a number is greater than another number, or <= and >= to determine whether a number is less than or equal to or greater than and equal to another number. You can use these symbols for strings as well, in which case they compare the strings and determine whether one comes before the other alphabetically.

You can also make more than one comparison at a time. For instance, you can test to see whether both "a" is equal to a number and "username" is equal to a string:

```
if ((a == 7) and (username == "Gary")) {
```

The previous line is only true if both conditions are met. On the other hand, you can use an *or* to see whether either one or the other condition is met:

```
if ((a == 7) or (username == "Gary")) {
```

These *if* statements are the fundamental building blocks of all programs. You can use them to change variables, branch to other frames, and decide whether a player is winning or losing a game. Loops are another important part of programs, as you'll see in the next section.

Lesson 11: Loops

Conditional statements are a necessary element of programming; however, you couldn't do much without loops either.

Computers excel at doing repetitive tasks. Loops are your way of making Flash do repetitive tasks. The most common type of loop is called the *for* loop. It allows you to perform a task an exact number of times. Here is a simple *for* loop:

```
for(i=0;i<10;i++) {
    trace(i);
}
```

NOTE

It has become traditional for programmers to use "i" as a generic program loop counter. In these cases, "i" stands for "increment." It is always a good idea to name your variables something that hints at what they are used for. However, in *for* loops, using "i" in a quick little loop is common.

The *for* loop looks cryptic at first. It is composed of three parts, all separated by semicolons. The first part lets you set a variable to a specific value. In this case, the variable "i" is set to 0.

The second part of the *for* syntax is a conditional statement, just like what would be used after *if*. In this case, the condition is false as long as "i" is less than 10.

The third part of the *for* syntax shows how the variable should be altered every time through the loop. In this case, "i" is incremented by 1 every time.

The result is that "i" starts at 0, gets 1 added to it every loop, and then the loop ends when "i" is no longer less than 10. So, "i" goes from 0 to 9 in 10 steps. If you run the previous code, you will see the numbers 0 through 9 placed in the Output window.

TIP

for loops should be used to process data inside programs, but not to animate objects on the screen. While a loop is in progress, the Flash screen is essentially frozen until the loop is complete. Short loops like the previous example run so quickly that they hardly affect the movie at all. However, long loops cause the movie to pause for seconds or longer.

Here's a more useful example of a *for* loop. Suppose you had 10 movie clips named "fox1" through "fox10" and you wanted to move them all 1 pixel to the left. This loop will do that for you:

```
for(i=1;i<=10;i++) {
    _root["fox"+i]._x++;
}
```

The *for* loop takes "i" from 1 to 10. It uses the *_root* object introduced in "Lesson 7: Letting the User Control Movie Clips." You can refer to any movie clip in the main timeline by using *_root[]* with the name of the movie clip inside the brackets. In this case, the code builds a string by combining the word "fox" with the number "i".

There are two other ways to create loops in ActionScript. The first is the *while* loop. Instead of having an incremental counter, such as "i", a *while* loop continues to loop as long as a condition at the beginning of the *while* statement is true. A *do* loop is the opposite, placing the condition at the end of the loop. Neither of these types of loops are used much by beginners, but you should be aware of them.

Lesson 12: Text and Strings

Using numbers in ActionScript is pretty straightforward. You can add, subtract, and perform other operations to wind up with another number. A lot of different things can be done with string values, however. Learning how to manipulate strings is an important step in learning how to program.

One of the simplest things you can so with strings is combine them. You learned how to do this in "Lesson 9: Performing Operations." In "Lesson 10: Conditional Statements," you saw how you can compare strings to determine whether they are equal to each other, or come before or after each other alphabetically.

Now, let's look at some more string functions. For instance, suppose you want to find out whether one string is contained inside the other. To do this, you can use the *indexOf* command. This command returns the position of the second string inside the first. If the second string is not found, it returns a -1. For instance, the following code finds the string "World" at character position 6 of "Hello World." If you try to search for "Earth" instead, you get a value of -1 because "Earth" is not in "Hello World."

```
myString = "Hello World.";
myPosition = myString.indexOf("World");
```

TIP

When ActionScript refers to character positions, it begins counting at 0. So the first character of a string is character 0. The string "Hello" would be found at character 0 of the "Hello World." string.

You can also find the number of characters in a string by using *length*:

```
myString = "Hello World.";
myStringLength = myString.length;
```

Sometimes it's useful to get a specific piece of a string. Two ActionScript commands can do this. The first is *substring*, which gets a piece of a string from one character position to another. In this example, the variable "mySubstring" ends up containing the text "lo Wo":

```
myString = "Hello World.";
mySubstring = myString.substring(3,8);
```

You can also use the *substr* function to perform the same task. Instead of getting the string from one position to the next, it gets a string starting at one position, and continuing for a specified number of characters. So the following code gets the string starting at character 3 and extending for 5 characters:

```
myString = "Hello World.";
mySubstring = myString.substr(3,5);
```

If you have two functions that perform basically the same task, then why not three? The *slice* function is identical to the *substring* function.

Eventually, you will want to display text information to the user. Doing so is easy. In Chapter 1, "Flash Elements Used to Make Games and Toys," you learned about dynamic text box. When you use the Text Options panel to make a text box dynamic, you can also set it to be linked to an ActionScript variable.

Figure 2.11 shows the Text Options panel with a text box that is now linked to the variable "mySubstring". The panel will now display the contents of "mySubstring" as long as the variable and the text box are at the same Flash level. It won't link the two if they are at different levels—for example, if one is inside a movie clip.

Figure 2.11

The Text Options panel can be used to link a text box to an ActionScript variable.

You can also link a variable to a text box that is set to be input text. In this case, the text box reacts to changes in the variable, but the variable also reacts to changes made when the user types in the input box.

In the next lesson, you'll learn about functions, and also see an example of a dynamic text box.

Lesson 13: Creating Functions

A function is a piece of code that can be used over and over again. You can pass values into it, and receive one value from it. For example, you could have a function that returns the sum of two numbers. Here's how that would look in ActionScript:

```
function sum(a,b) {
    c = a + b;
    return c;
}
```

Generally, you place functions in frame scripts of the main timeline. You define a function by using the *function* keyword. Then, you include the name of the function. That is followed by parentheses and then an open bracket }. Inside the parentheses, you can place nothing at all, or a comma-delimited list of variables that will be set when the function is called. These variables are called the function's parameters. For instance, the previous function can be called like this:

```
trace(sum(7,12));
```

The result of this call would be the number 19, which would be placed in the Output window by the *trace* command. When "sum" is called, the value 7 is passed into the function in the variable "a" and the value 12 is passed in as the variable "b". When the function is done, the *return* command sends the value of "c" back to the place where "sum" was called. So the result of "sum(7,12)" is 19, which the *trace* command uses to perform its duty.

You would use a function for two reasons. The first is to break your program into smaller pieces. If you have a 30-line program that performs three different tasks, you could instead have three 10-line functions that each performs a single task. This makes it easier to work with your code.

The other reason is that they are reusable. You can call a function as many times as you like in the rest of your program. So if you have a piece of code that needs to be used several times, you can place it into its own function and just call that function repeatedly. You can call it with different parameters.

Example file: Framelabeler.fla

Here's a function that takes the name of a frame label as a parameter. It then performs two tasks. First, it places this name into a text variable called "textFrameLabel". This text box is visible throughout the movie, so it acts as a sort of position indicator to tell the user where she is in the movie. The second task for the function is to *gotoAndStop* at the frame.

```
function gotoFrame(frameLabel) {
    frameLabelText = frameLabel;
    gotoAndStop(frameLabel);
}
```

This function gets placed in the first frame of the main timeline. Along with that function is one regular command line that will use this function to make the movie jump to the "introduction" frame. Because it's already there, the *gotoAndStop* command in the function only has the effect of a *stop* command, but the variable assignment works just as well.

```
gotoFrame("introduction");
```

The Framelabeler.fla example movie contains this function in the first frame, as well as four other labeled keyframes. Five buttons along the bottom take the user to each of the five frames. Instead of each button having its own *gotoAndStop* command, they all call "gotoFrame".

Figure 2.12 shows the example movie. You can see the dynamic text area in the upper-left corner of the Stage. It contains the temporary contents "frame label". This will be immediately replaced by "introduction" when the first call of "gotoFrame" is made.

Figure 2.12

This movie has five frames and five buttons to take the user to each frame. The text box displays the name of the current frame label.

The usefulness of having one function control all the navigation is more than just saving some keystrokes while programming. Suppose you have 100 calls to "gotoFrame" by the time you are done with your program. Then, you decide to take out the "textFrameLabel" box or display the frame label somewhat differently. If you didn't use a function, you would have to go through your program and remove or change code in 100 places. But because all your navigation buttons use "gotoFrame", you can just change "gotoFrame" and all the navigation buttons will perform differently.

Lesson 14: Arrays

No introduction to any programming language would be complete without discussing arrays. Although a lot of simple work can be done without ever using arrays, a programmer cannot be considered anything but a novice unless she can use arrays.

Arrays are another type of variable. The variables you have been using so far can contain a single value: a number or a string. An array can contain zero, one, or more values. Here's what an array looks like:

```
myArray = ["Apple", "Orange", "Peach", "Plum"];
```

You can then use some special syntax to access one item out of the array:

```
myItem = myArray[1];
```

The value of "myItem" is "Orange" because arrays, like strings, begin counting positions with 0.

As you might guess, arrays are useful for storing lists of data. Several special functions exist for dealing with arrays. First, let's look at how to build them. There are several approaches to building an array. So far, you've seen the all-at-once approach. The entire array is declared all at once. You can also create an empty array and add items to it:

```
myArray = new Array();
myArray.push("Apple");
myArray.push("Orange");
myArray.push("Peach");
myArray.push("Plum");
```

The first line in the previous code creates an empty array. Each of the next four lines adds one item to the array by using the *push* command. Although this seems more complex than the all-in-one-line approach, it is necessary to build arrays like this if you don't know what all the elements will be right away. For instance, you might want to allow the user to enter data and then add it to an array.

You can get the length of an array just like you can get the length of a string:

```
myLength = myArray.length;
```

You've already seen how to extract a single item from an array using bracket syntax. You can also use the *pop* command to remove the last item of an array and return it. The following piece of code adds four items to an array, and then uses a *while* loop to remove each item from the end of the array and send it to the Output window:

```
myArray = new Array();
myArray.push("Apple");
myArray.push("Orange");
myArray.push("Peach");
myArray.push("Plum");
```

```
while (myArray.length>0) {
    trace(myArray.pop());
}
```

In the Output window, the first line is "Plum" and the last "Apple", because *pop* takes the item from the end of the array.

You can also sort arrays. If the items in the array are numbers, Flash sorts them in numerical order. If they are strings, Flash sorts them in alphabetical order:

```
myArray = new Array();
myArray.push("Peach");
myArray.push("Orange");
myArray.push("Plum");
myArray.push("Apple");
myArray.sort();
trace(myArray.toString());
```

Notice that the last line of the previous code uses a *toString* function to convert the array to something that can be shown in the Output window. This can be useful when you want to make sure the array is what you expected it to be.

Lastly, the *splice* array function allows you to remove one or more elements from an array:

```
myArray = ["Apple", "Orange", "Peach", "Plum"];
myArray.splice(2,1);
```

The *splice* function can work in several ways. In this example, it is using two parameters. The first is the item position to start deleting items. The second parameter is the number of items to delete. In this case, "Peach" will be deleted, being the item at position 2. You could delete both "Peach" and "Plum" by changing the second parameter to 2. If you remove the second parameter altogether, you can delete all the items in the rest of the array.

You can also use *splice* to insert items. By including a third parameter, you can specify what to insert:

```
myArray = ["Apple", "Orange", "Peach", "Plum"];
myArray.splice(2,1,"Pear");
```

In this case, "Peach" is removed, and "Pear" is inserted into that position. You could include a fourth parameter to insert a second item, and even more parameters to insert more items. You could also use a 0 as the second parameter, which would mean that no items are deleted, but some are inserted at the position.

Now that you've had a sampling of all the basics of ActionScript, it's time to start applying that knowledge to building useful pieces of Flash movies. In the next chapter, you'll build some of these pieces, and then starting with Chapter 5, "ActionScript Design Effects," you'll build complete programs.

ActionScript Elements Used to Make Games and Toys

Now that you have learned the basics of ActionScript, let's look at some more advanced examples. The following 10 lessons show you some techniques that will be used in the games later in this book.

Lesson 15: Controlling the Playback of a Movie Clip

⊳Example file: Mcplayback.fla

Movie clips are like little Flash movies inside your Flash movie. They contain a complete timeline with layers and most of the elements of your main Flash movie. You can control your main Flash movie with commands such as *play()* and *stop()*. You can also control a movie clip with these commands.

On the Web site, in a file named Mcplayback.fla, you'll see a movie clip named MyMovieClip in the library. This movie clip contains 10 frames labeled with some text so that you know which frame of the movie clip is being shown at which time.

By dragging that movie clip from the library to the Stage, you are creating an instance of that movie clip. You can and should name these instances. To do this, use the "Instance" panel. In Figure 3.1, you can see the Instance panel used to name the instance myMovieClip.

Figure 3.1

The Instance panel allows you to name movie clip instances.

The example movie also has five buttons in the library. These have been placed on the Stage just under the movie clip instance. You don't need to name the button instances—in fact, you can't. Unfortunately, buttons by themselves cannot be referenced by code in any way, so there is no need for a name.

After the movie clip and the five buttons are on the Stage, you get something that should look like Figure 3.2. The buttons look like video tape recorder controls, and that's exactly how they will be used.

TIP

You might have noticed that the movie clip instance is named the same as the movie clip in the library. This is commonly done when you are creating exactly one instance of a movie clip and have no plans to create more. The name of the instance is easier to remember when it is the same as the library item.

Figure 3.2

The buttons allow you to control the playback of the movie clip above them.

The five buttons will have complete control over the movie clip. The play button starts the movie clip moving forward. The clip continues to move forward, looping around to the beginning when it reaches the end. The stop button halts the movie clip at its current frame. The rewind button takes the movie clip back to frame one and stops it. The previous and next buttons advance the movie clip one step and stop it there.

Before the movie turns over control of the movie clip to the user, it must tell it to stop moving. Movie clips naturally want to start going as soon as they appear on the Stage. To prevent this, the following frame script was placed on the first frame of the main timeline. It stops the movie clip from animating, and also tells the main movie to stop.

```
myMovieClip.stop();
stop();
```

By using the dot-syntax, the first line tells the movie clip instance named "myMovieClip" to obey the *stop()* command. The second line has no instance name before it, so the command is issued to the same place where the script is located—in this case, the main timeline.

The button scripts use the same dot-syntax to send their commands to the movie clip. Here is the play button's script, which tells the movie clip to *play()*:

```
on (press) {
    myMovieClip.play();
}
```

The stop button sends the *stop()* command to the movie clip.

```
on (press) {
    myMovieClip.stop();
}
```

The rewind button needs to tell the movie clip to return to the first frame and stop there. The *gotoAndStop()* command with the parameter 1 does just that.

```
on (press) {
    myMovieClip.gotoAndStop(1);
}
```

The previous and next buttons move the movie clip back or forward one frame. The *prevFrame()* and *nextFrame()* command can be used for this. Here are both scripts:

```
on (press) {
    myMovieClip.prevFrame();
}

on (press) {
    myMovieClip.nextFrame();
}
```

Although the purpose of this lesson is to teach you how to control the playback of movie clips, you can actually use this example as a way to play back an animation or even a slideshow with Flash.

Lesson 16: Controlling the Properties of a Movie Clip

⊕▷⋈Example file: Mcproperties.fla

In addition to controlling the insides of a movie clip, you can also control its external properties. For instance, you can control a movie clip's position, its rotation, and its scale.

The example movie Mcproperties.fla contains a sample movie clip of a fox in the middle of the screen. Both the library fox and the movie clip instance are named "fox".

In addition, there are eight buttons around the box. Each of these buttons sets a movie clip property of the fox. You can see how this screen appears in Figure 3.3. The first three are labeled "Left", "Middle", and "Right".

Figure 3.3

The fox movie clip in the center can be repositioned, scaled, and rotated by the buttons around it.

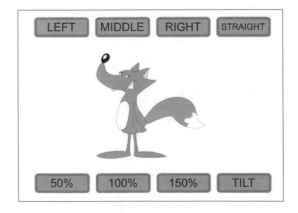

In "Lesson 6: Animating with ActionScript," of the previous chapter, you saw that the _x property of a movie clip can be used to set its horizontal location on the Stage. This is what the "Left", "Middle", and "Right" buttons will use. They could also use the _y property to set the vertical location of the movie clip, but that isn't needed in this example. Here is the code from the "Left" button. It sets the horizontal location of the fox to 200, which is slightly to the left of center considering that the movie is 550 pixels wide. The "Middle" and "Right" buttons only differ in the value that the _x property is set to.

```
on (press) {
    fox._x = 200;
}
```

To scale a movie clip, you need to use the _xscale and _yscale properties. If these are set to the same value, they provide a way to uniformly scale a movie clip. A value of 100 stands for 100% scale.

TIP

You can also change only _xscale or _yscale individually, or set them to different values to make a movie clip thinner or flatter.

Here is the button script for the "50%" button. The other two scaling buttons use the same code, but with a different value.

```
on (press) {
    fox._xscale = 50;
    fox._yscale = 50;
}
```

To rotate a movie clip, you need to use the _rotation property. It takes a value in degrees, so 0 is the same as 360. You can go higher than 360 or lower than 0, but Flash just interprets that into a reading between 0 and 360.

Here is the script for the "Tilt" button. It rotates the movie clip 30 degrees clockwise. The "Straight" button just sets the rotation back to 0.

```
on (press) {
    fox._rotation = 30;
}
```

By using these properties in more complex code to come later in this book, you'll be able to move movie clips around the Stage to create all sorts of games.

Lesson 17: Dragging and Dropping Movie Clips

Example file: Dragsimple.fla

An important part of many interfaces, whether it is a game or application, is the ability to drag elements around on the screen. This can be done several ways in Flash. Let's look at three of them.

The *startDrag* command tells Flash to make a movie clip automatically follow the cursor. The example movie Dragsimple.fla demonstrates how to use this command in the most basic way.

A movie clip with a circle drawn in it has been placed on the Stage and named "circle". As soon as the movie runs, the following command starts the circle following the cursor. It also tells the main timeline to stop animating so the movie doesn't continue past this frame.

```
startDrag("circle",true);
stop();
```

The *startDrag* command is using two parameters in this case. The first is the name of the movie clip to drag. The second is the keyword *true,* which in this case tells *startDrag* to lock the object's center to the cursor. If you used a *false* in this second parameter, the distance between the cursor and the center of the movie clip would remain the same as when the *startDrag* command was issued.

> **NOTE**
>
> The keywords *true* and *false* are called Boolean expressions. They can be used in cases in which an attribute is either on or off. They are also the results of comparisons, such as "a == b".

The example movie Dragsimple.fla forces the movie clip "circle" to follow the cursor. However, a more typical use of dragging is to have the user click an item to start dragging it, and then release the mouse to drop it.

Example file: Dragcomplex.fla

This can be done by making a movie clip that contains a button inside it. In Dragcomplex.fla, an invisible button has been placed in the same circle movie clip. The button was made invisible by only placing content on the "Hit" frame inside the button.

So the "circle" movie clip contains the same graphic as in Dragsimple.fla, but also a button. The following script has been attached to this button. It executes the *startDrag* command when the user presses down, and a *stopDrag* when the user lifts up the mouse button.

```
on (press) {
    startDrag("",false);
}

on (release) {
    stopDrag();
}
```

The empty quotes inside the *startDrag* command tell Flash that you want the current movie clip to be dragged. Because the button is inside the "circle" movie clip, that particular clip can be dragged. The *false* as the second parameter means that the movie clip will not lock its center to the cursor, but instead maintain the original distance between the cursor and the movie clip center. This makes it appear as if the cursor has grabbed a part of the circle and is dragging the circle by that point.

The *stopDrag* command needs no parameters. Only one movie clip can be dragged at a time, so all it needs to do is stop the current dragging action, which will return the movie clip to its immobile state.

One of the problems with the *startDrag* command is that only one movie clip can be dragged at a time. In addition, the dragging is happening automatically, which makes it hard for you to monitor the movie clip's progress as it is dragged. For these reasons, it is useful to know how to drag a movie clip without using the *startDrag* command.

Example file: Dragbetter.fla

The example movie Dragbetter.fla contains some code that will do this. The movie is set up the same way as Dragcomplex.fla with a movie clip that has an invisible button inside it. The script attached to this button, however, is different. All it does is set a variable called "drag" to *true* when the user presses down on the button, and *false* when the mouse button is lifted.

```
on (press) {
    drag = true;
}

on (release) {
    drag = false;
}
```

The "drag" variable becomes a global variable, which is shared by all the code associated with the movie clip. Therefore, the script attached to the movie clip can tell the value of "drag" and use it to determine whether of not the movie clip should follow the cursor.

The script attached to the movie clip sets the _x and _y properties of the movie clip to the _xmouse and _ymouse properties of the main timeline. These last two properties will give you the mouse location relative to the Stage.

```
onClipEvent (enterFrame) {
    if (drag) {
        this._x = _root._xmouse;
        this._y = _root._ymouse;
    }
}
```

The *this* keyword is used to indicate that the object being referred to is the current one. The script is attached to the "circle" movie clip, so *this* will refer to that clip. In the next section, you'll look at different ways of referring to movie clips at different levels.

Lesson 18: Movie Clips and Levels

The beginning ActionScript programmer might find it difficult to understand how movie clips and levels work. It helps to think of a movie clip as a Flash movie inside your main Flash movie. Although your main Flash movie has variables and properties, the movie clip inside it has its own world of variables and properties that are separate from the main Flash movie.

Whenever you place a movie clip on the Stage, you are creating a new world, also called an object. The main Flash movie is an object and the movie clip is an object inside that object.

Think of the Flash movie as a toy box full of toys. If you paint the toy box blue, it doesn't make all the toys inside it blue. Each toy maintains its original color. On the other hand, if you move the toy box across the room, all the toys come with it. However, they maintain their own properties, such as color and position inside the toy box.

Assuming the toy box was closed and you told someone in the room to get the toy truck, that person might have a difficult time if she hasn't been told that the toy truck is inside the toy box. "Get the toy truck," isn't enough. You would have to say, "Get the toy truck that is inside the toy box."

Movie clips work the same way. If you have a movie clip that is at the main level of the Flash movie, you can refer to it by name, such as "toyTruck". However, if you have a movie clip "toyTruck" that is inside another movie clip called "toyBox", then you'll have to refer to it as "the toy truck inside the toy box," or "toyBox.toyTruck".

⊕⊳Example file: Levels.fla

Figure 3.4 shows a situation like this. The source for this movie can be found as the file Levels.fla on the Web site.

Figure 3.4

The movie clip "secondMC" is inside the movie clip "firstMC", which is on the Stage.

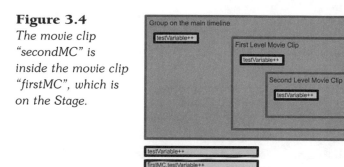

There are two movie clips in Levels.fla. However, only the movie clip called "firstMC" is on the Stage. The movie clip "secondMC" is actually inside "firstMC". A text box on the Stage and in each movie clip is linked to the variable "testVariable". These text boxes show you, at any time, the value of "testVariable" on the Stage in "firstMC" and in "secondMC".

The Stage and each movie clip contains a button that will increase the value of "testVariable". Here is the code inside each of these buttons:

```
on (press) {
    testVariable++;
}
```

The button changes the value of the variable "testVariable" found at the level of the button. So the button on the Stage changes the variable "testVariable" at the main level. The button in "firstMC" changes the variable "testVariable" in "firstMC". The button in "secondMC" changes the variable "testVariable" in "secondMC".

It is important to realize that these three variables named "testVariable" are actually three different variables. Because they are at different levels, they have no relationship to each other.

If you run this movie, you can see that pressing one of these small buttons changes the value of "testVariable" only at the level where the button is located.

You can also change the value of variables at levels other than the level where the code is located. By using ActionScript dot-syntax, you can force Flash to modify variables at different levels. The three larger buttons at the bottom of the screen show some examples.

All three of these buttons are on the Stage, not inside any movie clip. The first button changes the value of "testVariable" without specifying a movie clip. This results in the "testVariable" on the Stage being changed.

The second button specifies the variable "testVariable" inside the movie clip "firstMC". The code looks like this:

```
on (press) {
    firstMC.testVariable++;
}
```

The result is that the variable in the "firstMC" movie clip is changed. To change the variable inside "secondMC", you need to remember that "secondMC" is inside "firstMC". To get to this variable, tell Flash to look at "secondMC" that is inside "firstMC".

```
on (press) {
    firstMC.secondMC.testVariable++;
}
```

These three buttons are similar to saying, "paint the room blue," then "paint the toy box blue," and then "paint the toy truck inside the toy box blue."

In all the previous examples, the name of the movie clip instance has been used directly in the code. There is another way that you can refer to movie clips. You can use the _root property of the Flash movie to refer to a movie clip like this:

```
_root["firstMC"].testVariable++;
```

This comes in handy if you have a space in the name of the movie clip instance, because you can't use the other method with spaces in the name. This alternative method will also come in handy when you need to use more complex code to construct the name of a movie clip as a string, rather than having it hard-coded into the program. You'll see one use of that in the next section.

Lesson 19: Duplicating Movie Clips

Being able to manipulate movie clips is an important part of building games. However, you'll also need to be able to create movie clips. Although this is easy enough to do in Flash, you might want your code to be able to create the movie clips after the movie has started running.

Think about a game in which enemy spaceships are attacking the player. One ship comes, and then another, and then another, and so on. Instead of having to create dozens or hundreds of movie clips ready to be used by the game, you can have the code create them as necessary.

There are two ways to create movie clips. One is to duplicate a movie clip that already exists. Another is to create a movie clip from a symbol in the library.

To duplicate a movie clip, you'll need to use the *duplicateMovieClip* command. This command creates a carbon copy of an existing movie clip. Here is an example:

```
firstclip.duplicateMovieClip("newclip",0);
```

The command *duplicateMovieClip* must be triggered by the movie clip to be duplicated. So it starts with the name of that movie clip, in this case "firstclip". There are also two parameters. The first parameter is the name of the new movie clip instance. The second parameter is the level of this new movie clip.

This is where it can get a bit confusing. The *duplicateMovieClip* command uses the term level to describe the order in which movie clips are drawn. This is different than the use of the term level in the last section when it was used to describe which movie clips were inside other movie clips.

If a movie clip is drawn at level 0, like in the previous one-line code example, then it is drawn under a movie clip at level 1. Level 1 is drawn under level 2, and so on.

You don't have to worry about two movie clips being at the same level because they can't be. Flash won't let two movie clips be created at the same level. So with every use of *duplicateMovieClip*, you need to use a different level number.

Example file: DuplicateMovieClip.fla

The example movie DuplicateMovieClip.fla demonstrates this. In the first and only frame of the main timeline, the variable "level" is set to 0. On the Stage is a button labeled "New MC". There is also a movie clip with the name "firstclip". Each time the button is pressed, the following code is executed:

```
on (press) {
    // duplicate first clip
    firstclip.duplicateMovieClip("newclip"+level,level);

    // set a random position
    _root["newclip"+level]._x = int(Math.random()*550);
    _root["newclip"+level]._y = int(Math.random()*400);

    // increase level
    level++;
}
```

> **NOTE**
>
> Notice that for the first time, I've used comments in the ActionScript code. These comments start with two slashes. Everything else on a line after the two slashes is ignored by Flash and is only there to make it easier for you to understand what the code is doing. As the blocks of code in this book get longer and longer, you'll see comments to help you read through them. You should also use comments in your code to make it easier to edit later, or for a co-worker to be able to understand it easier.

The variable "level" is used in many ways in this handler. First, it is used to compose a name for the new movie clip. The first time the variable is used, the movie clip will be named "newclip0". The variable is also used as the level for the movie clip.

At the end of the handler, "level" is incremented by one. So the next movie clip created will be "level1" at level number 1.

This handler also sets the horizontal and vertical location of this new movie clip to a random spot on the Stage. Notice that the *_root[]* syntax is used to indicate which movie clip is being referred to.

Another way to create new movie clips is to use the *attachMovie* command. This command does not require that the movie clip already be on the Stage. Instead, it just needs to be in the library. However, if a movie clip is in the library and not used on the Stage, Flash automatically won't include it in the final .swf file. To force it to include this movie clip, you'll need to select it in the library and use the Options menu there to set the Symbol Linkage Properties. You can see this dialog box in Figure 3.5.

Figure 3.5

The Symbol Linkage Properties dialog box lets you include a movie clip in the .swf even if it isn't used on the Stage.

The Symbol Linkage Properties need to be set to Export This Symbol. Then, you have to come up with a name for the symbol that the code will use to refer to it. I usually use the symbol's name as it appears in the library.

Example file: AttachMovie.fla

The *attachMovie* command uses the name in the Symbol Linkage Properties dialog box as the first parameter. The second parameter is the name of the instance of the movie clip on the Stage and the third parameter is its level. The code for this button, found in the movie AttachMovie.fla, is almost the same as the code for the DuplicateMovieClip.fla movie, with the exception of one line.

```
on (press) {

    // duplicate first clip
    attachMovie("myMovieClip","newclip"+level,level);

    // set a random position
    _root["newclip"+level]._x = int(Math.random()*550);
    _root["newclip"+level]._y = int(Math.random()*400);

    // increase level
    level++;
}
```

⊕▷∢Example file: RemoveMovieClip.fla

You can also remove movie clips from the Stage by using the *removeMovieClip* command. For instance, the following code, found in RemoveMovieClip.fla, removes the previous movie clip before creating a new one:

```
on (press) {
    // remove previous movie clip
    _root["newclip"+(level-1)].removeMovieClip();

    // duplicate first clip
    attachMovie("myMovieClip","newclip"+level,level);

    // set a random position
    _root["newclip"+level]._x = int(Math.random()*550);
    _root["newclip"+level]._y = int(Math.random()*400);

    // increase level
    level++;
}
```

These techniques mean that your games and applications can create their own movie clips, adding them and removing them from the Stage as necessary.

Lesson 20: Creating an "Actions" Movie Clip

Now that you know how to create a bunch of movie clips with ActionScript, let's look at how to control them. You know that you can control one movie clip with code attached to it, but what if you have several movie clips that need to be controlled? What if these movie clips all need to behave in the same way?

If you place those movie clips on the Stage, you can copy and paste code from one movie clip on to the others. This has several disadvantages. First, there's the copying and pasting. Then, if you decide to change the code, you need to change it in all the instances of the movie clip.

One way to control several movie clips is to place code in one spot that controls all these clips. For instance, if you have 10 movie clips, you could place code on the first clip that will control all 10.

But rather than place the burden of control on one out of many clips, why not create a movie clip for the express purpose of controlling other clips. This common technique makes it easy to remember where you put your code. I call it the "actions movie clip".

Start by using the text tool to create a small text box on the Stage and write the word "actions" in it. This is just so it can be identified easily. Then, with this text box selected, choose Insert, Convert To Symbol and turn it into a movie clip named "actions". Move it to the gray area off the Stage, so the word "actions" isn't visible to the user.

This movie clip is used to attach a script that will control all sorts of things in the movie. For instance, suppose you want to have a movie that creates 10 movie clip instances from a library symbol, and then rotates them all a little each turn.

⊕▷ Example File:actionsMC.fla

First, create the symbol. Set its Symbol Linkage Properties to Export This Symbol with a name "sample". You can see this in the example movie ActionsMC.fla.

The only code needed will be attached to the movie clip "actions". There will be two parts to this code, each inside an *onClipEvent* handler. The first such handler will react to a *load* event. The *load* event occurs when the movie clip first appears. The code in it is executed once at this time. In this case, take the opportunity to create 10 new movie clips:

```
onClipEvent (load) {

    // create 10 movie clips
    for(i=0;i<10;i++) {
        _root.attachMovie("sample","sample"+i,i);

        // set the location
        _root["sample"+i]._x = i*50+50;
        _root["sample"+i]._y = 100;
    }

}
```

Not only are the movie clips created, but their locations are set. The vertical location is set to 100, but the horizontal location is set to different locations starting at 50 and continuing to 500. You can see what this looks like in Figure 3.6.

Figure 3.6
These 10 movie clips were created from a library symbol by using ActionScript.

The second part of the code is inside an *onClipEvent(enterFrame)* handler. The code here executes every time the "actions" movie clip loops. If the movie is set to run at 12 frames per second, then the code should run 12 times a second.

```
onClipEvent (enterFrame) {

    // loop through and rotate each movie clip
    for(i=0;i<10;i++) {
        _root["sample"+i]._rotation += 5;
    }
}
```

This code loops through all the movie clips and rotates each one by 5°. The result is that there will be 10 movie clips on the Stage and all 10 will be rotating.

Example file: Gears.fla

I've also created a more advanced version of this movie called Gears.fla. The movie is set up in exactly the same way, except for the code. In Gears.fla, the movie clips are placed close together so that the cogs on the gears touch. To make them act like gears, each movie clip starts rotated 15° more than the previous one. Because the cogs are 30° apart, it makes the cogs of one gear interlock with the cogs of the previous one. Then, instead of each gear rotating in the same direction, each gear rotates in the opposite direction of the one before it. Here is this code:

```
onClipEvent (load) {
    initialRotation = 0;

    // create 10 movie clips
    for(i=0;i<10;i++) {

        // attach the movie clip
        _root.attachMovie("sample","sample"+i,i);

        // set its position
        _root["sample"+i]._x = i*37;
        _root["sample"+i]._y = 100;

        // set initial rotation so each new one is off by 15 degrees
        _root["sample"+i]._rotation = initialRotation;
        initialRotation += 15;
    }
}

onClipEvent (enterFrame) {
    // loop through every other movie clip
    for(i=0;i<10;i+=2) {

        // make this one rotate clockwise
        _root["sample"+i]._rotation += 5;
```

```
        // make next one rotate counterclockwise
        _root["sample"+(i+1)]._rotation -= 5;
    }
}
```

To further understand how this code works, open the Gears.fla movie and play around with it. This code, like more code to come in this book, can only be explained so far with text. You'll need to open Flash and poke around at the examples to gain full understanding of how they work.

Lesson 21: Detecting Collisions

In games, things collide, usually with disastrous results for one or both objects colliding. You'll need to be able to write code that detects if two objects collide, or if the cursor location collides with an object.

In Flash, the primary way to determine if two objects collide, or an object is covering a certain point on the screen, is to use the *hitTest* function. You can feed the *hitTest* function either the location of a point, or another movie clip.

Let's start with testing for collision with a point. Suppose you have a movie clip on the screen and you want to determine whether the user's cursor is over it. You can attach this code to the movie clip:

```
onClipEvent (enterFrame) {
    if (this.hitTest(_root._xmouse,_root._ymouse,true)) {
        this._x = int(Math.random()*550);
        this._y = int(Math.random()*400);
    }
}
```

By using *this.hitTest()*, you are asking for the function *hitTest* to be used on the current movie clip. The three parameters passed into it are the horizontal location of the mouse, the vertical location of the mouse, and a *true*. This last parameter determines whether Flash uses the bounding box around the movie clip as the area for collision detection, or whether only the exact shape of the object is used. This code uses the latter by indicating *true*.

Example file: Runaway.fla

You can see this code in action in the sample movie Runaway.fla. When you move the cursor over the movie clip, it jumps to a random spot on the screen.

Example file: Collision.fla

To determine whether two movie clips intersect, you can instead use a single parameter—a pointer to the second movie clip—to see whether they both collide. In the movie Collision.fla, two movie clips are on the Stage. The larger is named "target" and the smaller is named "bullet". There is also an "actions" movie clip just off the Stage. The following code is attached to it:

```
onClipEvent (enterFrame) {

    // see if the bullet hit the target
    if (_root["target"].hitTest(_root["bullet"])) {

        // collision, so target grows
        _root["target"]._xscale += 5;
        _root["target"]._yscale += 5;

        // bullet resets
        _root["bullet"]._x = 350;

    } else {

        // no collision, continue to move bullet
        _root["bullet"]._x -= 5;
    }
}
```

This code moves the bullet to the left 5 pixels at a time. When the two movie clips collide, the target will grow slightly by having its scale increased by 5%. The bullet's horizontal position is reset so it can begin its approach again.

So far, you have learned how to scale a movie clip and change its position. Next, you'll learn how to change a movie clip's appearance in a more drastic way.

Lesson 22: Using Movie Clips to Change What's on the Screen

Unfortunately, in Flash you can't swap one movie clip for another on the Stage. One option to make up for this is to remove one movie clip and create another in its place. But when you have a single movie clip that needs to change its image often, you need a quicker way to do it.

Another method is to create a movie clip that contains all the different states of that object. For instance, if the object is a spaceship, I might have frames in that movie that represent the spaceship without any engines on, the spaceship with the main engine on, the spaceship with the left engine on, the spaceship with the right engine on, and a series of frames that make up an animation of the spaceship exploding.

⊕▷**Example file: Changingimages.fla**

The example movie Changingimages.fla shows this example. There are buttons on the left that allow you to select which part of the "ship" movie clip will be shown. Figure 3.7 shows you what this movie looks like. Check it out on the Web site as well.

Figure 3.7
Changingimages.fla lets you play with a single movie clip to have it show different view of the same object.

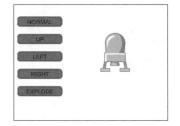

Each of the buttons in Changingimages.fla takes the movie clip to a different frame. For instance, this is the script on the Up button:

```
on (press) {
    ship.gotoAndStop("up");
}
```

The code on the Explode button is different than all the rest because it uses *gotoAndPlay* so that the movie clip jumps to the "explode" frame and continues to animate.

```
on (press) {
    ship.gotoAndPlay("explode");
}
```

The movie clip contains an eight-frame sequence starting with "explode" that shows the explosion. The last frame of this sequence has a *stop()* command placed on it so that when the explosion is done, the movie clip will wait on that last frame, which is blank, instead of looping back around to the first frame of the movie clip.

Check out Changingimages.fla on the Web site and pay special attention to the timeline inside the "ship" movie clip. This is where the frames are labeled so that the code can use frame names rather than numbers.

Lesson 23: Accepting Keyboard Input

The previous example used five buttons to allow you to test the five different portions of the movie clip. Although buttons are a primary source of input into Flash movies, in the world of games, you'll eventually want to accept input directly from the keyboard.

There are two ways to get keyboard input from the user. The first involves a special way to use buttons. The second method uses only code to test whether keys are pressed at any give time.

To use the button method, create a normal Flash button. It doesn't have to be anything special because you'll be hiding it off the Stage. The following sample code can be attached to that button to have it accept the "r" key and use it to move a movie clip:

```
on (keyPress "r") {
    circle._x++;
}
```

TIP

Note that *keyPress* actions attached to buttons are case sensitive. This means that if you are looking for the "r" key to be pressed, the button will not respond to Shift+R.

⊕▷ Example file: Keyboardbutton.fla

For movement, it is often better to look for the arrow keys to be pressed rather than letters. To do this, you can use some special syntax to indicate arrow keys rather than letters. Here is a longer script that will allow the user to move the movie clip in all four directions. You can find this script in the Keyboardbutton.fla movie on the Web site.

```
on (keyPress "<Right>") {
    circle._x++;
}

on (keyPress "<Left>") {
    circle._x--;
}

on (keyPress "<Up>") {
    circle._y--;
}

on (keyPress "<Down>") {
    circle._y++;
}
```

Although using buttons allows you to get individual keypresses, it does not work well in situations where you want fast and fluid movement. In these situations, the *Key* code object allows you to test the state of any key to see whether it is currently being pressed.

TIP

If you use a button to detect keypresses, you'll notice that the user can hold a key down and the action will take place repeatedly. This is because most computers are set to repeat keys if the user holds down the key. The delay between the first and second time the key is activated, and the delay between each successive key, is determined by the user's system keyboard settings. You should not rely on this keyboard functionality for games in which you want the user to be able to hold down a key to repeat an action. Instead, use the *Key.isDown()* function described in this section.

The *Key.isDown()* function allows you to test a key. For instance, if you want to see if the "r" key is pressed, you can do this:

```
if (Key.isDown("r")) {
    circle._x++;
}
```

Example file: Keyisdown.fla

This code does not have to be and should not be attached to a button. Instead, it should be attached to an "action" movie clip, as is the case in the movie Keyisdown.fla. The code is inside a *onClipEvent(enterFrame)* handler so that the keyboard is checked every frame. The code looks for the arrow keys again, which are signified by special constants, such as *Key.RIGHT*.

```
onClipEvent(enterFrame) {
    if (Key.isDown(Key.RIGHT)) {
        _root.circle._x++;
    }

    if (Key.isDown(Key.LEFT)) {
        _root.circle._x--;
    }

    if (Key.isDown(Key.UP)) {
        _root.circle._y--;
    }

    if (Key.isDown(Key.DOWN)) {
        _root.circle._y++;
    }
}
```

If you run this example movie, you'll see that the circle behaves in a much more fluid way. The frame rate of the movie was increased to 120fps to take advantage of as many frames per second as the computer can handle.

So when is it a good idea to use a button to accept keystrokes and when is it a good idea to use the *Key* object? If you are looking for a single keypress to trigger an event, then use a button. This will react to the keypress 100% of the time. The *Key.isDown()* function will only see the key pressed if the key happens to be down when the function is called. So if the user presses down and then lifts up quickly, the keypress could be missed. This can easily happen on slow computers.

The *Key.isDown()* function, on the other hand, is good for when you want the player to control movement. In this case, you want fluid movement that will continue at a constant rate as long as the player holds down the key. By using *Key.isDown()*, you can also test for more than one key being pressed at a time, whereas a button reacts to a single keystroke only.

Lesson 24: Playing Sounds

To conclude the ActionScript tutorial part of this book, you'll see how to use sounds. Flash has the capability to play sounds by placing them in the timeline of the movie, or a movie clip under it. However, you can also trigger sounds by using ActionScript commands.

Unfortunately, triggering a sound from the library is not as simple as on command. First, you have to make sure that the sound is included in the final .swf file. Do this by setting its Symbol Linkage Properties. The "Lesson 20: Creating an "Actions" Movie Clip" section showed how to do this. For this example, let's assume that the sound is linked with the name "beep".

You still have to use several lines of code to get the sound to play. First, you need to create a variable that is of type *Sound*. Next, you'll have to tell this variable that "beep" is the sound to play. Then, you'll have to trigger that sound. Here's how the code looks inside a button script:

```
on (press) {
    mySound = new Sound();
    mySound.attachSound("beep");
    mySound.start();
}
```

NOTE

The *start* command for sounds can also use two parameters. The first is the number of seconds into the sound before it should start. So if you wanted to skip the first 3 seconds, use a 3. For normal playback, use 0. The second argument is the number of times the sound would loop. So to get 10 "beep"s in a row, use 10.

You can also do many tricks with sound. The most useful is the ability to set the volume of the sound. This way, if you have a sound that is too loud, you can adjust the volume in your ActionScript rather than having to remake the sound.

To adjust the volume, use the *setVolume* command. This takes a value from 0 to 100. Here's the same code, but with the volume cut in half:

```
on (press) {
    mySound = new Sound();
    mySound.attachSound("beep");
    mySound.setVolume(50);
    mySound.start();
}
```

Another trick worth noting is the *setPan* command. This takes a value of -100 to 100. For stereo sounds, it works like a balance control with -100 being all left speaker and 100 being all right speaker. For monaural sounds, it will force the sound more from one speaker than the other. Here's a script that will play the sound only from the left speaker:

```
on (press) {
    mySound = new Sound();
    mySound.attachSound("beep");
    mySound.setPan(-100);
    mySound.setVolume(100);
    mySound.start();
}
```

One very frustrating thing about sounds is that when you set the volume or pan, it remains set, even when you want to play a completely different sound later. So if you use *setPan* or *setVolume* just once, get into the habit of setting them every single time. Otherwise, the previous setting will be used for the new sound.

Example file: Sound.fla

The example movie Sound.fla on the Web site has four buttons. The large middle one plays the sound normally. The large buttons to the left and right play the sound only from the left or right speaker. The smaller button in the middle plays the sound at 50% volume.

You can learn even more about sounds in Chapter 6, "Toys and Gadgets," in the section called "Jukebox." You can also learn more in Chapter 7, "Construction Toys," in the section called "Music Mixer."

This concludes the two-chapter tutorial that takes you through your first steps in ActionScript. In the next chapter, you'll learn about programming techniques such as planning, debugging, and testing. Then, beginning with Chapter 5, "ActionScript Design Effects," you'll begin to work through larger examples of programs.

The Game-Creation Process

4

Just knowing some ActionScript commands is not enough to enable you to make complete programs, such as games. You must learn some basic programming practices first, as well as some general information about how games are made. Let's start by considering how Flash measures up as a game-development environment.

Flash and Games

Flash did not start off as a program that you could use to make games. The initial uses for Flash were to make animations and Web site interfaces. Only with the addition of today's robust ActionScript can real games be created with Flash.

Weaknesses

Certainly Flash is far from an ideal game-development environment. Following are some reasons Flash makes it difficult to program games:

- **Timeline-based**—Flash movies are built around a timeline. Although Flash is ideal for animation, to make games you have to write code that actually fights Flash's normal state of moving forward through the timeline to get to the next frame.

- **Slow**—Flash is slow, there's no doubt about that. Compared to its older brother, Macromedia Director, it can be frustratingly slow for developers who use both. This limits Flash to turn-based games and arcade games with a small number of simple elements.

- **Flat**—Flash has no real capability to do any 3D graphics. Most major games today are 3D, even if they don't need to be. 3D has become the accepted standard for graphics in games. The good news is that this standard is usually not applied to Web-based games, for which Flash is usually used.

- **Limited feature set**—Suppose you want to add some functionality to your game and you determine that Flash doesn't have the capability to handle it. If you were programming in a lower-level language, such as C++ or Java, you could alter your game engine to include that new function. However, Flash is what it is. Only Macromedia can add new features to Flash. This means you have to make some compromises when you are building your game, especially if your game pushes the limit of what Flash can do.

Strengths

Flash also has many advantages over other game-development environments. Although programming in lower-level languages, such as C++ or Java, offers you a lot of power, it can't beat Flash in these areas:

- **Rapid development**—Flash allows you to work very fast to create a game from start to finish. You can create simple games in a matter of days or even hours.
- **Multimedia**—Flash allows you to import and use all sorts of different graphics and sound formats. You can work with artists and sound designers to quickly create your games without worrying about converting files or otherwise adjusting them to get them to work in your game.
- **Easy to use**—Flash is very easy to use. Features such as drag and drop, menus of ActionScript commands, and the panels and dialog boxes let you quickly add and modify elements with minimal time spent on tedious tasks.
- **Delivery**—Flash's greatest strength, without a doubt, is how you can deliver your content. Thanks to the Flash browser plug-in, almost all Web surfers can view your content directly on a Web page. In addition, you can also make standalone Flash projectors that allow you to deliver content to almost any Mac or PC.

It is almost more important to understand Flash's weaknesses than its strengths. Realize that you won't be able to create the next *Quake* or *Age of Empires*. However, also realize that you can create content that can be used by a much wider audience and distributed much more easily than those big-budget games.

Parts of a Game

Although each game is a little different, some parts of Flash games seem to be common to them all. Consider adding each of these parts when planning a game.

Loader Screen

Flash movies stream into the user's browser. This means they begin playing when only the first portion of the movie has arrived, hoping that by the time it gets to the next portion of the movie, it would have been downloaded. This happens automatically, whether you want it to or not.

Although streaming is great for animation, it is not always a good thing for games. In most cases, ActionScript will be controlling the appearance of items on the Stage, not the animation timeline. Flash isn't smart enough to know which items you need first, so sometimes those items aren't there yet when streaming is still going on.

For this reason, avoid streaming for most games. Instead, make the first frame or scene in a movie the loader screen. The loader screen displays a message to the user and waits until the entire movie has been downloaded before proceeding to the next screen. This gives you complete control over what the user sees, rather than leaving it up to which items have arrived and which have not. Figure 4.1 shows a loader screen.

Figure 4.1
The loader screen can be as simple as the game title and a message telling the user that the game is loading.

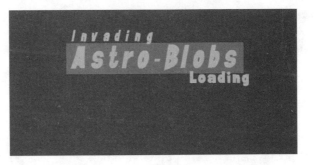

Chapter 17, "Advanced Techniques," goes into detail about how to build these loader screens.

Splash Screen

A splash screen, sometimes called a title screen, is a cool-looking screen that introduces the game to the user. I sometimes like to let my illustrators go wild on this screen, creating embellished views of the game play.

Think of those old arcade machines from the '80s. Although the graphics in the game itself might have been only blocky pixels, the artwork on the outside of the box was usually detailed and colorful. That's one way to do a splash screen.

Another method involves taking some of the graphics and movie clips that are already in the game and arranging them in an artistic way around the title. This is how Figure 4.2 was made. Using the graphics that are already in the game prevents you from having to make the file size of the game even bigger.

Figure 4.2
This splash screen also doubles as the instructions.

Instructions

Having game instructions is important. Most games should be easy to play without ever reading the instructions, but some people like instructions, so you should always provide them.

In some cases, such as Figure 4.2 shown previously, you can combine the splash screen and the instructions. Other games might have them on a separate screen. If the game is complex enough, you might want to stretch the instructions across several screens in a tutorial of some sort.

Another option for instructions is to not include them in the game at all. Some of my games feature instructions on a separate HTML page of the Web site. This allows users to open it in a separate window to view at the same time they are playing the game. It also allows you to easily provide instructions in other languages.

Backgrounds

Some games have graphics that cover the entire screen. Other games will take up only a portion of the screen at a time. This leaves room for you to create a colorful backdrop for the game.

For instance, Figure 4.3 shows a game in which you have to click the spaceships before they abduct the bunnies. The only active elements in the game are the ships and the bunnies. However, the interesting moonscape-and-stars background makes the game far more appealing.

Figure 4.3
The background for this game fits the game play very well.

Most of the games in this book involve a cartoon fox and his friends. To further accommodate the use of the fox, background images such as forests and trees are used. This helps create the setting for the game as much as the fox himself.

Game Over Screen

When the game is done, the player is usually taken to the "game over" screen. The words "game over" don't have to be there as long as there is some indicator to the player that he is done.

Sometimes, there is a screen for when a player wins a game, and another for when he loses. Of course, not all games have a win or lose option, as some are just played until the player runs out of ammunition, lives, or time.

Sometimes the "game over" screen includes a list of high scores and perhaps the ability for the player to submit a high score. Chapter 17 shows you how to set up a high score board.

How to Program

If you've already read Chapters 2, "An Introduction to ActionScript," and 3, "ActionScript Elements Used to Make Games and Toys," you might think you already know how to program. But there is a difference between knowing how to write some ActionScript and having learned the skill of programming.

Programming is hard for most people; it is easy for me. But I have a college degree in computer science and have been programming for 18 years. Don't expect programming to be as easy for you unless you have similar experience.

Here are some guidelines to help you learn to program. As with other skills, programming is something that takes time to learn. You'll find that the more programming you do, the easier it becomes.

Breaking Down Problems

Programming is not something you do all at one; it is a process. A large program can be broken down into parts. These parts can be broken into still smaller parts, and so on. To write a program, you must look at the problem in front of you and break it into the smallest pieces to solve it.

For instance, say you want to make a Space Invaders game. That's a big problem to solve. But if you break it down into smaller pieces, you'll find that it isn't so hard.

First, you would figure that there are several different elements in the game: the player's ship, the invaders, the bullets the ship is firing, and the bullets the invaders are firing.

Next, take one of those parts and break it down further. The player's ship moves horizontally across the screen, controlled by the arrow keys. This is a little more manageable problem.

You can break it down even further: How do you recognize when the user has pressed the left-arrow key? How do you move the ship to the left? How about the right-arrow key and moving the ship to the right? Solve these little problems and soon you'll solve the bigger problem of moving a ship. Then, move on to the next part of the program.

This process takes patience. That is a necessary part of programming. You must also be patient with yourself. Unless you are an expert at ActionScript, you might have to pause while writing a program to look up a command or examine some materials so that you can learn more before proceeding. You can't expect to be able to write a complex program without hitting some gaps in your knowledge.

The most important thing to realize is that if a problem seems too big to handle, then it probably is. Break it down into smaller problems and you'll have your solution.

Good Programming Practices

While learning to program, it's a good idea to get used to some practices that will make your life easier. These are practices used by programmers all over the world in every programming language:

- **Comments**—Get in the habit of adding comments throughout your code. Even passages that seem self-explanatory now might become confusing when you return to them a few months later.

- **Variable names**—Use variable names that describe what the variable is used for. This can complement your comments to help clarify your code when you return to it later.

- **Function names**—The same is true for function names. They should describe what the function does.

- **Smaller is better**—There is no limit on the length of functions in Flash. However, if you write a 100-line function, you'll find that it hard to modify later. Instead, break down the function into tasks and place each task into a different function.

- **Reusable is better**—While you are programming, always think about how a function can be used for a similar, if not exactly the same, task somewhere else in your program. For instance, if you have a function that adds one point to the user's score, make it so that the number of points added is taken from a parameter, allowing that function to be used to add 1 or any other number of points to the score.

- **Hard-coding is bad**—Hard-coding is the practice of including specific numbers in your code. For instance, if you place the number 550 in your code to describe the right side of the Stage, then 550 is said to be hard-coded into the program. If you decide to stretch the Stage to 600 pixels wide, you'll have to track down every instance of 550 in your code and change it to 600. Instead, set a variable called "screenRightSide" to 550 at the start, and use that variable throughout the program.

- **Organization is good**—Half of being a good programmer is being a good organizer. For instance, don't place functions in all sorts of different frames, but in one frame of your movie. Even then, try to group functions according to their tasks.

Debugging

All programmers need to do some debugging. It is impossible to write a complex program and have it work perfectly the first time you run it. To be a good programmer, you must be good at debugging.

Debugging doesn't always mean using the Flash ActionScript debugger either. You can debug in many ways. When you test a movie, you might get some error messages in the Output window. Usually, these messages are enough to point you to some problems in your program.

You can also use the *trace* command to place information about your program into the Output window. This helps you keep track of when your program hits certain points, and what the values of some variables are at these points.

If you do want to use the debugger, check out the information in the Flash 5 manuals. The debugger is a simple tool that allows you to see the values of variables as the Flash movie runs. It doesn't work magic, however. It is still up to your understanding of your own program to determine what is wrong.

Testing

Another stage of debugging deals with having other people test your games. Testing is important, especially if you are developing these games for professional purposes. As the programmer, you have a uniquely skewed view of how your program works and how it should work.

You might be surprised when someone who has never seen the game before sits down to play it for the first time. He might click things you never thought people would try to click. He might drag items off the Stage or place items in places they don't belong.

Often there are two stages of testing before a game is released to the general public. The first stage is called "alpha testing." This is when the game is tested by co-workers or people in some sort of private network. Then, "beta testing" is when the game is tested by people from outside your company or network. In both stages, you should have people report problems to you and then post updates of the game as you fix problems.

Bugs in a game can be more than just error messages. Playability issues and missing features can also be considered bugs. Try to make the game the best you can before declaring it done.

Games and Legal Issues

So now that you know some ActionScript, you plan to recreate your favorite game from the 1980s, right? Ever consider that it might be protected with a copyright?

After you place something on your Web site, or your company's Web site, you are now a publisher. In the world of publishing, people can protect works they have created from being copied by another. If you recreate an existing game and publish it on a Web site, you could be sued for copyright infringement.

I'm not a lawyer, but I do know that there is a lot of legal gray area in the realm of games and copyrights. Some companies are claiming to own the very ideas to which popular genres of computer games are based on. Other companies don't seem to care whether their games are copied even if they have the exact same name as the original.

If you feel that your game is close to one that has been previously published, you'll want to consult a lawyer. In my experience, lawyers give one of two responses. The first response is to explain to you that there is no simple answer and that you've got to be careful. This response is of little help. The other response that lawyers give is to play it safe and not publish your game at all. This response makes sense, because you are asking the lawyer how to stay out of trouble, and she is telling you how. However, the response doesn't help you much if you want to create any games at all.

One thing you should do is familiarize yourself with the game you are creating. For instance, the game Othello is made by a toy manufacturer who probably wouldn't appreciate it if you made a game of the same name. However, the game Reversi is the same game. Reversi is considered an "old standard" game like Chess and Checkers. Other games are more obvious: Scrabble is certainly off-limits unless you have a license from the owner. However, Backgammon is considered to be in the public domain. Another case is that of Yahtzee, which is a game owned by Milton Bradley, although the similar games Poker Dice and Yacht predate that one and are listed in many old game books as standards.

The purpose of this section is to make you aware of these issues. However, I can't offer any solutions other than to consult with a lawyer.

NOTE

Keep in mind that the games in this book are meant for you to use and alter for use on your Web sites and other projects. All these games are generic concepts, such as jigsaw puzzles and trivia games.

Altering the Games in This Book

One very good reason to buy this book is so that you can take these games and make your own. To this end, you will probably want to alter the games somewhat so that they fit your needs better and reflect your style.

Changing the Graphics

The easiest way to use the games in this book on your Web site is to just change the graphics. You can go in to the different symbols in the library and redraw graphics, or copy images from other Flash movies you have made. By keeping the code the same, it is possible to make usable games without doing any programming.

Altering the ActionScript

At the end of most examples in this book, you'll find suggestions on how the project can be improved. Think of these as exercises for you as you learn to program with ActionScript. Of course you can also come up with your own ideas for altering the games.

Be warned, however, that adding features or changing the game requires intermediate to advanced ActionScript programming. If you can't figure out how to make a change that you want, take the time to learn more about ActionScript before proceeding. Otherwise, changing the games can be frustrating.

Combining Games

A common technique for game programmers is to try to combine two games to make a new one. You can do this with the games in this book. However, such a task will require advanced programming skill, so don't get frustrated if you don't succeed immediately.

The next section will help anyone who wants to alter the games avoid some common problems.

Top Pitfalls

Whether you are altering a game from this book or creating your own, you'll occasionally hit pitfalls. These are usually little annoyances that are quickly discovered and corrected. Here are some that I came across while creating games in Flash.

Movie Clip Names

Every movie clip on the Stage has two names. The name by which it is called in the library makes no difference to your ActionScript code. However, the instance name applied to it by the instance of the movie clip on the Stage is all-important. However, it is easy to forget to name movie clip instances altogether.

Linkage Properties

To confuse things even further, if you want to use the *attachMovie* command to create instances of a movie clip, you need to set the Symbol Linkage Properties and include a name. So there are three possible places to name a movie clip: in the library, in instances on the Stage, and in the Symbol Linkage Properties dialog box.

Movie Clip Levels

Another pitfall is forgetting where variables are located. For instance, if a variable is in a script attached to a movie clip, it is at the level of that movie clip and not at the level of the main timeline. You can use dot syntax to access all the variables in your movie, but it's easy to forget where they are located.

Forgetting the Underscore

A minor annoyance is forgetting that most built-in Flash properties need the underscore (_) before them. If you have a movie clip named "myMovieClip", then "myMovieClip._x" is its horizontal position, but "myMovieClip.x" is just a variable called "x" inside "myMovieClip".

Splice and Slice

Another minor annoyance that can haunt you is accidentally using the *slice* function on an array rather than the *splice* function to delete an element from an array. That missing "p" can easily elude your eyes and the difference in functionality can create some puzzling bugs in your program.

Global and Local Variables

Remember that unless you use the keyword *var* before the first use of a variable in a function, the variable is a global variable. If you use this same variable name somewhere else, you might be stepping on the toes of the earlier variable. For instance, if you use "i" in a *for* loop, and then call another function inside the loop, and that function uses "i" for its own *for* loop, the two "i" variables will overwrite each other's values. To avoid this, use different variable names or the *var* syntax.

You have learned a lot about ActionScript in Chapters 2 and 3 and general programming techniques in this chapter. You are now ready to move on to Chapter 5, "ActionScript Design Effects," and beyond, where you will find complete examples of ActionScript programs.

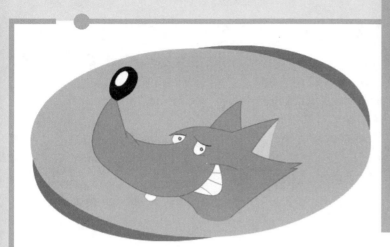

ActionScript Design Effects

- Expanding Buttons
- Randomness and the Old Film Effect
- Letter Movement
- 3D Illusions

Most of the chapters in this book deal with toys, gadgets, and games. Although toys, gadgets, and games all include some level of interactivity, I want to first talk about Flash movies that have little or no interaction. These non-interactive movies are similar to plain Flash animations, but are created with the use of ActionScript.

This chapter will also provide you with a few simple examples of ActionScript at work. Although many great effects can be created with Flash animation techniques only, ActionScript can also be used for design effects.

In this chapter, you will learn how to manipulate graphics and colors, change text, and move items around the Stage.

Expanding Buttons

▷÷Example File: Expandingbuttons.fla

Many sites use Flash as a way to navigate from page to page. Even a simple Flash movie with just one button can be an improvement to a static Web page. With ActionScript, you can make these buttons even more animated.

Project Goal

The goal is to create buttons that do more than just change colors when the user rolls the cursor over them. Instead, they expand and then return to normal when the cursor leaves. Figure 5.1 shows five of these buttons with the cursor over the second.

Figure 5.1
Each button expands as the cursor moves over it.

From the figure, you might think that when the cursor rolls over the button, it suddenly enlarges. However, the effect is more complex than that. Instead of just enlarging instantly, the button grows gradually, which is a much more pleasing visual effect. You can check out Expandingbuttons.fla on the Web site to see it in action.

Approach

Each button will react when the cursor rolls over it and when the cursor leaves. The reaction will be in the form of setting a target scale for the button to reach.

For instance, when the button starts, its scale will be 100%. When the user rolls the cursor over it, the target scale will then be 150%.

Then a script will act every frame to change the current scale to the target scale. So, the button will go from 100% to 150% in intervals of 10%.

When the user rolls the cursor off the button, the opposite occurs as the target scale is set to 100%. The button will shrink 10% every frame until it reaches that target.

Preparing the Movie

The example movie contains several buttons. Each button is actually a movie clip with a button inside it. I had just one button in the library, but created five different movie clips. Then, I placed the button in each movie clip along with a different piece of text to lay over the button. The result is five movie clips all with different text but the same button.

The button can be any sort of shape or color. I used a conservative style just to demonstrate the scripts at work.

Writing the Code

There are two types of scripts used in this movie—those attached to buttons, and those attached to movie clips. The first button scriptis attached to the button inside the movie clip. A script attached to a button can detect mouse events that occur only to that particular button. These are called event actions and they are defined by the word *on*.

In the button script, there will be three different event actions, two of which are *on(rollOver)* and *on(rollOut)*. These event actions both set a variable called "newscale" to the target scale for the button to enlarge or shrink to.

Here is what this script looks like for the button in the "Home" movie clip.

```
on (rollOver) {
    // set up for grow
    newscale = 150;
}
on (rollOut) {
    // set up for shrink
    newscale = 100;
}
on (release) {
    // do something
    trace("Home");
}
```

NOTE

The *on* declaration is used in button scripts to contain segments of code that should be executed when certain events concerning the button occur. Possible events are *press*, *release*, *releaseOutside*, *rollOver*, *rollOut*, *dragOver*, *dragOut*, and *keyPress*.

Each of the three event actions in the previous code segment contains a single line of code that runs when a specific event occurs to the button. For instance, when the user clicks and releases the button, the *trace* command executes. This places the word

"Home" in the Output window. In reality, you would probably use a *getURL* command to make the browser jump to a new page. *trace* is used here as a placeholder just for this demonstration.

The "newscale" variable is a custom variable created to store the value of what the scale of the movie clip should be. When the user rolls over the button, the new scale should be 150%. When the cursor leaves the button, it should be 100%. This variable is set here so that the movie clip script can use it.

The movie clip script is placed one level up on the overall movie clip in the main time-line of the movie. You can see a diagram that shows the main timeline, the movie clip, and the button inside it along with the two scripts in Figure 5.2.

Figure 5.2

This diagram shows where the two ActionScripts are located relative to the main timeline, the movie clip, and the button.

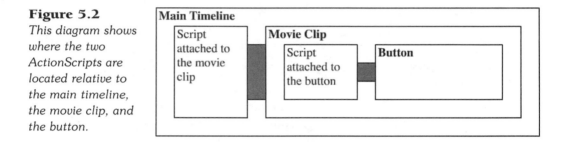

The movie clip script begins by setting the "newscale" variable to 100. Then, for each frame, the script checks this variable against the *_xscale* property of the movie clip. If they don't match, the *_xscale* is moved 10 closer to the "newscale" value. The *_yscale* property is also changed by the same amount.

```
onClipEvent(load) {
    // set initial scale to 100
    newscale = 100;
}

onClipEvent(enterFrame) {
    if (this._xscale > newscale) {
        // shrink
        this._xscale -= 10;
        this._yscale -= 10;
    } else if (this._xscale < newscale) {
        // grow
        this._xscale += 10;
        this._yscale += 10;
    }
}
```

NOTE

The *onClipEvent* declaration is used in scripts assigned to move clips. It will react to events like an event action, but to events happening to the whole movie, not just that single movie clip. The *enterFrame* event occurs every time a frame advances, or loops back, in the movie. A *mouseDown* event happens every time the user presses the mouse button, even if the cursor is not over that particular movie clip. Other events are *load*, *unload*, *mouseMove*, *mouseUp*, *keyDown*, *keyUp*, and *data*.

When the movie starts running, "newscale" is 100 and the *_xscale* property is also 100. On *every enterFrame* event, nothing happens. Then, when the user moves the cursor over the movie clip, and thus over the button inside the movie clip, the button's script changes "newscale" to 150.

NOTE

The *_xscale* and *_yscale* properties of a movie clip correspond to their horizontal and vertical size. A value of 100 for either of these means that the size is exactly equal to the original size of the movie clip instance. You can test and set these properties in ActionScript to stretch or shrink the movie clip. You can even use negative numbers, which would result in the movie clip image being flipped either horizontally, vertically, or both.

Now on *every enterFrame*, the value of *_xscale* and *_yscale* are less than "newscale". As a result, the scale is increased by 10. The button grows in size. When *_xscale* reaches 150, the growth stops as "newscale" and *_xscale* are once again the same. A similar process happens when the user moves the cursor off the sprite and "newscale" is set back to 100.

Loose Ends

To make a complete button bar, you must duplicate the movie clip several times. Inside each movie clip, you must alter the *on (release)* script to do something else, such as go to a different page than the other buttons. You also need to modify the text in the movie clip so that all the buttons look the same.

Each movie clip must have an exact copy of the same ActionScript. This is unfortunate because a single change to this script means that you need to change it in all the buttons.

TIP

To avoid copying and pasting the same script into all the buttons, use an *#include* command to have Flash read the script from an external file each time the movie is compiled. This way, you can change the script in the external file, and all the buttons will instantly use the new script. However, you still need to copy and paste the *#include* command onto each movie clip instance.

When complete, there should be as many movie clips in the library as there are buttons, but only one actual button is needed in the library. Each button inside each movie clip should have a slightly different script attached to it, whereas each movie clip on the main timeline will have a copy of the same movie clip script attached.

Take a look at Expandingbuttons.fla to see how all the pieces fit together.

Other Possibilities

You don't need to adjust both the _xscale and _yscale properties of the movie clip. You could just do one or the other to get a different effect. You also don't have to stick to my numbers. You could have the buttons expand to a smaller or larger size.

With a little more coding, you could make the buttons pulse instead of enlarge and hold their scale. Just check for when the scale expands to the maximum size, and then set the "newscale" variable back to 100. The result will be that the buttons expand and contract quickly as the user rolls over them.

Color Cycling Rotating Spiral

Example Movies: colorchange.fla, colortransform.fla, gradualchange.fla, spiral.fla

A movie clip's scale is not the only thing that you can alter with ActionScript. Just about every aspect of a movie clip can be changed. Scale is an easy example. To change something like the movie clip's color is a little more difficult. In this section, you will learn how to change a movie clip's color and rotate it.

Project Goal

The goal is to build a movie that features a rotating spiral that gradually changes colors. In doing so, you will learn about the Color object and the _rotation property.

Approach

You can use ActionScript to change most properties of movie clips on the Stage. In some cases, you just change the property directly. In other cases, you need to use functions to affect a change. This is the case when it comes to colors.

The Color Object

The Color object is what you use to change the color of a movie clip. Think of the color object as a set of commands that allows you to learn about and control the color of a movie clip.

TIP

A useful metaphor for objects such as Color is a television remote control. Think of the movie clip as your television and the Color object as a special remote control that adjusts the color setting on your television. You can use the buttons on the remote, like the commands of the Color object, to adjust or tint the colors on the television.

To use a Color object, you must first create one related to the movie clip you want to affect. You do that like this:

```
myColorObject = new Color("myMovieClipName");
```

There are a two ways to inspect and affect the color object. One is to look at the color directly. You can inspect the color of a movie clip with just two lines of code. First, create a new Flash movie and place one movie clip on the Stage. Name the instance "myMovieClip." Then, in the main timeline, place the following script:

```
myColorObject = new Color("myMovieClip");
trace((myColorObject.getRGB()).toString());
```

CAUTION

Remember that there is a difference between the name of the movie clip in the library, and the name of the instance of the movie clip on the Stage. ActionScript is always referring to the name of the movie clip instance. The library name is for your organizational purposes only.

When you test this movie, you will see that the Output window automatically opens and the value "0" is placed in it. This is the *trace* command telling you that the color value of your movie clip is 0.

NOTE

The *toString* function converts many kinds of ActionScript values to something you can see and understand. This is useful for converting things such as colors to numeric values for output using the *trace* command.

For a more interesting result, try changing the color of the movie clip. You can do this by selecting the movie clip and bringing up the Effect panel (choose Window, Panels, Effect). Then switch it to Advanced mode and change the R, G, and B fields to 128 as shown in Figure 5.3.

Figure 5.3

The Effect panel allows you to change the color of a movie clip. This example shows the R, G, and B values turned up to 128.

Now if you test the movie, you get the value of 8421504 placed in the output window. This corresponds to R, G, and B values of 128. With a slight tweak to the *toString* function, you can get a hexadecimal value instead of a decimal one. This means that it will look like the RGB values that Web designers use to define colors.

```
myColorObject = new Color("myMovieClip");
trace((myColorObject.getRGB()).toString(16));
```

NOTE

The *new* declaration allows you to create new instances of objects such as the Color object. You can also use it to create new arrays or sounds, as well as your own object constructs. If this seems confusing at this point, don't worry about it. A thorough understanding of how *new* works is not needed to be able to use it.

The output is now "808080" which is a hexadecimal number representing middle gray, or red, green, and blue values of 128—halfway between 0 and 255. The value of 16 tells it to convert numerical values into hexadecimal, as it did here.

Now that you know how to get the RGB value of a movie clip, the next step is to change it. This is done, not surprisingly, with the *setRGB* function. It accepts one parameter: the hexadecimal color you want to use. Here is an example that uses the same movie as the previous example, but with two new lines of code:

```
myColorObject = new Color("myMovieClip");
myColorObject.setRGB(0xFF0000);
```

The "0x" in front of the number tells Flash that what follows is a hexadecimal number. This number, "FF0000", is red. The movie clip, regardless of its starting color, will change to red when the movie runs. A sample movie on the Web site named Colorchange.fla demonstrates these two lines of code in action.

Transforming Colors

Using the color transformation object is another way to change the color of a movie clip and it has more versatility. This is sort of like an object inside an object. A transformation includes separate numerical values for red, green, and blue, as well as numerical values for the brightness of each of these colors. Figure 5.3 showed all six of these values, plus two values for the alpha channel, or transparency, of the image.

A color transformation object can include new values for each of these eight items. You define a color transformation object by creating a new variable. In this variable, you will place up to eight values as a single object. Here is an example:

```
myColorTransform = {rb:255, bb:0, gb:0};
```

This color transformation object can be used to tell any color object to change to red. It uses only three properties: the red, green, and blue color offsets. In addition to these properties, you can also set the red, green, and blue brightness with the "ra", "ga", and "ba" properties. To round off the properties, "aa" and "ab" are the alpha channel brightness and offset.

When it comes to colors in Flash, both the brightness and offset of the red, green, and blue colors are used to compute the final color. This means there are many ways to combine values to create the same color. In Figure 5.3, shown previously, you can see an example of how these number can be set.

After you have a color object and a color transform object, you can use them to change the color of a movie clip. These three lines will change a movie clip to red:

```
myColor = new Color("myMovieClip");
myColorTransform = {rb:255, bb:0, gb:0};
myColor.setTransform(mycolorTransform);
```

This example does essentially the same thing as the previous example, just in a different way. You can examine the sample movie on the Web site named Colortransform.fla to see it in action.

The advantage of the *setTransform* function over the *setRGB* function is that you have more control over the color values. For instance, the numbers can be ActionScript variables rather than hard-coded numbers. You can then change these values over a period of time, thus changing the color over time.

The following movie clip script takes the red value of the movie clip from 0 to 255 and beyond. The result is that the clip starts as a black oval, and then gradually changes to red. The "load" event is used to set up the color object and the color transform object. The variable "n" is created there too. The "enterFrame" event is then used to set the color transformation, apply it to the color, and then increment the variable "n".

```
onClipEvent(load) {
    myColor = new Color(this);
    myColorTransform = {rb:255, bb:0, gb:0};
    n = 0;
}

onClipEvent(enterFrame) {
```

```
myColorTransform.rb = n;
myColor.setTransform(myColorTransform);
n++;
}
```

NOTE

The operator "++" increments any variable by one. So, if "n" is equal to 7, and Flash encounters a "n++" line, then "n" increases to 8. You can also use "--" to decrease a variable by one.

In this example, the value of "n", and thus the value of the color red, is taken from 0 to 255 and beyond. When it is greater than 255, then value of red is at its maximum and doesn't change. You can see this script in action on the Web site by viewing the Gradualtransform.fla movie.

Although all this information about colors and transformations is interesting, it has yet to give you a useable special effect. So let's try something a little more mesmerizing.

For the main example in this section, we will make a movie clip cycle through most of the colors of the rainbow. To do this, we need to change the red, green, and blue color components. The same *setTransform* function will be used, but the way that the values change will have to be more complex than in the previous example.

The values of red, green, and blue will all start at 255 and work like this:

1. Red will be decreased until it hits 0.
2. Blue will be decreased until it hits 0.
3. Red will be increased until it hits 255.
4. Green will be decreased until it hits 0.
5. Blue will be increased until it hits 255.
6. Green will be increased until it hits 255.

This sequence will take the colors from black to cyan, cyan to green, green to yellow, yellow to red, red to magenta, and magenta to black. This hits all the colors except pure blue. This is how we will make our color cycling spiral.

Preparing the Movie

The only element that you need in this movie is a spiral shape. Place that on the Stage in the middle. To take the color transformations well, the spiral should be black, and the background color of the Stage should be black.

Color Cycling and Rotation

There will be just one script in this movie, which is attached to the spiral movie clip.

In this script, we will have a variable "n" that contains the mode of the color change. Its number will correspond to the number in the previous list. So, for instance, when "n" is 3, then the change occurring will be that red is increasing.

The variable "n" will start at 1 and go through 6 and then repeat. Here is a code segment that shows the long *if...then* sequence that uses "n" and changes the color transform object.

```
if (n == 1) {
    colorTransform.rb -= 5;
    if (colorTransform.rb == 0) n = 2;
} else if (n == 2) {
    colorTransform.bb -= 5;
    if (colorTransform.bb == 0) n = 3;
} else if (n == 3) {
    colorTransform.rb += 5;
    if (colorTransform.rb == 255) n = 4;
} else if (n == 4) {
    colorTransform.gb -= 5;
    if (colorTransform.gb == 0) n = 5;
} else if (n == 5) {
    colorTransform.bb += 5;
    if (colorTransform.bb == 255) n = 6;
} else if (n == 6) {
    colorTransform.gb += 5;
    if (colorTransform.gb == 255) n = 1;
}
```

NOTE

The operator "+=" takes a variable and adds a certain number to it. So "n += 5" adds 5 to n. This is the same as coding "n = n + 5". You can also use "-=" to subtract a certain number from a variable.

In each part of the *if...then* statement, the value of "n" is checked. According to which line it matches, one of the three color components of the "colorTransform" object will be changed. If the change is complete, then "n" itself is changed to the next value.

The full program will be a simple movie clip ActionScript with both an *onClipEvent(load)* and *onClipEvent(enterFrame)* function. The first will set up the color and transformation objects and the second will perform the color cycling, step-by-step.

As an added bonus, we will also make the movie clip rotate. This is done by increasing the _rotation_ property of the movie clip each time.

```
onClipEvent(load) {
    // create the color object and transform
    spiralColor = new Color(this);
    colorTransform = {rb:255, bb:255, gb:255};

    // start in mode 1
    n = 1;
}


onClipEvent(enterFrame) {
    // depending on which mode we are in, alter the transformation
    if (n == 1) {
        colorTransform.rb -= 5;
        if (colorTransform.rb == 0) n = 2;
    } else if (n == 2) {
        colorTransform.bb -= 5;
        if (colorTransform.bb == 0) n = 3;
    } else if (n == 3) {
        colorTransform.rb += 5;
        if (colorTransform.rb == 255) n = 4;
    } else if (n == 4) {
        colorTransform.gb -= 5;
        if (colorTransform.gb == 0) n = 5;
    } else if (n == 5) {
        colorTransform.bb += 5;
        if (colorTransform.bb == 255) n = 6;
    } else if (n == 6) {
        colorTransform.gb += 5;
        if (colorTransform.gb == 255) n = 1;
    }

    // set the new color
    spiralColor.setTransform(colorTransform);

    // rotate the spiral too
    this._rotation = this._rotation += 5;
}
```

NOTE

The _this_ object allows a movie clip to refer to itself. Because this script is attached to a movie clip, using _this_ inside the movie clip will mean that the command affects the movie clip itself, as opposed to another movie clip or the movie in general.

NOTE

The _rotation property of a movie clip can be used to turn the movie clip a number of degrees. You can use both positive and negative numbers. If you exceed 360, Flash wraps the values around; so, for instance, 370 is the same as 10.

Figure 5.4 shows a screen grab of the Web site sample movie Spiral.fla in action. The spiral cycles through the colors and spins at the same time.

Figure 5.4
The spiral changes colors and spins.

The importance of this example is not the result itself, which can also be done with animation techniques, but the fact that it is all done with ActionScript. This makes the result much easier to achieve.

Loose Ends

The frame rate of this movie determines how fast the spiral rotates and changes colors. In Flash 5, you can go up to 120 frames per second. However, a slow computer might not be able to keep up with a fast frame rate, resulting in different speeds between fast and slow computers.

Other Possibilities

You can make the spiral rotate in the opposite direction by changing the "+=" to a "-=" in the last line of code. You can also change the way in which the colors shift by changing the red, green, and blue values in the code.

Randomness and the Old Film Effect

Example movies: randomlocation.fla, randommovement.fla, oldfilm.fla

When you use Flash purely as an animation tool, you can create some amazing-looking effects. However, the animation plays back the exact same way each time. With ActionScript, you can use random numbers to vary what goes on in the movie.

Project Goal

The goal in this section is to learn about using random numbers to create visual effects. You eventually will use this to create an "old film effect" that puts random scratches and dots on top of any Flash movie.

Approach

There are two ways to generate random numbers in Flash 5. The old Flash 4 method is to use the *Random* function. This returns a value from 0 to one less than the number passed in. So *Random(5)* will return a value from 0 to 4.

In Flash 5, the new *Math.random()* function is recommended by Macromedia. It is possible that the old *Random* function will disappear in future versions of Flash. *Math.random()* returns a floating point number from 0.0 to 1.0.

The way to use *Math.random()* is to multiply the result by a larger number. For instance, multiplying the result by 500 gives you a result between 0.0 and 500.0. Using the *int* function rounds the result down and gives you an integer value from 0 to 499. Here is an example:

```
n = int(Math.random()*500);
```

The following short function takes a movie clip and repositions it anywhere on a 550×400 screen.

```
onClipEvent(load) {
    this._x = Math.random()*550;
    this._y = Math.random()*400;
}
```

The movie Randomlocation.fla on the Web site demonstrates the use of the previous function. Try running it several times to see how the oval moves to a different location each time.

The next step in using random numbers is to record their values and use them to affect movie clips over a period of time, rather than in just one instant.

The following short movie clip script moves a movie clip in a random direction. It sets the value of "dx" and "dy" to a number from -5 to 5 and then changes the _x and _y properties of that movie clip by those amounts. In addition, 10% of the time the values of "dx" and "dy" are changed to new random values.

```
onClipEvent(load) {
    dx = Math.random()*10-5;
    dy = Math.random()*10-5;
}

onClipEvent(enterFrame) {
    this._x += dx;
    this._y += dy;
```

```
    if (Math.random() > .9) {
        dx = Math.random()*10-5;
        dy = Math.random()*10-5;
    }
}
```

The movie Randommovement.fla shows this script in action. The oval moves around in a random manner. It might even actually leave the Stage area because nothing has been placed in the code to make sure that it does not exceed these bounds.

Preparing the Movie

As an example of using random numbers, let's create a common Flash special effect: the look of old movie film. This is typically done with animation only. The animator places little nicks and marks on different frames of the movie, as well as a line that moves from side to side, representing a scratch in the film.

You can do all these effects more easily with ActionScript. First, the moving scratch can be accomplished by placing a vertical white line down the side of the movie.

To take this knowledge of random numbers and apply it to a movie to make an "old film effect," you first need some old film. By that, I mean that it helps to have an image that you can place the scratches and spots on top of.

Figure 5.5 shows such an image. It is not static either: The propeller on the plane is rotating and the eyes of the fox are blinking. Your movies will probably have even more animation in them.

Figure 5.5

A simple animated movie that could use some random spots and scratches to make it look more authentic.

In addition to this background art, we will need a scratch and a spot movie clip to place on top. In the example movie, Oldfilm.fla, the scratch is a simple vertical line inside a movie clip. The spot is a small oval inside another movie clip.

Writing the Code

First, you need to write the code for the scratch. Place the scratch movie clip on the Stage and attach this ActionScript to the movie clip instance:

```
onClipEvent(load) {
    wanderAmount = 300;
    leftLimit = 10;
    rightLimit = 540;
    chanceOfJump = 50;
    xPosition = 275;
    speed = 10;
    chanceOfChange = 0;
}

onClipEvent(enterFrame) {
    xPosition += speed;
    this._x = xPosition;
    chanceOfChange++;
    if ((Math.random()*wanderAmount < chanceOfChange) or (xPosition < leftLimit)
        or (xPosition > rightLimit)) {
        speed = -speed;
        chanceOfChange = 0;
    }
    if (Math.random()*chanceOfJump == 1) {
        xPosition = Math.random()*(rightLimit-leftLimit)+leftLimit;
    }
}
```

NOTE

When you use math functions on numbers, Flash calculates the result with a specific precedence for operations: Multiplication and division are done before addition and subtraction. So 2×3+4 equals 10. If you want to force a different order of operations, you must use parentheses. For example, 2×(3+4) equals 14.

The first part of the script sets up some variables. The "leftLimit" and "rightLimit" variables are the horizontal boundaries of the line. The code won't let it go beyond these value. The "speed" variable will be used to determine how much the line moves each frame. The rest of the variables are amounts that are used to determine changes during the animation.

Every time the frame loops, the horizontal position, "xPosition" of the movie clip is changed by the "speed" variable. This will move it left or right 10 pixels. The "chanceOfChange" is incremented, and then used to determine if a change should occur. When "chanceOfChange" is 1, there is a 1 in 300 chance that there will be a change in that instant. By the time "chanceOfChange" equals 150, there is a 150 in 300, or 50% chance that there will be a change in that instant. This is a good way to manage the change so that it rarely happens right away, and also rarely waits a long time to happen.

In this case, "a change" is a reversal of direction. This is done by changing "speed" from a positive to negative number, or vice versa. This change also happens if the line hits the left or right horizontal limit.

Another type of change is determined by the "chanceOfJump" variable. This change actually repositions the line to a new location entirely. The reason for this is that real film scratches behave in this way. So, it more closely simulates reality.

The movie Oldfilm.fla shows this line effect, as well as the random spot effect we will look at next. Figure 5.6 shows what this looks like. You can see the random spots and the line over the image.

Figure 5.6
The old film effect is the line and two dots on top of a normal Flash animation.

The spots on the image are two movie clips that are constantly changing position. Basically, they use the same technique as the random location movie from earlier in this chapter. However, we will throw in a random chance of the scratch appearing at all. This chance will build from 0% to 100% just like the chances in the previous script.

```
onClipEvent(load) {
    chanceOfAppearing = 10;
    chance = 0;
}
```

```
onClipEvent(enterFrame) {
    chance++;
    if (Random(chanceOfAppearing) < chance) {
        this._x = Random(550);
        this._y = Random(400);
        chance = 0;
    } else {
        this._x = -100;
    }
}
```

When the movie clip starts, it has a 1 in 10 chance of appearing at a random spot on the Stage. If it doesn't, it has a 2 in 10 chance next time. This continues until it appears.

Loose Ends

Both of the spots and the line are best put off the Stage to the right, out of the visible area, so they are not seen when the movie starts. Then, they will appear at random times and places.

Make sure the scripts are in the right places. Remember that you don't have to rely on recreating the entire movie from the text in the book. You also have the example on the Web site. With all the different elements in the Flash movie, such as movie clip instance, script locations, and object names, I recommend that you use the example on the Web site before you try to create your own example from scratch.

The end result of this exercise is a pair of movie clips and ActionScripts that you can place in any Flash animation to give that old film effect.

Other Possibilities

You can have more spots on the screen by duplicating the spot movie clip, making sure that both copies have the same ActionScript attached to it. This means there can be as many spots on the Stage at once as you want.

You can also have two scratches on the screen. Different segments of your animation can have different numbers of scratches and spots to represent better or worse portions of film.

Letter Movement

⊕▷⊰Example movie: textfly.fla

There seems to be a lot of Flash movies out there that include text flying around in all sorts of different ways. There are many ways to accomplish effects like this, and each example on the Web probably does it a different way.

Project Goal

In this section, you will make a movie that takes a text phrase and creates a bunch of independent letters in random positions on the screen. Then, those letters fly across the screen to join together to make that phrase.

Figure 5.7 shows four screen shots of the example movie on the Web site in action. The letters come down from the top, all scrambled, and then assemble at the bottom in the correct order.

Figure 5.7

These four screen-shots show how the ActionScript anima-tion progresses.

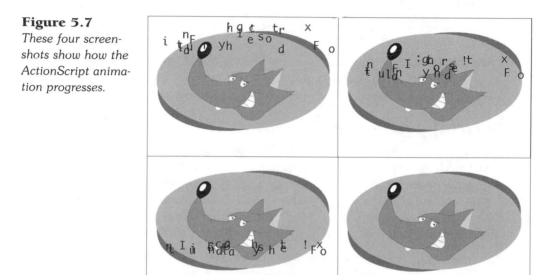

Introducing: Flashy the Fox!

Check out the Textfly.fla example movie on the Web site. In this case, it's helpful to see exactly where the following scripts belong, and how the whole movie is put together.

Approach

The approach here will be to divide the text into individual letters, each in its own movie clip. Then, these movie clips will be moved from a random location on the screen to a location that matches its position in the original text.

Preparing the Movie

The example movie includes a graphic in the middle of the screen that is completely independent of the text effect.

There is a single movie clip with the letter "A" inside it. This movie clip was created by first making a small text field. This field is set to Dynamic Text in the Text Options panel, and is assigned the variable name "letterText" in the same panel (see Figure 5.8).

Figure 5.8

In the Text Options panel, you can set a text area to Dynamic Text and assign it a variable name. This allows ActionScript to control the contents of the text.

Then the text field is converted to its own movie clip by choosing Insert, Convert To Symbol. This symbol instance is given the name "letter0" and positioned where the first letter in the phase should end up—in this case, in the lower-left corner.

Writing the Code

This program works by creating a collection of movie clips from a single movie clip. The collection is made by looping and creating a new movie clip for each letter with *duplicateMovieClip*. As each movie clip is created, the custom variables "endx" and "endy" are set in the movie clips. This is the location where the letters need to end up at the end of the animation. The "endy" variable is set to the _y location of the "Letter0" movie clip, whereas the "endx" is set to an increasing number from left to right.

The script only creates new movie clips for letters 1 and greater. The first letter, letter 0, uses the already existing "Letter0" movie clip.

```
text = "Introducing: Flashy the Fox!";
for (i=0;i<text.length;i++) {
    if (i > 0) duplicateMovieClip("Letter0","letter"+i,i);
    this["letter"+i].letterText = text.charAt(i);
    this["letter"+i].endx = this["Letter0"]._x + i*19;
    this["letter"+i].endy = this["Letter0"]._y;
}
```

> **NOTE**
>
> The *charAt* function returns the character at a specific spot in a string. The first character in a string is character 0. You can also use *substr* to get a range of characters.

NOTE

The *for* command creates a short loop. The code inside the loop executes a set number of times. The first parameter after the *for* command is used to set a variable. The second parameter is the test that should be performed before every loop to determine if the loop should continue. The third and last parameter is a command to execute every time through the loop. For instance, "for (i=0; i<text.length; i++)" means that the variable "i" should start at 0, it should increase by one every loop, and the looping should continue while "i" is less than the length of "text".

The number 19 appears at the end of the fifth line to indicate that the letters are spaced 19 pixels apart from each other. You will have to adjust this if you are using a different font or font size.

TIP

This type of effect works best when you use a monospaced font, which is a font in which each letter is the same width. Monaco, Courier, and Courier New are good examples of such fonts. If you use a variable-width font, letters such as "w" and "l" can vary greatly in width. In that case, a fixed width in your code, such as the 19 in the previous code, can cause the text to fit together strangely.

The other part of this movie is the ActionScript attached to the "Letter0" movie clip. This script starts the movie clip at a random position at the top of the screen, and gradually moves the letter to its final position a little each frame.

Because the script is attached to "Letter0", every time the preceding script duplicates it, a duplicate of the script comes along with it. So each movie clip has a copy of the same code.

The first part of this script sets "startx" and "starty" variables to a random location just above the top of the Stage area. It then sets the location of the movie clip itself to these values. Remember that "endx" and "endy" were set by the main timeline script when it created each of these movie clips. So, the movie clips now have a random starting point in "startx" and "starty", as well as a fixed end point in "endx" and "endy".

The variable "n" counts from 0 to 100 in steps of 5. This corresponds to the percent of the letter's journey that is complete. At 0, "n" signifies that the letter's position is at 0% of the end point and 100% of the start point. At 5, "n" signifies that the letter is at 5% of the end point and 95% of the start point. With each jump of 5, the letter gets 5% closer to the goal. The location is only updated if "n" is less than or equal to 100.

```
onClipEvent(load) {
    startx = Math.random()*550;
    starty = -Math.random()*100;
    this._x = startx;
    this._y = starty;
```

```
    n = 0;
}

onClipEvent(enterFrame) {
    n += 5;
    if (n <= 100) {
        this._x = endx*n/100 + startx*(100-n)/100;
        this._y = endy*n/100 + starty*(100-n)/100;
    }
}
```

Loose Ends

The position of the "letter0" movie clip determines the position of the first letter of the final text, so place it carefully and experiment with its positioning. You will also want to alter the font with care, noting that using a variable-width font could cause trouble with some letters being wider than others.

Other Possibilities

You easily can vary this script in many ways. You can have the letters start from other areas of the screen, increment "n" slower or faster, or even have the letters stack vertically instead of horizontally.

3D Illusions

Example Movies: 3d.fla, 3dcubepoints.fla, 3dcube.fla, 3dspaceship.fla

Another common Flash special effect is to simulate a small 3D object. Some developers say that Flash is not capable of real 3D, but then again, neither is any computer program because computer monitors are only 2D.

All 3D computer graphics are just illusions. Although Flash and ActionScript don't have much that can help you create 3D illusions, some special effects are still possible. By using trigonometry, you can convert 3D coordinates to 2D screen coordinates and simulate simple objects such as cubes.

Project Goal

In this section, you will learn how to convert 3D coordinates into 2D screen locations. You will then use this knowledge to make a simple 3D cube and then a more complex model. The user will be able to manipulated these models to see that they are true 3D, and not just a 2D drawing.

Approach

To learn how to use 3D coordinates, a little background in 3D mathematics in needed. This is one of the most complex sections in this book, so feel free to skip it and go on to the next chapter if learning some new math is not your idea of a good time.

Preparing the Movie

In each of the examples to follow, all that is needed are some dots and lines. Creating a dot is easy, but the line needs to fit specific specifications. More on that to follow.

Writing the Code

The following sections describe, step-by-step, one way to make 3D models come alive in Flash 5. We'll start with code to convert 3D coordinates to 2D screen locations.

Converting Coordinates

The location of objects on the Stage is represented by two coordinates: x and y. Objects in a 3D space, however, need to have x, y, and z coordinates. "z" represents depth.

To draw these objects on the Stage, you must have a function that converts x, y, and z to just a screen x and y. In addition, you will want to rotate and tilt the objects. So, the conversion function should take into account a base rotation and tilt.

Note that this is certainly the most complex script in the book so far. It is probably one of the most complex in the entire book.

The math function *Math.atan* is used to convert coordinates to an angle, and the *Math.sin* and *Math.cos* functions are used to convert angles back to coordinates. In this way, the point is converted from an x, y, and z position to an angle and distance from the center of a plane. Then the point is rotated and converted back to coordinates. This is done once for rotation and once for tilt. The result gives you x and y coordinates that can be used on the computer screen.

The comments in the following code explain what each section does. A step-by-step explanation follows.

```
   // take 3d coordinates and convert to screen location
   function plotPoint(object) {
①▶     // get coordinates from object
       x = object.x;
       y = object.y
       z = object.z;

②▶     // determine distance from center
       radius = Math.sqrt (x*x+y*y);

③▶     // compute first angle
       if (x == 0) angle = Math.atan(1000000);
```

```
        else angle = Math.atan(y/x);
        if (x < 0) angle += Math.PI;
```

(4)→
```
        // add rotation
        angle += rotation;
```

(5)→
```
        // compute new coordinates
        realx = radius*Math.cos(angle);
        realz = radius*Math.sin(angle);
        realy = z;
```

(6)→
```
        // determine new distance from center
        radius = Math.sqrt(realy*realy+realz*realz);
```

(7)→
```
        // compute second angle
        if (realz == 0) angle = Math.atan(1000000);
        else angle = Math.atan(realy/realz);
        if (realz < 0) angle += Math.PI;
```

(8)→
```
        // add angle of plane
        angle += plane;
```

(9)→
```
        // compute screen coordinates
        screenx = realx;
        screeny = radius*Math.sin(angle);
        screenz = radius*Math.cos(angle);
```

(10)→
```
        // center on screen
        screenx += 275;
        screeny += 200;
```

(11)→
```
        // return object
        return({x:screenx,y:screeny,z:screenz});
    }
```

NOTE

The *Math.atan()* function converts a line to an angle, in radians. You need to feed it the vertical difference between the start- and end points of the line, divided by the horizontal difference of the start- and end points of a line. For instance, if a line went from 200,200 to 275,250, then you would use "Math.atan(75/50)" to get the angle. The result is .9828 radians, which is about 56 degrees. Real-life use of the *Math.atan()* function is a little more complex, but this gives you the basic idea.

Here are the steps for the previous code:

① The 3D coordinates are placed in x, y, and z.

② The distance from the center of the world to the object on the xy plane is determined.

③ The angle on the xy plane is determined.

④ The amount of rotation is added to this angle.

⑤ A new x, y, and z are determined that take into account this angle change.

⑥ The distance from the center of the world to the object on the yz plane is determined.

⑦ The angle on the yz plane is determined.

⑧ The tilt of the plane is added to this angle.

⑨ A new x, y, and z are determined that take into account this tilt.

⑩ The new coordinates assume that 0, 0 is the center of the screen. So, the actual center of the screen (275,200 in this case) is added to them to correct it.

⑪ The x and y coordinates can now be used to display the object on the screen. The z coordinate can also be used to fade the color of objects that are farther from the user.

The "plotPoint" object will convert points with 3D coordinates to points with 2D coordinates using orthographic projection. This means that there is no sense of perspective, so objects that are farther away do not shrink. This works great for small objects and special effects like this one, but will not work well for large 3D scenes.

Cube Corners

Now, we will go about creating the eight corners of the cube. We'll store each point in its own small object with an x, y, and z property. The whole list of objects is stored in an array.

```
// create an array of the 8 points in a cube
function makePoints() {
    points = new Array();
    points[0] = {x: 30, y: 30, z: 30};
    points[1] = {x: -30, y: 30, z: 30};
    points[2] = {x: -30, y: -30, z: 30};
    points[3] = {x: 30, y: -30, z: 30};
    points[4] = {x: 30, y: -30, z: -30};
    points[5] = {x: 30, y: 30, z: -30};
    points[6] = {x: -30, y: 30, z: -30};
    points[7] = {x: -30, y: -30, z: -30};

    // create eight movie clips for cube corners
    for(i=0;i<points.length;i++) {
```

```
        attachMovie( "point", "point"+i, i )
    }
}
```

This function also creates eight movie clips from a clip stored in the library. Each clip is named starting with the word "point" and ending with a number from 0 to 7. This number corresponds to the point in the array that the clip represents.

NOTE

The *attachMovie* command makes a new movie clip from one stored in the library. However, for this to work in the Flash player or a Web page, you need to get the linkage property of the movie clip to Export This Symbol. Do this by going to the Library window Options menu, and choosing Linkage. You will also need to assign an identifier to the movie clip. In this case, call it "point".

Now that you have the points and a function to convert them to screen display locations, all you need is a small function that loops through the points and plots each one. In addition to setting the _x and _y properties of each point's movie clip, the _alpha property is set so that points fade a little according to their depth into the screen.

```
// loop through points and set corners of cube
function drawPoints() {
    for(i=0;i<points.length;i++) {
        loc = plotPoint(points[i]);
        this["point"+i]._x = loc.x;
        this["point"+i]._y = loc.y;
        this["point"+i]._alpha = loc.z+100;
    }
}
```

All the previous functions should be placed into the main timeline. In addition, after the functions, the following lines will set up the model and prepare the "rotation" variable.

```
// call initial functions and stop on this frame
rotation = 0;
makePoints();
stop();
```

Now, only the call to "drawPoints" remains. This is done from inside a small "reposition" function. It changes the "rotation" variable depending on whether the cursor is to the right side or left side of the screen. The function will also set the "plane" variable according to how high or low the cursor is. The function will then call "drawPoints" to set the current position of each point.

```
// reposition cube every frame
function reposition() {
    rotation += (275-_xmouse)/1000;
    plane = -(200-_ymouse)/100;
    drawPoints();
}
```

The "reposition" function is called each frame from inside another movie clip. This movie clip is an off-stage clip that exists to run this piece of code as it loops.

```
onClipEvent(enterFrame) {
    _root.reposition();
}
```

Now the movie is somewhat complete. The eight points show a cube on the screen that rotates and angles itself according to mouse movement. Check out 3dcubepoints.fla on the Web site to see it in action. Figure 5.9 shows what this looks like.

Figure 5.9
A 3D cube repre-sented by eight points on the screen. The illusion is far more complete while the movie is running, because the cube spins.

Adding Edges

Although the eight points of the cube create a nice illusion, you can go further. By adding a line for each edge of the cube, it begins to appear much more cube-like, even while not rotating.

In Flash, dynamic lines are created by making a library movie clip of a simple line. This line needs to start at the center of the movie clip and extend down and to the right. It also needs to be a hairline width and extends exactly 100 pixels horizontally and verti-cally. Figure 5.10 shows the main Flash window with such a line being created. Note that the grid is set to 50×50 pixels.

Figure 5.10

A simple line movie clip can be used to create dynamic lines on the Stage with ActionScript. The line extends exactly 100 pixels horizontally and vertically.

A cube has 12 edges, so you need 12 lines. Instead of specifying the x, y, and z coordinates of both ends of each line, you can use two of the points that are already in our "points" array. So each line has "p1" and "p2" properties.

```
/ create an array of the 12 lines in a cube
function makeLines() {
    lines = new Array();
    lines[0] = {p1: 0, p2: 1};
    lines[1] = {p1: 1, p2: 2};
    lines[2] = {p1: 2, p2: 3};
    lines[3] = {p1: 3, p2: 0};
    lines[4] = {p1: 4, p2: 5};
    lines[5] = {p1: 5, p2: 6};
    lines[6] = {p1: 6, p2: 7};
    lines[7] = {p1: 7, p2: 4};
    lines[8] = {p1: 0, p2: 5};
    lines[9] = {p1: 1, p2: 6};
    lines[10] = {p1: 2, p2: 7};
    lines[11] = {p1: 3, p2: 4};

    for(i=0;i<lines.length;i++) {
        attachMovie( "line", "line"+i, 50+i )
    }
}
```

The 12 movie clips are also created by the previous function. Each movie clip is named "linex", where "x" is the number that corresponds to the "lines" array.

In Flash, lines are dynamically drawn by setting the location of the line to the first point, and setting the scale of the line to the second. Because the line inside the movie clip starts at the center of the movie clip, setting the location sets the upper-left corner of the line to the first point. Then, because the scale the line determines the horizontal and vertical stretch of the line, setting the scale to the x and y difference between the second and first points positions the line perfectly.

For example, if you want a line from 50,80 to 170,210, you first set the location of the line to 50,80. Then, you calculate that the horizontal difference for the line is 170-50=120. The vertical difference is 210-80=130. By setting the _xscale and _yscale to 120 and 130, respectively, you get a line from 50,80 to 170,210.

CAUTION

It is crucial that the line movie clip be 100 pixels in width and height. This makes it so that a scale of 100% equals 100 pixels in width and height, a scale of 200% equals 200 pixels in width and height, and so on. The line also needs to be hairline width, so that the scaling never affects the width of the line. Any other line width, such as 1, is scaled as you use the _xscale and _yscale properties.

```
// loop through lines and set edges of cube
function drawLines() {
    for(i=0;i<lines.length;i++) {
        loc1 = plotPoint(points[lines[i].p1]);
        loc2 = plotPoint(points[lines[i].p2]);
        this["line"+i]._x = loc1.x;
        this["line"+i]._y = loc1.y;
        this["line"+i]._xscale = loc2.x-loc1.x;
        this["line"+i]._yscale = loc2.y-loc1.y;
        this["line"+i]._alpha = loc1.z+100;
    }
}
```

All that is left to do to add edges to the cube is to set call the "makeLines" function when the movie starts, and the "drawLines" function from inside the "reposition" function. Figure 5.11 shows the result. This can be found on the Web site as 3Dcube.fla.

Figure 5.11
A 3D cube is shown here with both points and lines.

Other Possibilities

You can create objects that are more complex than a cube, of course. Figure 5.12 shows a small model of a spaceship. This program, which can be found in 3Dspaceship.fla on the Web site, dispenses with the "drawPoints" function altogether, although it still uses the "points" array to define each corner so that lines can be drawn between them.

Figure 5.12
This is a simple 3D model of a spaceship; the ship rotates in the actual program.

By playing with the lists of points and lines, you can create any number of different 3D models. You can give the user control of the rotation and tilt, or have the tilt fixed, and the model rotating at a constant speed. You can even change the center point of the screen to give the illusion that the model is moving.

Toys and Gadgets

- The Magic Crystal Ball
- Music Jukebox
- Analog Clock
- Lava Lamp

Before looking at full games, you should take a look at toys and gadgets. These are not quite games, because they don't have objectives or scores, but they are full applications that can stand alone.

First, you will look at a few interactive gadgets: a magic crystal ball and a music jukebox. Then, you will look at two more complex but non-interactive movies: a clock and a lava lamp.

The Magic Crystal Ball
⊕▷⊰Example File: Crystalball.fla

Random answer prediction machines are perhaps the most common interactive gadget found on the Internet. They are usually called Magic Eight Balls, after the popular real-world Tyco toy.

Figure 6.1 shows how a gadget of this sort might look.

Figure 6.1
The fox will answer your question after you click the crystal ball.

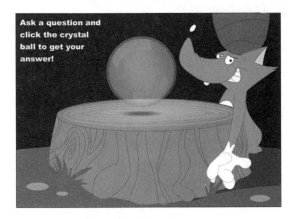

Project Goal

When the user clicks, the fox will wave his hands and invoke the crystal ball into giving an answer. The answer will be taken at random from a list of text responses.

Approach

Most of the effort going into this movie is actually the drawing and animation itself. The ActionScript is simple.

Preparing the Movie

Take a look at the animation first. There will be two stages to the movie. The first is a static frame that looks just like Figure 6.1. The movie is waiting for the user to click the crystal ball.

The only element needed to accomplish this is a simple *stop()* command placed in any layer. Figure 6.2 shows the main timeline for this movie. A little "a" in the first frame of the second "Text" layer shows that an ActionScript is attached to that frame. This is the *stop()* action.

Figure 6.2

The main timeline shows the complete crystal ball animation.

The way the main timeline is set up is completely at the discretion of the animator. In this case, the fox is broken into a main layer, and one layer for each hand. The ball is broken up into several layers as well.

It is more important to note how the animation unfolds over time. The first frame is a static frame in which no animation takes place, but text is displayed and a button is present. The text is the same text you can see in Figure 6.1. The button is actually an invisible button placed over the crystal ball.

To create an invisible button, you create a new button member, use any colored area to create the button shape, and drop it on to the main timeline in a layer near the top. At this point, the button will be visible, as it is in Figure 6.3.

Figure 6.3

The first frame of the crystal ball movie shows the central button over the crystal ball.

The desire is to have the button invisible to the user while at the same time making it an active button that can be clicked. To do this, go to the Effect panel, choose Alpha as the effect, and set it to 0%. Figure 6.4 shows this panel.

Figure 6.4
The Effect panel allows you to set the Alpha of an element to 0%, thus making it invisible.

NOTE

The Alpha effect relates to the term *alpha channel* when it comes to images. A graphic image is said to have four channels: red, green, blue, and alpha. The first three channels determine the color of a pixel. The last channel determines its transparency. When the alpha channel is 0, the pixel is completely transparent. Setting the Alpha of a Flash element to 0 will make that element completely transparent.

Even though the button is completely transparent, Flash still considers it to be on the Stage. Thus, the button is 100% active and will respond to mouse clicks. This is one way to make an invisible button. Another way is detailed in the "Memory Game" in Chapter 14, "Brain Puzzles."

When the user clicks the button, the movie jumps to frame 2 and continues playing. This will play out the rest of the animation until the end of the movie.

From frames 2 to 22 you can see that the hands animate with a little bit of tweening. At frame 20, the "Ball Effect" layer animates, creating a flash inside the ball. The actual movie can be seen on the Web site in the file Crystalball.fla.

The most important change in the time span of the animation is the appearance of a second text area in frame 23. This is the text area that will hold the answer to the user's question. The text in it will be set when the button is first clicked, but the text will not become visible until frame 23.

So, the movie consists of one frame at the beginning that waits for user input, and then a series of frames that animates, showing the text midway. When the animation is done, the movie loops back to the first frame to await the next question.

Writing the Code

The actual "magic" for this movie is all done in the ActionScript for the button. You've already learned that it will jump the movie to frame two and get it animating. That's the last thing it actually does. Before that, it will generate the answer and place it in the text area.

Because it is a button that activates the response, you need to place all the code in a button event. This always starts with *on* and then specifies the event. The most commonly used event is *release*.

First, the script creates an array and fills it with a list of responses. There are many ways to do this. One way would look like this:

```
responses = new Array("Yes", "No", "Ask again later","It is certain",
"Doubtful", "Probably", "The answer is unclear","Of course not!","Certainly!",
"It looks positive", "It looks negative");
```

This is the most compact way of declaring the array and filling it at the same time. However, it is a bit messy as the text runs off the right side of the screen. Here is another way of doing it:

```
responses = new Array();
responses[0] = "Yes";
responses[1] = "No";
responses[2] = "Ask again later";
responses[3] = "It is certain";
responses[4] = "It is certain";
responses[5] = "Doubtful";
responses[6] = "Probably";
responses[7] = "The answer is unclear";
responses[8] = "Of course not!";
responses[9] = "Certainly!";
responses[10] = "It looks positive";
responses[11] = "It looks negative";
```

This way is a lot neater, because each answer is on its own line. It is much easier to see what is there. However, you have to individually enter each element number in the brackets. Make a mistake and you might miss a possible answer, or leave a space blank. But there is yet another way to do this, which is even better:

```
responses = new Array();
responses.push("Yes");
responses.push("No");
responses.push("Ask again later");
responses.push("It is certain");
responses.push("Doubtful");
responses.push("Probably");
responses.push("The answer is unclear");
responses.push("Of course not!");
responses.push("Certainly!");
responses.push("It looks positive");
responses.push("It looks negative");
```

By using *push*, each answer is added to the array one after the other. It looks neat and is easy to see on the screen, plus it's easy to add new answers or remove answers.

> **NOTE**
>
> A quick and easy way to add an element to the end of an array is to use *push*. You can actually add more than one element by including more than one parameter to *push*. You can also use it as a function at the same time, because it returns the new length of the array. For instance *newLengthOfArray = myArray.push("Gary", "Debby")*.

After an array has been filled with potential responses, all that is needed is to pick one at random. You can get the number of items in an array with the *length* property of an array. Then, you can use the *Math.random* function to choose a random number that fits a random element in the array. You can read more about the *Math.random* function in the "Randomness and the Old Film Effect" section in Chapter 5, "ActionScript Design Effects."

After you have a random number, you can use it to set the text in a text area. Remember to set up the text area as a Dynamic Text, with a variable name, in this case "fortune." You can see how the Text Options panel should look in Figure 6.5.

Figure 6.5

This Text Options panel specifies that the text area is dynamic and linked to the variable "fortune."

Here is the complete code for the button. After the text has been set, the movie jumps to frame 2, which begins the animation. The text area actually doesn't appear until frame 23.

```
on (release) {
    // make list of possible responses
    responses = new Array();
    responses.push("Yes");
    responses.push("No");
    responses.push("Ask again later");
    responses.push("It is certain");
    responses.push("Doubtful");
    responses.push("Probably");
    responses.push("The answer is unclear");
    responses.push("Of course not!");
    responses.push("Certainly!");
```

```
responses.push("It looks positive");
responses.push("It looks negative");

// get number of responses
n = responses.length;

// pick random response
r = Int(Math.random()*n);

// place response in text area
fortune = responses[r];

// start animation
gotoAndPlay(2);
}
```

NOTE

The two commands that you will use to move around in a Flash movie are *gotoAndPlay* and *gotoAndStop*. The main difference is that the second command will jump the movie or movie clip to the specified frame or label, but it will not trigger any code in that frame, nor will it continue to advance any animation. The *gotoAndPlay* command, on the other hand, will run any code in that frame and keep the animation going. If you want to run any code in that frame, but not advance to the next, then use *gotoAndPlay*, but include a *stop* command in that frame.

When the animation is complete, the text appears in the middle of the crystal ball. Figure 6.6 shows what the screen now looks like.

Figure 6.6
At the end of the animation, the answer appears for a few seconds before the movie loops back to the beginning.

Loose Ends

You might want to place a *stop()* at the end of the animation so that the movie does not loop. You could place another button there to allow the movie to jump back to frame 1 if the player wants to ask another question.

Other Possibilities

It is easy to go into the code and change the list of possible responses. You don't even have to follow the positive/negative/undecided model used here. Instead, you can customize it to a particular subject, such as whether the local sports team will win today or what the weather will be like.

Music Jukebox

Example File: Jukebox.fla

Adding sound to Web pages has never been straightforward. Either you need to use obscure HTML tags that work on only one browser, or you need to use one of many plug-ins, none of which ever caught on as the standard. However, if you are using Flash anyway, you might as well leave all the sound playing up to your Flash.

Project Goal

An obvious way to demonstrate Flash's music-playing capability is to build a jukebox. This is just a simple movie that will play some songs.

Figure 6.7 shows the jukebox. It contains up to 10 different songs. A song can be played by clicking its selection box.

Figure 6.7

The jukebox is reminiscent of the type found at each table in a diner from the 1950s.

Approach

It's tempting, when building a movie like this, to create 10 different buttons, with 10 different pieces of code in each, to play the 10 different songs. This would work, but it would be hard to build and harder to modify.

A better way is to create 1 button and use it 10 times, once for each of the songs. Each "button" will actually be a movie clip with a button inside it. There will be only 1 movie clip and 1 button in the entire movie library. This one movie clip will be placed on the Stage 10 times, each of those being identical.

When the movie runs, the first thing that will happen is that the text for each movie clip instance will be changed. This is done with this piece of code:

```
// set the song names
this["1"].text = "Song Name 1";
this["2"].text = "Song Name 2";
this["3"].text = "Song Name 3";
this["4"].text = "Song Name 4";
this["5"].text = "Song Name 5";
this["6"].text = "Song Name 6";
this["7"].text = "Song Name 7";
this["8"].text = "Song Name 8";
this["9"].text = "Song Name 9";
this["10"].text = "Song Name 10";
```

The movie clips are all named "1" to "10" just to make things simple. After the above code runs, each movie clip instance displays a different song name. So even though there is one movie clip in the library, each instance now looks different.

Not only that, but the names of all 10 songs are in a single script. Had there been 1 song name in each movie clip, you would have to do quite a bit of work to open and close each movie clip to make 10 changes. This way, you can quickly change all 10 song names.

The other piece of code that helps keep the number of movie clips to 1, is the one attached to the button inside the movie clip.

```
on (release) {
    _root.playSong(this._name);
}
```

This one line of code takes the name of the movie clip, which could be anything from "1" to "10", and sends it to a "playSong" function at the root level. This same piece of code can be used in every movie clip because it uses the name of the movie clip instance, which will be different in each case. As long as you remember to change the instance name every time you create a new instance of the movie clip, this code will get a different result for *this._name*.

The result of using this code is that you can make only one movie clip and use it as many times as you want in the movie. Now if changes are needed to the movie clip, either graphical or functional, you only need to make those changes one time. In addition, the final .swf file will be smaller than one that had 10 copies of a similar movie clip in the library.

Preparing the Movie

After you have your 10 movie clips in place and your songs titled by the ActionScript of the first frame in the main timeline, you just need to add the sound.

Star by importing the 10 songs and naming those library items "song1" to "song10". After each is imported, you must change the Linkage property of each sound so that it is included when an .swf is made. You need to change it to Export this Symbol and include an identifier for each song. Figure 6.8 shows this dialog box. You can get to it by going to the Library window and choosing Linkage in its Options menu.

Figure 6.8

The Symbol Linkage Properties dialog box allows you to include sounds with the .swf file even when they are not in any timeline.

Unfortunately, there is no way to use true external sound files for the sounds. The only way to make a jukebox like this is to import all the songs and set their Linkage properties so that they are included with the .swf file. Perhaps in future versions of Flash, you will be able to access external files and play them.

Writing the Code

The code to play a sound is simple, but unfortunately not as simple as it should be. Instead of a single command to tell a sound to play, you need to have three lines. The first creates a sound object. The second associates a sound from the library to the object. The third tells the sound to play.

```
song = new Sound();
song.attachSound("song1");
song.start();
```

The "playSong" function must do a little more than this, however. First, it must tell any previous song to stop. The *stop* command will do that. Assume that a previous song is playing, and that it is still assigned to the global variable "song." Here is a simple version of the function:

```
function playSong(songnum) {
    // stop the previous song, if any
    song.stop();

    // play new sound
    song = new Sound();
    song.attachSound("song"+songnum);
    song.start();
}
```

One special effect to add is a light behind the selections on the jukebox. The selection movie clip is set up to have two frames: the first with the light off, and the second with the light on. You can see the light on in Figure 6.9.

Figure 6.9
The jukebox is playing song 2.

When each song begins, you should make sure that all the lights are off, and then turn on only the light behind the proper selection:

```
function playSong(songnum) {
    // stop the previous song, if any
    song.stop();

    // turn off all lights
    for(i=1;i<=10;i++) {
        this[i].gotoAndStop(1);
    }

    // play new sound
    song = new Sound();
    song.attachSound("song"+songnum);
    song.start();
```

```
    // turn light on
    this[songnum].gotoAndStop(2);
  }
```

Check out jukebox.fla on the Web site to see how all the pieces fit together.

Other Possibilities

The scripts in this section work pretty independently of the jukebox design. You could create something that looks like a floor model jukebox, or something that looks completely unlike a jukebox. You could even create a jukebox with multiple "screens" representing different song banks. Forward and Back buttons could be used to go frame to frame where different songs are listed.

Analog Clock

Example File: Simpleclock.fla
Example File: Betterclock.fla

One of Flash 5's new capabilities is its ability to use ActionScript to get the user's computer's time and date. This is done by using the Date object. Although there are many uses for this, you can tackle a simple one here by building an animated analog clock.

Project Goal

This clock should take the user's computer's time and display it like a wall clock or wristwatch. It should have hour, minute, and second hands. The hands should use any movie clip, not just a simple line, so that odd and interesting clocks can be created.

Approach

To learn how to make a clock, you will first need to learn how to use the Date object. This is where you will get the current time to display.

Using the Date Object

Think of a Date object as a small array that holds several pieces of information about a moment in time. When you create a Date object, it captures the current time, according to the user's computer.

CAUTION

Remember that relying on the date and time on a user's computer to be correct can be a bad idea. You would be surprised how many people have their clocks set to the wrong time. However, I usually don't hesitate to use their clock anyway, especially for gadgets and games. These people will probably have bigger problems than your Flash movie showing the wrong time, such as all their email being sent with the wrong time stamp.

The elements in a Date object include the date, month, year, hour, minute, and second. To get any of these, all you need to do is use the proper function, such as *getDate()*. The following handler shows all the functions you can use to get information from a Date object:

```
on (release) {
    now = new Date();

    trace("toString:" + now.toString());

    trace("getDate:" + now.getDate());
    trace("getDay:" + now.getDay());
    trace("getFullYear:" + now.getFullYear());
    trace("getHours:" + now.getHours());
    trace("getMilliseconds:" + now.getMilliseconds());
    trace("getMinutes:" + now.getMinutes());
    trace("getMonth:" + now.getMonth());
    trace("getSeconds:" + now.getSeconds());
    trace("getTime:" + now.getTime());
    trace("getTimezoneOffset:" + now.getTimezoneOffset());
    trace("getYear:" + now.getYear());

    trace("getUTCDate:" + now.getUTCDate());
    trace("getUTCDay:" + now.getUTCDay());
    trace("getUTCFullYear:" + now.getUTCFullYear());
    trace("getUTCHours:" + now.getUTCHours());
    trace("getUTCMilliseconds:" + now.getUTCMilliseconds());
    trace("getUTCMinutes:" + now.getUTCMinutes());
    trace("getUTCMonth:" + now.getUTCMonth());
    trace("getUTCSeconds:" + now.getUTCSeconds());
}
```

There are a few things to note about the various functions. All the "UTC" functions rely on the user having his system properly configured with the correct time zone. The number of hours is added or subtracted to get universal time. The *getTime* result is the number of milliseconds since January 1, 1970. The "day" is a number from 0 to 6 representing the day of the week. The month is a number from 0 to 11. However, the date is a number from 1 to 31. This might be hard to understand and remember, but it is not unique to Flash; other programming languages, such as C and JavaScript, are the same way.

Here's the result of all these `trace` commands:

```
toString:Sat Oct 14 18:47:06 GMT-0600 2000
getDate:14
getDay:6
getFullYear:2000
getHours:18
```

```
getMilliseconds:0
getMinutes:44
getMonth:9
getSeconds:7
getTime:971570647000
getTimezoneOffset:360
getYear:100
getUTCDate:15
getUTCDay:0
getUTCFullYear:2000
getUTCHours:0
getUTCMilliseconds:0
getUTCMinutes:44
getUTCMonth:9
getUTCSeconds:7
```

You can also set any portion of a Date object. Each "get" function has a matching "set" function. So, for instance, to set the hour, use *setHour(newHour)*. Note that this will change the Date object only, but not the user's system clock. The next time you create a fresh Date object, it will match the system clock.

Preparing the Movie

One cool thing that can be created with the Date object is a clock. By translating the hour, minute, and second of the current time to degrees, you can set the *_rotation* property of three different movie clips to look just like the hands of a clock.

Figure 6.10 shows what this clock might look like. The shorter arm represents the hour, the longer arm represents the minute, and the tail is the second hand.

Figure 6.10
The clock shows 9:20 and 35 seconds.

What you can't see in Figure 6.10 is that the hands (and tail) of the clock move just like a real clock. This is accomplished in three steps. First the current time is read and placed into "hour", "minute", and "second" variables. Next, these numbers are converted into angles. Then, these angles are used to set the *_rotation* property of the three movie clips that represent the arms and tail.

Writing the Code

The code that does all this is an *onClipEvent (enterFrame)* script that is placed in an otherwise unused movie clip, as shown here. You can see exactly how that is set up by checking out Simpleclock.fla on the Web site.

```
onClipEvent (enterFrame) {
    // get current time
    now = new Date();
    hour = now.getHours();
    minute = now.getMinutes();
    second = now.getSeconds();
    // convert to 12-hour clock
    if (hour > 12) {
        hour -= 12;
    }

    // determine angle of hands
    hourAngle = 360*hour/12;
    minuteAngle = 360*minute/60
    secondAngle = 360*second/60;

    // set angles of hands
    _root["hour hand"]._rotation = hourAngle;
    _root["minute hand"]._rotation = minuteAngle;
    _root["second hand"]._rotation = secondAngle;
}
```

The time is converted to angles by dividing it by the highest value and multiplying by 360. For instance, the minutes are divided by 60, giving a value between 0 and 1, and then multiplied by 360, giving a value between 0 and 360. Also note that 12 is subtracted from the hour so that it is a 12-hour clock rather than a 24-hour one.

The result of each operation is an angle from 0 to 360. 0 represents 0 (or 12) hours, 0 minutes, or 0 seconds. This corresponds to a hand on the clock being straight up, or at 0 degrees. This being the case, the three movie clips that represent the hands of the clock should be drawn pointing straight up, as in Figure 6.11. Then, when the *rotation* is set, the hand points to the proper place.

Figure 6.11
The hands (and tail) of the clock should be drawn straight up to represent 12:00:00. Then, when the _rotation of the hands is set, they will point to the right place.

A problem with the code so far is that the clock does not operate completely like a normal clock or watch. For instance, the hour hand in Figure 6.10 is pointing at 9 o'clock. It will continue pointing at 9, even when it is 9:59, then it will instantly change to 10 at 10:00.

A real clock, however, will move the hour hand gradually throughout the hour, eventually getting to 10 at 10:00. You need to add a slight amount to the angle of the hour hand for each minute, and a slight amount to the angle of the minute hand for every second. Here is a piece of code that does this:

```
// add fractions of hour and minutes
hourAngle += minute/2;
minuteAngle += second/10;
```

The minute is divided by 2, which gives you 30 additional degrees for every hour. The second is divided by 10, which gives you 6 additional degrees for every second. Do the math: At 9:59, the angle will be 9*30 + 59/2 = 270 + 29.5 = 299.5. At 10:00, the angle will be 10*30 + 0/2 = 300 + 0 = 300.

Likewise, for the minute hand, at 20 minutes and 59 seconds, the angle will be 20*6 + 59/10 = 120 + 5.9 = 125.9. After one more second, the angle will be 21*6 + 0/10 = 126 + 0 = 126.

Figure 6.12 shows the clock with this piece of code inserted. Compare it carefully to Figure 6.10 to see that the hour and minute hands are a little more accurate.

Figure 6.12
This clock has new code to make the hour and minute hands more accurate.

The Betterclock.fla file has this extra bit of code in it to smooth out the hand movements. Note that you can actually see the minute hand move slightly as the time changes.

Other Possibilities

Of course, you can substitute anything you want for the clock hands. It can be as simple as lines, or as complex as your own character. You can also color up the rest of the clock with numbers or background images.

One fun possibility would be to create a clock that runs backward. You can see this sort of novelty clock in stores and restaurants sometimes. You can also add a chime sound to be played when the hands strike the hour or every 15 minutes.

Lava Lamp

Example File: Lavalamp.fla

The last movie in this chapter recreates the classic lava lamp. There are many lava lamp-like things on computers and the Web. Most of these are simply animations. You could make a great lava lamp animation with Flash and not need to have one piece of code.

However, that sort of defeats the purpose of a lava lamp. You are supposed to be able to stare at it for hours and never see the same pattern repeat. With an animated lava lamp, the pattern must repeat when the full length of the animation runs out.

Project Goal

In this section, you will create a truly random lava lamp. This means that the code must decide when and where new bubbles appear. The result will be a lava lamp that never repeats itself.

Approach

To create a truly random lava lamp, you need to use ActionScript. You will create 20 movie clips that represent bubbles in the lava lamp. Then, you will continuously call a function that moves the bubbles up and down the screen. Figure 6.13 shows what the lava lamp will look like.

Figure 6.13
The lava lamp is made up of a top and bottom, a transparent glass piece, and red bubbles.

Preparing the Movie

The graphics for the lava lamp movie need to be created with care. For instance, the bubbles themselves are filled circles with no stroke and a radial fill. The fill, however, is not a usual one. It is between a solid red and a transparent red. The transparent red is created by setting the Alpha of the color to 0%. Figure 6.14 shows the movie clip, plus the Fill and Mixer panels displaying the settings for the red to transparent red gradient.

Figure 6.14

The Fill panel shows a fill between a solid red and a transparent red. The Mixer panel shows the transparent red, which is obtained by setting the Alpha to 0.

Writing the Code

The lava lamp will use 20 movie clips created from a single library clip. The *attachMovie* command will be used to bring these instances into the movie. To read more about the *attachMovie* command, see the "3D Illusions" section in Chapter 5.

When the movie begins, the first and only frame in the timeline will execute the "initLamp" function. This will not only create the 20 bubble clips, but also an array full of objects that will represent the speed of each bubble.

In addition to the bubbles, the movie will have an opaque top and bottom that will hide the bubbles as they rise from the bottom or descend from the top. There will also be a semitransparent glass graphic that should go on top of the bubbles.

This brings about a problem. When the *attachMovie* or *duplicateMovieClip* command is used, you must specify the level for the new movie clip. This level is used to determine which elements the clip is in front of and which elements the chip is behind. Because these are new movie clips, they will all be in front of existing movie clips. That means the bubbles will be in front of the top, bottom, and glass graphics. You can use the *duplicateMovieClip* command to create new instances of these three graphics that will be on top of all the bubbles.

Here is the "initLamp" function:

```
function initLamp () {
    // present and remember top and bottom
    top = 0;
    bottom = 300;

    // generate movie clips for bubbles
    numBubbles = 20;
    for (i=0; i<numBubbles; i++) {
        attachMovie("bubble", "Bubble"+i, i);
    }

    // duplicate top, bottom, and glass so they are above bubbles
    duplicateMovieClip("Glass", "Glass", i++);
    duplicateMovieClip("Top", "Top", i++);
    duplicateMovieClip("Bottom", "Bottom", i++);

    // generate objects for bubbles
    bubbles = new Array();
    for (i=0; i<numBubbles; i++) {
        bubbles[i] = {speed:0};
    }
}
```

NOTE

You can create quick little objects by just using brackets as shown in the last line of the "initLamp" function: "bubbles[i]= {speed:0}." You can then refer to the contents of this object with dot syntax such as "bubbles[0].speed". This makes your code more readable, and also allows you to have more than one piece of information as a single element in a variable or array. For instance, you could use "myObject = {speed: 6, weight: 40, clipname: "clip1"}" and then use syntax such as "myObject.speed" to get the values.

After all the elements are ready, the movie works off the principle that a function will be called every so often to update the position of the bubbles and create new ones. An off-screen movie clip will call the "moveBubbles" function on *every enterFrame* clip event.

The "moveBubbles" function will move bubbles either up or down, stopping them at the top or bottom. It will also, based on a 1 in 30 chance, call "newBubble" to create a new bubble.

```
// move all existing bubbles
function moveBubbles () {
    for (i=0; i<numBubbles; i++) {
        // get current location
        y = _root["Bubble"+i]._y;
        // stop if at bottom
```

```
        if ((bubbles[i].speed > 0) and (y > bottom)) {
            bubbles[i].speed = 0;
        // stop if at top
        } else if ((bubbles[i].speed < 0) and (y < top)) {
            bubbles[i].speed = 0;
        // keep moving
        } else {
            // move
            _root["Bubble"+i]._y  = y+bubbles[i].speed;
            // shape
            height = _root["Bubble"+i]._yscale;
            width = _root["Bubble"+i]._xscale;
            if (height > width) height -= 1;
            _root["Bubble"+i]._yscale = height;
        }
    }


    // 1 in 30 chance of a new bubble
    if (Math.random()*30 <= 1) {
        newBubble();
    }
}
```

The "newBubble" function will search through the "bubbles" array to find a bubble that is not in use. It will then start the bubble from either the top or bottom. The size of the bubble will also be set by a random number. It will always be three times longer than it is wide. This difference will slowly close as the bubble moves.

```
function newBubble () {
    for (i=0; i<numBubbles; i++) {
        // find an unused bubble
        if (bubbles[i].speed == 0) {
            // start it at the top
            if (Math.random() < .5) {
                bubbles[i].speed = 1;
                _root["Bubble"+i]._y = -40;
            // start it at the bottom
            } else {
                bubbles[i].speed = -1;
                _root["Bubble"+i]._y = 340;
            }
            // shape it
            size = 40+ Math.random()*40;
            _root["Bubble"+i]._xscale = size;
            _root["Bubble"+i]._yscale = size*3;
            _root["Bubble"+i]._x = 10+Math.random()*80;
            // done
```

```
        break;
    }
  }
}
```

These three functions make up the heart of the lava lamp movie. To see how it all comes together, check out Lavalamp.fla on the Web site.

Loose Ends

The glass graphic was created with alpha transparency in a similar fashion as the bubbles so that the bubbles will show through. You might want to spruce up the exterior of the lava lamp with a label or logo to make it fit your site or project.

7

Construction Toys

- Drag-and-Drop Games
- Click-and-Switch Games
- Sketchbook
- Music Mixer

In this chapter, you'll take a look at Flash movies that allow the user to create things. These types of toys appeal to the creative side of users. There are no goals or score, just infinite possibilities.

First, you'll make a program that allows users to build an image from various parts. Making something like this as a computer program can be done in a number of ways. On the one hand, you can allow the user to drag and drop pieces onto a fixed body. Another way is to fix the position of the pieces, but allow the user to change the shape of each one.

Next, you'll make a program that allows the user to draw lines and shapes on a canvas. Finally, switching from the visual to the aural, you'll make a program that allows the user to build a song from various music pieces.

Drag-and-Drop Make-A-Fox

⊕▷⊱**Example File: Makeafox-drag.fla**

Many computer toys and games have origins in precomputer era toys. One of these old toys is the Mister Potato Head. This was a collection of plastic body parts that kids could stick on a potato and make a funny-looking person. Later, the potato was replaced with a plastic body.

Project Goal

The goal here is to create an application in which the user can drag and drop pieces of a fox onto a fixed body to create their own fox. The drag and drop must be very natural for anyone accustomed to using other computer programs.

Approach

The program needs to recognize when the mouse button is pressed and when it is released. It will need to decide which movie clip the cursor is over and allow that movie clip to be dragged throughout the duration of the mouse action.

This is not as easy as it sounds. To determine which movie clip the user clicked, you have to compare the location of the click with the area of each movie clip.

Preparing the Movie

To create a drag-and-drop construction toy, you first need to make various graphics pieces. Figure 7.1 shows the main body to the right, and various arms, legs, mouths, and eyes to the left.

Figure 7.1
The pieces on the left are moveable and can be dragged to the body on the right.

You can find the sample movie on the Web site by looking at Makeafox-drag.fla. Click any piece to the left and you can drag it around the screen to any position.

Writing the Code

If you have done a little work with Flash before, you might recognize that this should be easy—just make the pieces movie clips and use the *startDrag* and *endDrag* commands, right? This will actually make things complex. I'm not a fan of the *startDrag* command, and will not use it here. One reason is that you cannot easily use it to click and drag something around the Stage.

If you make each piece a button, then you can place an *on(press)* function on it and issue a *startDrag* command. However, you cannot specify the button as a target of the *startDrag* command because it must be a movie clip for that. If you make it a movie clip, then you cannot have an *on(press)* function attached to it, as that is only for buttons. Instead, you must make each piece a movie clip with a button inside the movie clip. This can be a mess. Any time you want to add a new part to the movie, there are several steps to follow.

A better way to do this is to write the drag-and-drop code yourself. This will involve no code at all on the individual pieces, making them easy to create and add.

The only code needed is on a movie clip that exists only to hold this code. You can see it in the example movie as a clip beyond the upper-left corner of the movie with the text "Actions" placed in it.

This movie clip will have an ActionScript attached to it that controls dragging for all the pieces. To do this, it needs to have several *onClipEvent* functions. Here is a run-down of what each must do:

- *load*—Set a variable to indicate that no dragging is going on yet.
- *mouseDown*—Identify which piece has been clicked and set a variable to indicate that this piece is now being dragged. Also, get the offset between the place the user clicked and the center of the piece.

- ***mouseUp***—Reset the variable to indicate that no piece is being dragged.
- ***enterFrame***—Change the position of the piece being dragged to correspond to the cursor position minus the offset.

There are two things in the previous list that might confuse nonprogrammers. The first is the recurring mention of a variable. This variable will be called "dragPart" in the code and will be set to 0 at the start. When it is set to 0, no dragging is taking place. However, when the user clicks a piece, "dragPart" will be set to the number of that piece. When it is set to a number, dragging takes place. When the user drops that piece, the variable is set to 0 again.

The other complex feature of this code will be the offset. When a user clicks a piece, chances are he will not click the center of it. For example, the user might click the spot 10 pixels to the right and 5 pixels below the center. When the code starts repositioning the piece as the user drags, it could attempt to set the position of the piece to the exact position of the cursor.

However, if the user did not click the center of the piece, the piece would appear to immediately jump so that the center of the piece is directly under the cursor. But if you subtract the 10 horizontal pixels and 5 vertical pixels from the position, then the piece will not jump at all. In fact, it will appear as if the user has grabbed the piece at the exact spot that he clicked it.

Now, take a look at each part of this ActionScript. First comes the *onClipEvent(load)*. This simply needs to initialize the "dragPart" variable.

```
// start with nothing dragging
onClipEvent (load) {
    dragPart = 0;
}
```

The *onClipEvent(mouseDown)* is the most complex piece of code. It will loop through all 13 pieces and use *hitTest* to determine which one the cursor is over. It will then set the "dragPart" variable as well as the "offsetx" and "offsety" variables.

Note that the movie clips that contain the pieces are named "Part1" to "Part13" to make this code simple.

```
// start drag
onClipEvent (mouseDown) {
    // get current location
    x = _root._xmouse;
    y = _root._ymouse;

    // find which, if any, part the cursor is over
    for(i=1;i<=13;i++) {
        if (_root["Part"+i].hitTest(x,y, true)) {
```

```
            // set to drag this part, remember offset
            dragPart = i;
             offsetx = _root["Part"+i]._x - x;
             offsety = _root["Part"+i]._y - y;
            break;
        }
    }
}
```

NOTE

Instead of getting the *_xmouse* and *_ymouse* properties, the code above uses
_root._xmouse and *_root._ymouse*. This is because the basic properties will return the
x and y position of the cursor relative to the movie clip, not the Stage. So, unless your
movie clip happens to be at the exact upper-left corner, the values will not be what you
want. Adding *_root* before these properties forces ActionScript to give you the mouse
position relative to the Stage.

When the user releases the mouse button, the "dragPart" variable is set back to 0.

```
// end drag
onClipEvent (mouseUp) {
    dragPart = 0;
}
```

The workhorse of this ActionScript is the *onClipEvent(enterFrame)* function. It tests
"dragPart" to make sure it is not 0, and then resets the position of the part being
dragged to the current mouse position plus the offset.

```
// if dragging, set new position
onClipEvent (enterFrame) {
    if (dragPart > 0) {
        _root["Part"+dragPart]._x = _root._xmouse + offsetx;
        _root["Part"+dragPart]._y = _root._ymouse + offsety;
    }
}
```

In the example movie, graphics, as opposed to movie clips, are used in the library.
However, when each movable part is placed on the Stage, the behavior of each element
is changed to "Movie Clip" and then named. Figure 7.2 shows the Instance panel with
these settings. You can see that the library name is "Arm 1", but the instance name is
"Part1". You can also see by the icon next to "Arm 1" that the library item is a graphic,
but its behavior has been changed to that of a movie clip. With these settings, as far as
the Flash movie is concerned, it is a movie clip named "Part1".

Figure 7.2
The Instance panel allows you to make Flash treat graphic elements as movie clips with names different from the names used in the library.

The layering of each element was adjusted appropriately as well. You can do this by choosing Modify, Arrange with an item selected. All the parts were made to float on top of the stationary head and body, except the legs, which would be behind them. This is the way the artist intended them to be used.

Figure 7.3 shows a sample use of this movie. A handful of items have been moved by the user from the left to the right to create one version of the fox.

Figure 7.3
The Make-A-Fox movie allows the user to drag fox parts around the screen.

Click-and-Switch Make-A-Fox

Example File: Makeafox-switch.fla

Another type of image construction program is one that keeps all the parts in the same position but allows the user to switch parts. This is a "Click-and-Switch" version of the previous example. No dragging is used at all, just clicks.

Project Goal

The image would start off complete, but the user could click a part and it would swap itself out with another version of that part. For instance, the user could click the eyes, and a different set of eyes would appear.

Approach

To do this, the movie library would have to be arranged differently. Instead of individual graphics for each version of each part, there would be movie clips. In each movie clip would be every version of that part, one per frame. For instance, the "Eyes" movie clip would have three frames, each with a different version of the eyes.

Writing the Code

Because no dragging and dropping are needed here, the script is a little simpler. It is just a *onClipEvent(mouseDown)* script placed on an "Actions" movie clip that is off the Stage. This script will search for the movie clip that was clicked in the same way that the Makeafox-drag.fla movie did, with *hitTest*.

However, instead of using names such as "Part1" to "Part13" for the movie clips, names such as "Eyes" and "Head" are used. To make sure that the script checks all these movie clips, they are specified in a list and the code loops through each element in that list.

When the appropriate movie clip is found, the code will advance it one frame. If this takes it beyond the number of frames available in the movie clip, it loops back to frame 1.

```
onClipEvent (mouseDown) {
    // get current location
    x = _root._xmouse;
    y = _root._ymouse;

    // see if this is over any parts
    list = ["Eyes", "Mouth", "Head", "Legs", "Left Arm", "Right Arm", "Body"];
    for(i=0;i<list.length;i++) {
        if (_root[list[i]].hitTest(x, y, true)) {
            // over a part
            with (_root[list[i]]) {
                // go to next frame or loop back to first frame
                if (_currentFrame == _totalframes) {
                    gotoAndStop(1);
                } else {
                    nextFrame();
                }
            }
            break;
        }
    }
}
```

NOTE

The _currentFrame and _totalFrames properties of a movie clip return the values you would expect. They are particularly useful in situations like this where there could be any number of frames in the movie clip and you want your code to handle all variations.

NOTE

The *with* action will allow you to specify that you want the code to consider all commands and functions inside it to act as if they apply to a specific movie clip. This saves you from having to specify _root[movieClip] for each command or function.

The Makeafox-switch.fla movie on the Web site shows this code in action. Figure 7.4 shows one possible outcome of the user's clicks. Note that no matter how many times and in what combination the user clicks, the fox will always appear whole and intact.

Figure 7.4
The user can click any single part to change it.

Loose Ends

There are a few details about the Makeafox-switch.fla that are needed to bring it together. First, there must be a *stop()* command in the first frame of every movie clip. This is to prevent it from just animating through all the variations when the movie is first run. There is also the matter of placing each movie clip on the Stage and naming each instance to match the items in the list in the script.

Other Possibilities

This type of program can be adapted for almost any object. For instance, you could have a car where the user can swap out tires and accessories. You could also just center in on the face to allow the player to swap eyes, noses, ears, mouths, hair, and so on. This could make a good cosmetics game.

Sketchbook

⊕⊳⊰Example File: Drawing-justline.fla
⊕⊳⊰Example File: Drawing-full.fla

Although the previous two examples allow for a lot of creativity, they do not allow the user to create just anything. Now, you'll see a drawing program that starts users with a blank canvas and allows them to draw anything they want.

Project Goal

The goal of this section is to create a program that allows users to draw like they would in a simple paint application. They should be able to paint lines and some simple shapes. They should also be able to select from a variety of colors.

Creating a Simple Drawing Program

Although the final movie will allow the user to draw with different shapes and colors, you'll start out by just allowing the user to draw a continuous line.

This is done with only two movie clips. The first is a large white rectangle that will be the drawing canvas. The second is a hairline-width line exactly 100 pixels by 100 pixels. This line is the same element used in the 3D example in Chapter 5, "ActionScript Design Effects." By using a 100×100 line, you can set the location and scale of the line and precisely control its placement on the Stage.

The ActionScript will be placed on the canvas movie clip. When the user presses the mouse button down, a variable called "draw" will be set to true. This will then be used in the *onClipEvent(enterFrame)* function to draw a line. When the user lifts up the mouse button, "draw" is set to false again.

```
// init variables
onClipEvent (load) {
    // drawing or not?
    draw = false;

    // increment shapeNum every time to use as name and level
    shapeNum = 0;
}

onClipEvent (mouseDown) {
    // remember starting spot
    startx = _xmouse;
    starty = _ymouse;

    // ok to draw
    draw = true;
}
```

```
onClipEvent (mouseUp) {
    // stop drawing lines
    draw = false;
}
```

NOTE

The ActionScript constants *true* and *false* can be used by *if* and *for* commands to determine whether to execute code. You can also use them as values in your variables to represent on and off states.

The work is actually done by the *onClipEvent(enterFrame)* function. The function reads the current location of the mouse and then determines whether that is at least one pixel away from the previous location of the mouse, stored in the "startx" and "starty" variables.

If the mouse has moved, a new movie clip is added using the *attachMovie* command. For this to work, the shape has to be present and properly set up in the library for export. You have done this for several previous examples.

The location and scale of this movie clip are set so that the line stretches perfectly between the two locations. The variable "shapeNum" is incremented each time this happens so that each new movie clip has a different name and level.

```
onClipEvent (enterFrame) {
    if (draw) {
        newx = _xmouse;
        newy = _ymouse;
        dx = startx-newx;
        dy = starty-newy;

        // only draw if cursor moved
        if (Math.sqrt ( dx*dx + dy*dy ) > 1.0) {
            this.attachMovie("Line", "Shape"+shapeNum, shapeNum);
            this["Shape"+shapeNum]._xscale = dx;
            this["Shape"+shapeNum]._yscale = dy;
            this["Shape"+shapeNum]._x = newx;
            this["Shape"+shapeNum]._y = newy;
            shapeNum++;
            startx = newx;
            starty = newy;
        }

    }
}
```

Figure 7.5 shows this movie after the user has clicked and dragged the mouse around a bit. Note that the drawing takes place only as fast as the frame rate of the movie, so you want to set it to a maximum of 120 frames per second to make the drawing as smooth as possible. You can see this movie on the Web site as Drawing-justline.fla.

Figure 7.5

The simple drawing program allows the user to draw a long black curve.

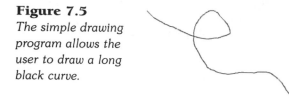

Creating a Complete Drawing Program

Although the previous program demonstrates some advanced ActionScript, it does not make a very exciting toy. You can add some other shapes and colors to the program.

First, go in an update the previous ActionScript to support ovals, rectangles, and colors. To this end, you will add the variables "shapeType" and "brushColor". The *onClipEvent(load)* needs to be changed to initialize them.

```
// init variables
onClipEvent (load) {
    // drawing or not?
    draw = false;

    // increment shapeNum every time to use as name and level
    shapeNum = 0;

    // what shape is being drawn
    shapeType = "line";

    // set brush color
    brushColor = {rb: 0, bb: 0, gb: 0};
}
```

When the user clicks down, the "startx" and "starty" variables are set, as before. However, if the "shapeType" is an "oval" or "rect", then the new shape is instantly added as a movie clip. The position of the shape is also set, with the scale being left up to the *onMovieClip(enterFrame)* function. At this point, the user is actually dragging to define the size of the shape.

```
onClipEvent (mouseDown) {
    // remember starting spot
    startx = _xmouse;
    starty = _ymouse;
```

```
// make sure that this is inside canvas
if (this.hitTest(startx+this._x,starty+this._y,false)) {
    // ok to draw
    draw = true;

    // start drawing an oval or rect
    if ((shapeType == "oval")  or (shapeType == "rect")) {
        this.attachMovie(shapeType, "Shape"+shapeNum, shapeNum);
        this["Shape"+shapeNum]._x = startx;
        this["Shape"+shapeNum]._y = starty;
    }
}
}
```

The *onClipEvent(mouseDown)* function also checks to see whether the user clicked within the canvas movie clip before starting the draw. This new piece of code will encourage users to draw only within the canvas, although Flash will automatically expand the boundaries of the movie clip if the user drags a line or shape over the edge.

When the mouse button is lifted, there also needs to be some special code for handling the shapes. A new shape is created every time the mouse button is pressed, so somewhere along the way the "shapeNum" needs to be incremented. With the drawing of the line, a new line is added every frame, so "shapeNum" is incremented every frame. With ovals and rectangles, however, a single shape is added when the user clicks, and this shape is resized as the user drags. So the "shapeNum" is incremented when the shape is complete.

```
onClipEvent (mouseUp) {
    // stop drawing lines
    if (shapeType == "line") {
        draw = false;

    // stop drawing the oval or rectangle
    } else if ((shapeType == "oval") or (shapeType == "rect")) {
        shapeNum++;
        draw = false;
    }
}
```

The workhorse here, as before, is the *onMovieClip(enterFrame)* function. You will recognize the following code to draw the continuous line. In addition, there is code to set the scale of an oval or rectangle if that is what is being drawn. Another element added in the following code is the color being set for the current shape. This is done with the same commands from the "Color Cycling Spiral" section in Chapter 5.

```
onClipEvent (enterFrame) {
    if (draw) {
        // draw a new line
        if (shapeType == "line") {
            newx = _xmouse;
            newy = _ymouse;
            dx = startx-newx;
            dy = starty-newy;

            // only draw if cursor moved
            if (Math.sqrt ( dx*dx + dy*dy ) > 1.0) {
                this.attachMovie("Line", "Shape"+shapeNum, shapeNum);
                this["Shape"+shapeNum]._xscale = dx;
                this["Shape"+shapeNum]._yscale = dy;
                this["Shape"+shapeNum]._x = newx;
                this["Shape"+shapeNum]._y = newy;
                myColor = new Color(this["Shape"+shapeNum]);
                myColor.setTransform(brushColor);
                shapeNum++;
                startx = newx;
                starty = newy;
            }

        // update drawing of oval or rectangle
        } else if ((shapeType == "oval") or (shapeType == "rect")) {
            newx = _xmouse;
            newy = _ymouse;
            dx = newx-startx;
            dy = newy-starty;
            this["Shape"+shapeNum]._xscale = dx;
            this["Shape"+shapeNum]._yscale = dy;
            myColor = new Color(this["Shape"+shapeNum]);
            myColor.setTransform(brushColor);
        }
    }
}
```

Now that the main ActionScript can handle different shapes and colors, all that is needed is a way for the user to select which shape and color she wants to use. Figure 7.6 shows the new movie, called Drawing-full.fla on the Web site. You can see a series of buttons on the left side of the screen that allow the user to select color and shape.

Figure 7.6
*The buttons on the
left allow the user
to select the color
and shape to draw.*

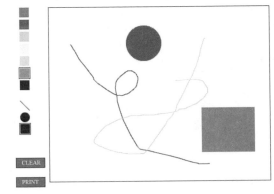

Each of the color buttons is made from a single movie clip. When the clip is placed on the Stage, the Effects panel is used to tint it. In addition, there is a button inside the movie clip that reacts to the user's clicks. Here is the code in that button. It will take the color tint of the movie clip and store it in the "brushColor" variable.

```
on (release) {
    // get color
    myColor = new Color(this);

    // set global color
    _root.Canvas.brushColor = myColor.getTransform();

    // set the selection box
    _root["Color Selection"]._x = this._x;
    _root["Color Selection"]._y = this._y;
}
```

The button script also sets the "Color Selection" movie clip, a simple square box, to the location of the clip that was clicked. This causes the color button to be outlined the same way that the black color button is in Figure 7.6 (shown previously).

The shape buttons work in a similar way. Each shape button is made from a single movie clip in the library. Each of the three instances of this button are named for the shape: "line", "oval", and "rect". The actual shape icon you see on the Stage is a completely separate graphic that has no script at all—it's just cosmetic.

The code in the button inside the shape button movie clip takes the name of the movie clip and stores it in the "shapeType" variable. It also places the "Shape Selection" box around the new shape button.

```
on (release) {
    // set the shape
    _root.Canvas.shapeType = this._name;
```

```
    // set the selection box
    _root["Shape Selection"]._x = this._x;
    _root["Shape Selection"]._y = this._y;
}
```

When you run the Drawing-full.fla movie, try clicking the shapes and colors. The selection box for each will follow your clicks. The drawing will then reflect those selections.

Adding Clear and Print Buttons

The lines and shapes for the drawing program are actually made of different movie clips. These clips are being added, one after the other, as the user draws. The number of the next clip to be drawn is stored in the "shapeNum" variable.

This makes it easy to add a clear button. All you need to do is loop from 0 to the last movie clip created, remove that movie clip, and then set "shapeNum" back to 0.

```
on (release) {
    // loop and delete all shapes
    for(i=0;i<_root["Canvas"].shapeNum;i++) {
        Canvas["Shape"+i].removeMovieClip();
    }

    // reset the shapeNum
    _root["Canvas"].shapeNum = 0;
}
```

The print button is even easier. All you need to do here is issue the *print* command with the name of the movie clip to be printed.

```
on (release) {
    // send a simple print instruction
    print("Canvas","bframe");

}
```

NOTE

The *print* command will send the movie clip you specify to the user's operating system to be printed. You can specify _root to print the entire Stage. The second parameter defines the bounding box for the print area. See the manuals for more details on that.

Figure 7.7 shows the movie in use. It would be nice to allow the users to save their creations, but that would require some complex code to link to either your server or JavaScript. The print option is a simple alternative.

Figure 7.7
The sketch program is shown after being used by an artist.

Other Possibilities

This program can continue to be expanded by adding more colors and more shapes. In addition to colors and shapes, you can also add the option to draw filled or hollow shapes. This could be done by providing hairline-thin hollow movie clips instead of filled ones.

You could also add a white color to the palette so the user can draw in white, effectively erasing what is already there.

Music Mixer

Example File: Musicmixer.fla

Graphics are not the only things that can be constructed with Flash. You can also play several sounds together to create a mix of music. You can allow users to choose which pieces of music they want to play and when.

Project Goal

This project creates a toy that will allow users to mix various drum loops, bass loops, and single-instance sounds to create their own songs. It should be easy to swap sound samples in and out of the program. It should also provide some feedback to the user about which samples are playing. Figure 7.8 shows what this application might look like.

Figure 7.8
This music mixer is made up of six drum loops, six bass loops, and six instance sounds.

Approach

You will use six drum loops, six bass loops, and six single-instance sounds. Only one drum loop should be playing at a time, so when the user selects a second drum loop, it needs to turn off the first. Multiple bass loops can be played at the same time. Single-instance sounds do not loop, but simply play once when selected.

There will be three different sets of switches. The first will represent the drum loops. Turn one on, and any one previously on will automatically turn off. The second set will represent bass loops, you can turn one, several, or all of them on at the same time. Pressing a button that represents a drum or bass loop when it is already on will turn it off.

The third set of buttons will play a single-instance sound. They will turn on only for a short period of time, while the sound plays. Whereas the drum and bass loops will loop forever, single-instance sounds play only once per button press.

Preparing the Movie

The main element here is the 18 sounds needed. The example movie on the Web site, Musicmixer.fla, used sounds created by a professional composer. You will need to compose the sounds yourself, find a friend or co-worker to help, or license some music from elsewhere.

The drum and bass loops are short sounds that create perfect loops. They should be short enough that the file size does not become huge, but long enough so that the loop produces interesting sounds.

After you import all 18 sounds into Flash, you must set their Symbol Linkage Properties to Export This Symbol, and the Identifier to something the code will understand. Figure 7.9 shows this dialog box.

Figure 7.9

The Symbol Linkage Properties of this sound have been set so the sound will be included with the Flash movie.

There need to be three different types of buttons created. These are actually not buttons, but movie clips. So to avoid confusion, this book calls them "switches." Inside the movie clips are invisible buttons that react to mouse clicks. The movie clips themselves have at least two frames. The first represents the "off" state of the switch, whereas the rest of the frames are an animation representing the "on" state. Because the drum and bass sounds are loops, the animation loops in those two switches, although it plays once and then goes back to the "off" state in the instance sound switch. Check out the Musicmixer.fla movie on the Web site to see what the animation sequences consist of.

The buttons in the movie clips are just plain white shapes that will be placed behind the other graphics in the movie clip so they are not visible. For the example movie, a small circular button was created to be placed in the drum and bass switches, and a triangular one was created to be used by the instance switches. Only two different types were used so they would be easier to hide behind the shape of the graphics for each one. Six copies of each of the switches are placed on the Stage. Arrangement can be anything you want. The arrangement was kept simple in the example movie, which looks like Figure 7.8.

Writing the Code

All the code is attached to the buttons inside the switches. The first frame of every switch contains code to start the sound. In addition, this code will also advance the movie clip to the next frame. The button also appears in the rest of the frames of the movie clip. For the drum and bass loops, different scripts will stop the sound.

The simplest ActionScript is the one in the instance sound switches. All these scripts need to do is start a sound playing and go to the next frame.

```
on (press) {
    // play the sound that matches
    // the name of this movie clip
    instanceSound = new Sound();
    instanceSound.attachSound(this._name);
    instanceSound.start();

    // start this movie clip animating
    gotoAndPlay(2);
}
```

Notice that the name of the sound is specified as *this._name*. This will take the name of the movie clip and use it as the name of the sound. So if the movie clip is "instance 1", it will attempt to play the sound "instance 1". The first "instance 1" is the name of a movie clip instance on the Stage, the second "instance 1" is the name of a linked sound in the library. This will work as long as you take special care to make sure these names match exactly.

The advantage of doing it this way is that you can use the same movie clip many times on the Stage, with each one playing a different sound. The sound name is taken from the movie clip instance name, not from a hard-coded string inside the ActionScript.

When the movie clip advances to the next frame, an animation begins. At the end of the animation, the movie clip will loop back to the first frame, where a *stop()* command will prevent it from looping.

For the single-instance sounds, the same button appears across all frames, so the user can trigger another sound even if the animation is currently playing.

The bass loop switch movie clips are almost the same as the single-instance sounds. The main difference is that the sound must loop. This is done by adding an extra two parameters to the *start* command. The first is the sound offset and the second is the number of loops. Because you don't want a sound offset, leave that at 0. But you do want the sound to loop, so set that to a very high number.

```
on (press) {
    // play the sound that matches
    // the name of this movie clip
    bassloop = new Sound();
    bassloop.attachSound(this._name);
    bassloop.start(0,9999);

    // start this movie clip animating
    gotoAndPlay(2);
}
```

The other difference between the single-instance sounds and the bass loops is that you can turn a bass loop off. To do this, there will be a different ActionScript on the button inside the bass loop switch for frames 2 and on. This will turn off the sound and send the movie clip back to frame 1.

```
on (press) {
    // stop the sound with the
    // same name as this movie clip
    bassloop = new Sound();
    bassloop.stop(this._name);

    // turn this animation off
    gotoAndStop(1);
}
```

The button scripts for the drum loop are just a bit more complex. When you turn a drum loop on, it must make sure that all the other drum loops are off. To do this, it loops from "drum loop 1" to "drum loop 6" and turns each sound off. It will also set each switch movie clip back to frame 1. After that, it starts the new drum loop sound.

```
on (press) {
    // stop any other drum sound
    // and set any other drum switch to off
    drumloop = new Sound();
    for(i=1;i<=6;i++) {
        _root["drum loop "+i].gotoAndStop(1);
        drumloop.stop("drum loop "+i);
    }

    // play the sound that matches
    // the name of this movie clip
    drumloop.attachSound(this._name);
    drumloop.start(0,9999);
```

```
    // start this movie clip animating
    gotoAndPlay(2);
}
```

The other button code for a drum loop is the same as it was for a bass loop. It just turns off the sound and sends the movie clip back to frame 1.

```
on (press) {
    // stop the sound with the
    // same name as this movie clip
    drumloop = new Sound();
    drumloop.stop(this._name);

    // stop this animation
    gotoAndStop(1);
}
```

Loose Ends

Remember to name each of the 18 buttons something different and match the name to that of a linked sound in the library. Even if the sound is named in the library, you also have to have it in the Symbol Linkage Properties dialog box (refer to Figure 7.9).

The animations for each button type are up to you. In the example movie, I simply have it flashing from white to black for the drum loops, an expanding circle for the bass loops, and three expanding lines for the single-instance sounds. The drum and bass loops need to have a *gotoAndPlay(2)* command in the last frame so that they will loop. The single-instance sounds can just be left to finish and return to frame 1. All these movie clips need to have a *stop()* command on frame 1 so they don't start animating when the movie is first loaded.

Other Possibilities

Swapping out the sounds for your own is an easy modification, as long as you have sounds. Just delete the old sounds from the library and import your own. Remember to set the Symbol Linkage Properties.

You can also have more or less sounds. You might want to have fewer drum loops, but more single-instance sounds. As long as the instance names of the movie clips match the link names of the sounds in the library, you can have as few or as many sounds as you want.

The animation inside each switch can also be varied. If you have a lot of time to animate, you might want to abandon the idea of reusable movie clips and have a different clip for each switch. This will make it harder to modify the movie in the future, but allow you to have an individual animation for each switch.

Hunt and Click Games

- Find-A-Fox
- Whack-A-Fox
- Shoot-A-Fox

Perhaps the simplest and most common game on the Web is the type in which a player is expected to click a target and score points. This type of game varies in difficulty depending upon how the target moves, if at all.

In this chapter, you will look at three major variations of the hunt and click game, the first is a game in which the targets don't move but are instead hidden in a complex picture. This is a little like the popular series of books *Where's Waldo?* We will hide images of the fox in a drawing of trees and such.

In the second game, the foxes will not always be on the screen. Instead they will appear and disappear at random times. This is similar to the Whack-A-Mole game.

In the third game of this series, the foxes will run, jump, duck, and hide in complex animations. Players must try much harder to hit the foxes. A game like this is usually called a shooting gallery.

These three games are similar because the player's main action is to click a target. The only difference is how the target moves, if at all. However, this minor difference is enough to create games that seem to be completely different to the player.

We'll start with the simplest game, which I've called Find-A-Fox.

Find-A-Fox

⊕▷⋉Example file: Findafox.fla

The Find-A-Fox game presents an image to the player and asks him to locate certain objects in it. In the case of the example movie, Findafox.fla, the scene is a forest and the objects the player is looking for are foxes.

This sounds like an easy game, but the idea is that the objects are supposed to be cleverly disguised and hidden. Figure 8.1 shows the example movie with seven foxes hidden in the forest.

Figure 8.1
The forest scene includes seven hidden foxes for the player to find.

Project Goal

When the player finds a fox in the picture, she should click it to select the fox. When this happens, there should be some feedback to let the player know that she guessed right. There also needs to be a way to let the player know which foxes have been found.

When all seven foxes have been discovered, the game should automatically go to a new screen. This means that the program needs to keep track of what has been found and what has not.

Approach

It might seem that this game would be ridiculously simple to create. In fact, it would be nothing more than a few buttons if it weren't for two factors: You want feedback concerning which objects have been found, and you want the game to recognize when all the objects have been found.

The feedback feature can be accomplished by applying a color transformation to the object movie clips. If done with the right color, the hidden foxes will stand out.

To determine whether all the foxes have been found, we'll use an array of true and false values. The array will start with seven false values, and each one will change to true as the player finds the foxes. When all seven values in the array are true, it means that the player has found all the foxes.

Instead of using buttons, we'll use movie clips plus an ActionScript control clip that looks for mouse clicks. When a mouse click is detected, the code will loop through all the movie clips using *hitTest* to determine which one was clicked. This is similar to how the Make-A-Fox game in Chapter 7, "Construction Toys," determines which movie clip was clicked.

Preparing the Movie

Most of the effort to make this game actually involves drawing the background scene. In the example movie on the Web site, there are nine layers of graphics that make up the ground, trees, and other forest elements. Different things are on different layers to allow some of the foxes to be partially hidden behind trees and such.

Two movie clips are foxes. One uses thin lines so the fox can be hidden in tree bark. The other is a solid-shaped fox that can appear in the background. You can see these two movie clips in Figure 8.2. These two clips are placed several times each onto the Stage. They are in one of four different layers, positioned so they are behind some layers and in front of others.

Figure 8.2

Here are two movie clips used to hide foxes among the trees. The appropriate one is used depending on the background behind the fox.

In addition to the main frame where the game is played, we'll fill out this game with a start screen and an end screen. Both of these will have a button to allow the player to start the game.

The code will all be attached to a movie clip that is just off the Stage. This code will assume that the fox movie clips are named "fox0" to "fox6".

Writing the Code

When the movie clip loads, all the movie clip needs to do to start is set up the "found" array. The code fills the array with seven *false* values:

```
onClipEvent (load) {
    // create array to keep track of
    // which ones found
    found = [];
    for (i=0; i<7; i++) {
        found[i] = false;
    }
}
```

When the player clicks, the location is recorded in the variables "x" and "y". Then, these values are checked against the fox movie clips using *hitTest*. When a match is found, the color of the movie clip is transformed to a red tint. This is enough to make the hidden foxes stand out from the background.

After every click, the "found" array is searched for a *false* value. This would indicate that there is at least one fox not yet found. However, if all the foxes have been found, then the movie will be sent to another frame:

```
onClipEvent (mouseDown) {
    // record location of click
    x = _root._xmouse;
    y = _root._ymouse;

    // loop through all foxes to see if any hit
    for (i=0; i<7; i++) {
```

```
        if (_root["fox"+i].hitTest(x, y, false)) {
            // change color of fox
            myColor = new Color(_root["fox"+i]);
            myColor.setTransform({rb:128, bb:0, gb:0});
            // record that this one was found
            found[i] = true;
            break;
        }
    }

    // see if all foxes found
    gameover = true;
    for (i=0; i<7; i++) {
        if (found[i] == false) {
            // this fox not found, game not over
            gameover = false;
        }
    }

    // go to end frame if all foxes found
    if (gameover) {
        _root.gotoAndPlay("Game Over");
    }
}
```

NOTE

The *break* command can be used inside *for* loops and other types of loops to tell the code to break off the loop instantly. This comes in handy when there is more than one reason why the loop might end. In the previous code, the loop goes from 0 to 6, but it could also end if the *hitTest* returns *true*.

Loose Ends

The only other code in the game are the two "Play" buttons, one on the start screen and one on the end screen. In addition, there is a *stop()* command on all the frames so that the movie does not advance to the next frame.

The choice of the color transformation for the found foxes depends on your background. In this example, the background has a lot of greens, browns, and blues. I chose a medium red for the found foxes to contrast these colors.

Other Possibilities

The example described here is nothing more than a game for young children. However, the concept can be used for more sophisticated games.

For older children, you could have a math game in which they have to find certain types of numbers or words. For instance, they could have to pick the verbs out of an assortment of verbs, nouns, and adjectives. You could also do a geography quiz in which the player has to pick out certain countries or locations.

Whack-A-Fox

Example file: Whackafox.fla

One of the earliest arcade games was called Whack-A-Mole. This was a physical game, not a computerized one. There were holes in a platform through which appeared little mole-like objects. You used a soft mallet, usually tied to the machine, to hit the moles. They appeared in a random order at random times, so you had to be quick to hit them.

Whack-A-Mole games also appear in many forms on computers. They are very popular on the Web. Although they rarely look like a Whack-A-Mole game, the functionality is the same: Objects appear at random times and at random places and the player has to click them before they disappear.

In this example, found on the Web site as Whackafox.fla, you'll look at a more tradition implementation of this game. Figure 8.3 shows the play area: a log with 18 holes. At different times, a fox will pop up out of one of those holes and remain there for a second or so. Clicking the fox will result in a "hit" animation and the player will score points.

Figure 8.3
The Whack-A-Fox game features a log with 18 holes. The fox could pop out from any one of them.

Project Goal

The game requires that the objects appear at random times and places. We'll have 18 holes through which a fox can pop out. After the fox appears, it quickly disappears again. This is an animation, part of which can be seen in Figure 8.4. However, while the fox is visible, the player can click it to "hit" it and score points.

Figure 8.4
One of the foxes has come out of a hole.

The game should run for a limited amount of time and keep track of how many objects the player hit.

Approach

Each hole in the log will be the instance of a movie clip. This clip can be just a hole at times, and can also show an animation of the fox popping up out of the hole.

Another movie clip, called "actions," will signal the hole movie clips when it is their turn to act at regular time intervals. At first, the foxes will pop up every 2 seconds. With each appearance, the time until the next fox will decrease slightly.

When the player clicks the screen, the "actions" movie clip will determine which fox was clicked. That movie clip will be told to play another animation that will show the fox a bit dazed.

Every time a fox appears, a counter will increase by one. Every time a player hits a fox, another counter will increase by one. The score will then be displayed as the number hit, then a "/", and then the number that have appeared. In other words, "5/12" means that the player hit 5 out of 12 foxes.

Preparing the Movie

The 18 holes in the log are actually instances of a movie clip. The movie clip features a frame 1 that is just a hole. Later in that movie clip's timeline is an animation sequence that adds the fox popping out of the hole, hesitating, and then going back in. There is another sequence in the movie clip that shows the fox getting hit and then seeing stars. We'll use this one when the player gets the fox. You can see a part of it in Figure 8.5.

Figure 8.5
This fox has just been hit.

The 18 movie clip instances will be named "fox 0" to "fox 17" so the code can identify them. There will also need to be a text area set to "Dynamic Text" and named "showScore". Figure 8.6 shows the Text Options panel for this text area.

Figure 8.6
The Text Options panel shows a text area set to be linked to the ActionScript variable "showScore".

Writing the Code

All the code for this game lies in the script attached to our "actions" movie clip that sits just off the Stage. It begins by initializing all the global variables. The time for the appearance of the first fox is set for 2 seconds, or 2000 milliseconds, from the start of the movie.

```
onClipEvent (load) {
    // how much time between fox appearances
    timeBetweenFoxes = 2000;

    // calculate time until next fox
    nextFox = getTimer() + timeBetweenFoxes;
```

```
    // init scores
    score = 0;
    numFoxes = 0;
}
```

NOTE

The *getTimer()* function returns the number of milliseconds since the Flash movie
began. This clock constantly counts upward, so this is a good function to use to add
time intervals to your games.

The task of the *onClipEvent(enterFrame)* function is to determine whether it's time for
a new fox to appear. If so, a new hole is picked that is not already in use. The time gap
between fox appearances is shortened by 10 milliseconds, causing the game to get faster
and faster as time goes on. If the gap is less than 1,000 milliseconds, the game ends.
This will give the player 100 opportunities to hit a fox, spread out over 150 seconds.

```
onClipEvent (enterFrame) {
    // see if it is time for the next fox
    if (getTimer() >= nextFox) {

        // shorter wait next time
        timeBetweenFoxes -= 10;

        // see if the game is over
        if (timeBetweenFoxes < 1000) {
            _root.gotoAndPlay("End");

        // new fox
        } else {

            // increase count and update score
            numFoxes++;
            _root.showScore = score + "/" + numFoxes;

            // loop until a fox is found that is
            // not in use
            while (true) {
                fox = Int(Math.Random()*18);
                if (_root["fox "+fox]._currentFrame == 1) break;
            }

            // tell fox to pop up
            _root["fox "+fox].gotoAndPlay("popup");
```

```
            // set time for next fox to appear
            nextFox = getTimer() + timeBetweenFoxes;
        }
    }
}
```

The next function handles the player clicks. It uses the same technique as the Find-A-Fox game by looping through all the movie clips and using *hitTest* to determine the correct one.

The function also has to make sure that the fox is animating through the pop-up sequence at the time of the click. Frame 1 of the movie clip is the static frame of just a hole. Frames 2 through 24 are the animation of the fox getting hit. Frame 25 and on are the pop up animation that is the only time that the player should be able to click the fox. Therefore, if the frame number is more than 24, the click is allowed. Otherwise, it is ignored.

```
onClipEvent (mouseDown) {
    // get the location of the click
    x = _root._xmouse;
    y = _root._ymouse;

    // loop through all 18 foxes to see which was clicked
    for (i=0;i<18;i++) {

        // only look at clips that are doing the
        // pop up animation
        if (_root["fox "+i]._currentFrame > 24) {

            // see if this was the one clicked
            if (_root["fox "+i].hitTest(x,y,false)) {

                // have the clip play the "whack" animation
                _root["fox "+i].gotoAndPlay("whack");

                // increase score and show it
                score++;
                _root.showScore = score + "/" + numFoxes;
            }
        }
    }
}
```

Loose Ends

As usual, you need a few extra scripts here and there. Small *stop()* commands need to be placed on the main game frame, as well as a start frame and end frame. In the example movie, these are in three different scenes.

Other Possibilities

Note that all the movie clips in this game do not have to use the same movie clip. The script only cares if there are "whack" and "popup" labels and that the pop-up animation starts after frame 24. You could conceivably make several different movie clips to use, each with a slightly different fox. Just make sure they are similar enough for the code to handle and that the movie clip instances are named properly when you place them on the Stage. This would add some variety to the game.

The end of the game can be determined in many different ways. The example movie waits until the time delay between foxes is less than a second. This corresponds to 100 foxes. You could, instead, use a fixed number of clicks by the player to determine the end of a game. You could also have levels. The player might need to get a certain number of hits in a level to be allowed to advance to the next.

Shoot-A-Fox

⊕▷<**Example file: Shootafox.fla**

Next comes the ultimate hunt-and-click game: the shooting gallery. Like the first game in this chapter, Find-A-Fox, the goal is to click objects on the screen. Like the second game, Whack-A-Fox, the objects will appear on the screen at random times and places.

However, in this game the objects will move. Instead of the fox merely popping up out of a hole, he will run, swing, or peek out from behind a tree. The player must have quick reflexes to catch a fox before he disappears again.

Figure 8.7 shows the scene, which is much like the scene for Find-A-Fox. However, this time the fox won't be standing still waiting for the player to discover him. The figure shows one of the animations in which the fox is dashing from side to side.

Figure 8.7

In the Shoot-A-Fox game, the fox will move around the screen, making him harder to hit.

Project Goal

This project builds on the Whack-A-Fox game. It features foxes that run through a whole animation sequence that could take them from one part of the screen to another. We'll have one animation that shows the fox running from place to place, one that shows him swinging from a tree, and one that shows him peeking out from behind a tree. Each animation will be used two or three times, for a total of seven possible sequences that can occur during the game.

Every two seconds or less, one of these animation sequences will be triggered and the player will have a chance to click and hit the fox. The animation sequence should continue, but there should be some indication of a hit, if there is one.

The game should keep track of how many shots were fired and how many hits there were, and then limit the player to a certain number of shots. The cursor should look like a gun crosshairs, rather than just a plain arrow cursor.

Approach

To create this game, I started with Whack-A-Fox, so a lot of this code should look familiar. However, there are some major improvements and feature additions.

The first change is the way that the movie clips are arranged. They need to animate to show movement, and also change to show that they have been hit. This calls for a movie clip inside a movie clip. The inner clip can be switched between not-hit and hit states. The outer clip dictates the movement of the fox.

This game will keep track of both the shots taken, and the hits. Both of these numbers will be displayed on the screen for the player to see. When the player has used up all his shots, the game ends.

Another improvement in this game will be the use of a custom cursor. We'll actually hide the computer's cursor when it is over the game, and replace it with a movie clip that floats above the scene. You can see this cursor as the crosshairs at the bottom of Figure 8.7.

Preparing the Movie

The trickiest part of creating this game is making the movie clips. Unfortunately, this is also difficult to explain here. I strongly recommend taking a look at the example movie, Shootafox.fla on the Web site now.

In the library, you will see three movie clips: "Peeking Fox", "Running Fox", and "Swinging Fox." Each of these features either a single frame or short animation of the fox, followed be a short animation that has the fox looking surprised and outlined in yellow. The first part is for the normal animations, whereas the second part shows that the player has hit the fox. The second part starts with the frame label "hit".

There are also seven movie clips labeled "fox0" to "fox6". These clips contain one of the previous three movie clips, but are animated so that they move across the screen or peek out from behind a tree. The inner clips in each of these movie clips are all labeled "fox" so the code can address them. When the code needs to show that a fox has been hit, it tells the movie clip instance "fox" inside the movie clip instance "fox0" to "fox6" to go to frame "hit".

The layers in this movie play a big part. There are 15 layers that represent either scenery or foxes. This allows the foxes to appear behind some items and in front of others. There is also a layer for the "actions" movie clip and the "cursor" movie clip.

The cursor is a movie clip of some crosshairs. Past frame one is a short animation of a blast that will play whenever the player takes shot. The movie clip will loop back to frame 1 which has a *stop()* command.

Like the other two movies in this chapter, this one will have a "start" scene, a "play" scene, and an "end" scene.

Writing the Code

The "actions" movie clip contains most of the code as it did in the previous example. It starts with the *onClipEvent(load)* function. In addition to setting the score to 0, it will also set the "shotsLeft" to 50, giving the player 50 shots to hit as many foxes as he can. In addition to "showScore" being used to relay the score to the screen, a variable called "showShotsLeft" will link to a text area to show the player how many shots remain.

The *onClipEvent(load)* code also hides the mouse with the *Mouse.hide()* command.

NOTE

The *Mouse* object allows you to control the visibility of the cursor while it is over the Flash movie Stage. You can use *Mouse.hide()* to make the cursor invisible, and *Mouse.show()* to make it visible again.

```
onClipEvent (load) {
    // how much time between fox appearances
    timeBetweenFoxes = 2000;

    // calculate time until next fox
    nextFox = getTimer()+timeBetweenFoxes;

    // init scores
    score = 0;
    shotsLeft = 50;
    _root.showScore = "Score:"+score;
    _root.showShotsLeft = "Shots Left:"+shotsLeft;

    // hide cursor
    Mouse.hide();
}
```

Because the real cursor is hidden, you need to replace it with something to indicate to the player where she is clicking. In this case, a movie clip called "cursor" will be set to the mouse location.

Besides this, the *onClipEvent(enterFrame)* function is the same as in the Whack-A-Fox game.

```
onClipEvent (enterFrame) {
    // set the cursor
    _root["cursor"]._x = _root._xmouse;
    _root["cursor"]._y = _root._ymouse;

    // see if it is time for the next fox
    if (getTimer()>=nextFox) {

        // shorter wait next time
        timeBetweenFoxes -= 5;

        // see if the game is over
        if (shotsLeft < 1) {
            _root.gotoAndPlay("End");

        // new fox
        } else {

            // loop until a fox is found that is
            // not in use
            while (true) {
                fox = int(Math.Random()*7);
                if (_root["fox"+fox]._currentFrame == 1) {
                    break;
                }
            }

            // tell fox to move
            _root["fox"+fox].gotoAndPlay(2);

            // set time for next fox to appear
            nextFox = getTimer()+timeBetweenFoxes;
        }
    }
}
```

The *onClipEvent(mouseDown)* function needs to take into account some of the improvements in the Shoot-A-Fox game over the Whack-A-Fox game. First, it will use the "cursor" movie clip location as the click spot, not the actual mouse location, which might have changed slightly since the frame updated.

Then, it searches through the seven movie clips to find one that might have been hit. If one has, the "fox" movie clip inside that movie clip is told to play the "hit" animation. The "score" variable is incremented if there is a hit, and the "shotsLeft" variable is incremented in either case.

The game ends when the *onClipEvent(enterFrame)* function attempts to move a new fox, and discovers that the player is out of shots. This prevents the movie from ending the instant that the last shot is fired, but rather delays the end for about a second or so.

```
onClipEvent (mouseDown) {
    // show blast
    _root["cursor"].gotoAndPlay("blast");

    // get the location of the click
    x = _root._root["cursor"]._x;
    y = _root._root["cursor"]._y;

    // loop through all 18 foxes to see which was clicked
    for (i=0; i<7; i++) {

        // only look at clips that are doing the
        // pop up animation
        if (_root["fox"+i]["fox"]._currentFrame <= 1) {

            // see if this was the one clicked
            if (_root["fox"+i].hitTest(x, y, false)) {

                // have the clip play the "hit" animation
                _root["fox"+i].fox.gotoAndPlay("hit");

                // increase score and show it
                score++;
            }
        }
    }

    // take away one shot
    shotsLeft--;

    // update score
    _root.showScore = "Score:"+score;
    _root.showShotsLeft = "Shots Left:"+shotsLeft;
}
```

This code also advances the cursor movie clip to the "blast" frame, which shows a yellow blast for a few frames and then returns to frame 1. Even if the player misses a fox, she at least has some feedback that a shot was fired.

A new function here, *onClipEvent(unload)*, runs when the movie clip is about to disappear from the Stage. This will happen when the game is over. In this case, all it does is make the cursor visible again.

```
onClipEvent (unload) {
    // game over, so return cursor to normal
    Mouse.show();
}
```

Loose Ends

After all the code is in place, the movie clip instances need to be named "fox0" to "fox6" to match their library names exactly. The example movie is built so that all fox animations assume that the center of the movie clip is at the center of the Stage. This was done by adding the animation to the main timeline, selecting the animation sequence, choosing Edit, Copy Frames, and pasting these frames into a blank movie clip. Check the example movie on the Web site to see how it all fits together.

Other Possibilities

The gameplay can be altered in many ways. There can be a timer, rather than a set number of shots. You can build levels that the player attains by getting a certain number of shots in a simple round.

Note that in this game it is possible to score more than 50 points. How? Well, if you wait long enough, the foxes appear pretty rapidly. Soon, there are more than one on the screen at the same time. When two foxes cross each other's paths, it is possible to shoot once and hit two foxes. I consider this a game feature that rewards an experienced player. You might want to find a way to prevent this.

This game can also use some sound effects and maybe some background sounds. You might also want to add some distracting animation, such as a bird flying by or the wind blowing some branches.

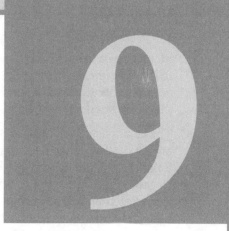

Catch and Avoid Games

- Apple Catch
- Apple Letter Catch
- River Rafting Game

Many games on the Web can be classified as catch and avoid games. They all share a few characteristics. The player controls an object or character that moves left and right across the bottom of the screen. Other objects fall from the top of the screen. The player must either catch or avoid these objects.

These games vary, however, in how the player's character is controlled, what the objects are, and other aspects. In this chapter, you will look at three different games. The first is a basic catch-the-objects game. The second builds on that and adds new features, such as some objects that are to be avoided rather than caught. The last game doesn't look like a catch and avoid game at all, but rather a movement-based game. However, it will use almost exactly the same code as the original game, just different graphics.

Apple Catch

Example file: Applecatch.fla

In the first game, Apple Catch, the fox will move along the bottom of the screen and try to catch apples that are falling from the tree. Figure 9.1 shows how the game will look. The game can be found on the Web site as Applecatch.fla.

Figure 9.1
The Apple Catch game features a fox at the bottom of the screen and apples that fall from the top.

Project Goal

The fox will be controlled by the left- and right-arrow keys. Instead of responding to a single key press, the fox should move as long as the player holds down one of those two arrow keys. The fox should stop automatically before going beyond the left or right side of the screen.

The apples should fall from a random place at the top of the screen. They should fall at random times, but not come too quickly. They should begin falling slowly, and then fall faster and faster as the game goes on.

After a certain number of apples have fallen, the game should end. The score should be equal to the number of apples that the fox has caught.

Approach

To move a fox, you'll use the Key object. This allows you to detect whether a key on the keyboard is being held down—in this case, the left-arrow key and the right-arrow key.

At the start of the game, no apples will be present. You'll use *attachMovie* to create new apples. These apples will be placed at random spots at the top of the screen, and then fall down until they're either caught by the fox or hit the bottom of the screen.

After an apple is created, a counter, "timeSinceLastApple" is reset to 0. This counter is then incremented once per frame. Only when the counter reaches 20 can another apple be created. This assures that an apple cannot be created until 20 frames have passed since the last apple was created.

The speed at which apples fall will depend on an "appleSpeed" variable. Each time an apple is dropped, the "appleSpeed" variable is increased. So, as the game goes on, the apples fall faster and faster.

An apple clip will be removed when it either hits the bottom of the screen or goes in the fox's basket. To determine when an apple hits the fox's basket, we will look at the position of the apple relative to the position of the basket. The fox movie clip is centered on the basket to make this calculation easier. Figure 9.2 shows the fox movie clip with the center marked by a cross.

Figure 9.2
The fox movie clip is centered on the basket.

When a certain number of apples have been dropped, the game ends. The number of apples caught will be displayed in the upper-right corner and serve as the player's score.

Preparing the Movie

The background image in the example movie is complex, but doesn't matter as far as the game is concerned. Only the apples and the fox matter. Both of these movie clips are stored in the library, but neither appears on Stage. They are created by the code as needed.

The apple movie clip is just a static image of an apple. The fox, however, is a little more complex. The first frame, labeled "stand", is a drawing of the fox standing still. The second frame, "run", is the start of an animation that shows the fox's feet moving. It has a *gotoAndPlay* command in the last frame so that it loops back to the "run" frame. This provides two modes for the fox clip: The first has it just sitting on frame 1; the second has it animating in a loop through all the frames starting at frame 2.

Because neither the fox nor the apple clip appears in the movie until the code asks for it, we'll need to set the Linkage properties of both to "Export this symbol". The apple is given the identifier "apple" and the fox is given the identifier "running fox".

Writing the Code

As with most of our games, the trigger for all events occurs in an "actions" movie clip. You can find this clip just beyond the upper-left corner of the Stage in the example movie.

The ActionScript attached to this clip calls functions in the main timeline of the movie. This makes the code simpler because "_root" doesn't have to be placed in front of all the movie clip names.

The code calls the "initGame" function when the clip loads, and then calls three functions every frame.

```
onClipEvent (load) {
    _root.initGame();
}

onClipEvent (enterFrame) {
    _root.moveFox();
    _root.dropNewApple();
    _root.moveApples();
}
```

So all the work is really done in four functions declared in the main timeline. Let's look at them one by one.

The first function, "initGame", sets up a whole bunch of variables at the start of the game. It also creates the fox movie clip. The reason the fox must be created by the code, rather than just put in place while building the movie, is so the fox appears on top of the apples. If we created the fox when building the movie, then each apple created by the code would appear on top of the fox. Doing it this way allows us to control the level at which the fox resides, relative to the level of the apples. You can see that the fox is assigned to level 999,999. The apples will start at level 1 and so appear under the fox.

```
function initGame() {
      // the range of falling apple clips
      firstApple = 1;
      lastApple = 0;

      // init the score
      score = 0;

      // set the number of apples to fall
      totalApples = 20;

      // init the speed and time delay
      timeSinceLastApple = 0;
      appleSpeed = 5;

      // create the fox so that it is on top of the apples
      attachMovie( "running fox", "fox", 999999 );
      fox._x = 275;
      fox._y = 300;
}
```

To move the fox, you must use the *Key* object to examine the state of the keyboard. You use *Key.isDown(Key.RIGHT)* to see if the right-arrow key is down, and *Key.isDown(Key.LEFT)* to see if the left-arrow key is down. The variable "dx" is set to 10 or -10 to indicate how much and in what direction the fox should move.

 NOTE

The *Key.isDown()* function allows you to determine whether a specific key is currently held down. This is particularly useful in arcade games that need keyboard control. To specify a key, you need to use its key code. In addition to numbers, such as 65 for the letter "A", you can also use constants such as *Key.UP* to specify special keys such as the up arrow. The ActionScript Reference Guide that comes with Flash 5 lists all these codes in its Appendix B.

As well as setting "dx", the function will also set the *_xscale* of the fox clip. The actual value of *_xscale* is kept the same, but sometimes it is negative and sometimes it is positive. This will make the movie clip flip horizontally so that the fox is facing the direction of movement.

After "dx" is set, the fox movie clip is moved by the value of "dx". Then, this new position is checked against the left and right limits of movement.

If there is movement going on, and the fox movie clip shows the fox standing still, then the clip is sent to the "run" frame so it will appear as if the fox is running. On the other hand, if the fox isn't moving, but it isn't on frame 1, then it's sent there so the fox appears as if it is standing still.

```
function moveFox() {
    // check for arrow keys
    if (Key.isDown(Key.RIGHT)) {
        dx = 10;
        // fox faces right
        fox._xscale = -Math.abs(fox._xscale);
    } else if (Key.isDown(Key.LEFT)) {
        dx = -10;
        // fox faces left
        fox._xscale = Math.abs(fox._xscale);
    } else {
        // no movement
        dx = 0;
    }

    // move the fox and limit that movement
    fox._x += dx;
    if (fox._x < 30) fox._x = 30;
    if (fox._x > 520) fox._x = 520;

    // make the fox run or stand still
    if ((dx != 0) and (fox._currentFrame == 1)) {
        fox.gotoAndPlay("run");
    } else if ((dx == 0) and (fox._currentFrame != 1)) {
        fox.gotoAndPlay("stand");
    }
}
```

Once every frame, the "dropNewApple" function is called. A set of three nested *if* statements determines whether a new apple needs to be created.

First, the "timeSinceLastApple" variable is examined. The code continues only if the variable is greater than 20. This variable is incremented by 1 at the end of this function.

The next test is whether the number of apples dropped so far is less than the total number of apples to be dropped during the game.

Finally, the *Math.random()* function is used to give an apple a 10% chance of being dropped. This will prevent the apples from being dropped at exact time intervals.

To create a new apple, the *attachMovie* function is used to create a new apple clip. The horizontal location of that clip is randomly chosen from between 30 and 520. Every time a new apple is created, the "appleSpeed" variable is increased slightly.

```
function dropNewApple() {
    // only drop if it has been long enough
    if (timeSinceLastApple > 20) {

        // only drop if there are more apples
        if (lastApple < totalApples) {

            // only drop 10% of the time
            if (Math.random() < .1) {

                // create next apple and set its locations
                lastApple++;
                attachMovie( "apple", "apple"+lastApple, lastApple );
                _root["apple"+lastApple]._x = Math.random()*490+30;
                _root["apple"+lastApple]._y = 0;

                // reset time delay for next apple
                timeSinceLastApple = 0;

                // increase apple speed
                if (appleSpeed < 10) appleSpeed += .5;
            }
        }
    }

    // even if no apple dropped, get closer to next drop
    timeSinceLastApple++;
}
```

The function to move the apples needs to do a lot more than just change the vertical location of the apples. It also needs to check whether the apple has hit the ground or landed in the basket.

To see whether the apple hit the ground, the function only needs to determine whether the position of the apple is below the bottom of the screen. Checking for a catch is a little harder, because the function has to find the difference from the position of the apple to the position of the fox, and see whether that falls in an acceptable range. If it is within 10 vertical pixels and 25 horizontal pixels of the fox, then the apple has been caught. Remember, the fox movie clip is centered on the basket, so the location of the fox is actually the location of the basket. Figure 9.3 shows the fox movie clip again, with a box representing the catch area.

Figure 9.3
When the center of an apple comes within the 50×20 pixel box around the center of the basket, it has been caught.

> **NOTE**
>
> The *Math.abs()* function is useful for determining collisions between objects. If you take the position of one object and subtract the position of another, you can get either a positive or negative number. For instance, if the first object is 7 pixels to the right of the second, then you get a 7, whereas if the first object is 7 pixels to the left you get a –7. The *Math.abs()* function strips the sign so that you get a 7 in either case. This way, you can test to see whether an object is a certain number of pixels away from another object, regardless of which side it is on.

If a catch is made, or the apple hits the ground, it will call the function "removeApple". In the case of the apple being caught, the score is also incremented.

```
function moveApples() {
    // loop through all existing apple clips
    for (i=firstApple;i<=lastApple;i++) {

        // get apple location
        x = _root["apple"+i]._x;
        y = _root["apple"+i]._y + appleSpeed;

        // see if apple reached ground
        if (y > 400) {
            removeApple(i);

        // see if apple hit basket
        } else if ((Math.abs(y-fox._y) < 10) and (Math.abs(x-fox._x) < 25)) {
            removeApple(i);
                score += 1;

        // continue to move apple
        } else {
            _root["apple"+i]._y = y;
```

```
            }
        }
    }
```

The "removeApple" function uses *removeClip* to delete the apple clip. It also increments "firstApple" so that the "moveApples" function no longer needs to try to move that apple down.

If the apple is the last one, the movie jumps to the "game over" frame. The fox movie clip is also removed so that it does not remain on the screen.

```
function removeApple(n) {
    // take away apple movie clip
    _root["apple"+n].removeMovieClip();

    // reset range of apples to move
    firstApple = n+1;

    // see if this was the last apple
    if (n == totalApples) {
        fox.removeMovieClip();
        gotoAndPlay("game over");
    }
}
```

Loose Ends

The previous code assumes that your Stage is 550×400, Flash 5's default size. You should adjust those numbers in the code if your Stage size is different. You can also adjust the margin on the left or right. The previous code limits the apples and fox to between 30 and 520, a 30-pixel margin. You can make that more or less.

The fox movie clip needs a *stop()* in the first frame to prevent it from automatically animating. Don't forget about the *gotoAndPlay* command in the last frame of that movie clip either.

There is also a text area set to Dynamic Text and linked to the variable "score". This makes the display of the score effortless.

The complete game in example Applecatch.fla contains three frames. The first is a start frame that has a *stop()* command on it. The button there will take the game to the "Play" frame where the action occurs. Then, of course, there is a "Game Over" frame after that. This is done differently than in some of the previous games in this book that use different scenes for the frames. I kept them in the same scene so I could use a single instance of the background graphic across all three frames. However, it can also be done in separate scenes if you like that better.

Other Possibilities

This game can be adjusted in a number of ways. You can start the apples at a faster speed or adjust the delay between apples. You can easily change the number of apples that fall in the game.

You can also adjust the fox graphic and the *moveApples* function so that the player has a larger or smaller basket with which to catch the apples.

A clever programmer could also show the basket getting fuller and fuller as more apples are caught and possibly require the fox to go to a place on the screen to dump the apples from time to time.

The next section in this chapter will build on this game by adding bad apples to avoid.

Apple Letter Catch

⊕▷Example file: **Applelettercatch.fla**

The point of this next example is to add a "bad apple" to the previous game. This is actually simple to do. So, to add to that challenge, let's also introduce the idea of different good and bad apples so they don't all look alike. In fact, let's make the appearance of the apples important to the game.

Each apple that falls will have a letter inside it. Depending on whether the letter is a vowel or a consonant, the apple will be good or bad. The player will try to catch only the good ones.

Figure 9.4 shows this new game with a few apples in the air. The example on the Web site is named Applelettercatch.fla.

Figure 9.4
The Apple Letter Catch game features apples with either vowels or consonants on them.

Project Goal

The goal here is to modify the Apple Catch game to allow for apples with different letters on them. Any apple with a vowel on it will give the player points, whereas any apple with a consonant on it will give the player negative points. The score should not be allowed to dip below 0, however.

Approach

In the Apple Catch game, a single library movie clip contained a single-frame static image of an apple. To accommodate different types of apples, we'll have two different movie clips, one for good apples and one for bad. In addition to that, each movie clip will have many frames, each representing a different apple. The good apple movie clip will have 5 frames, each showing a vowel. The bad apple movie clip will have 20 frames, each showing a consonant. We'll leave the letter "y" out of this game.

When it's time to drop a new apple, there will be a chance that it will be a good apple, and a chance it will be a bad one. Regardless of which, the code will display a random frame from the appropriate apple movie clip.

Then, when the player catches an apple, the code will determine which type it was, and award points accordingly.

Preparing the Movie

If you look at the example movie on the Web site, you will see two apple movie clips in the library. The first is "bad apple" and it contains 20 frames. Each frame has the apple, plus a consonant over it. The other movie clip, "good apple", has 5 frames for the 5 vowels. Figure 9.5 shows the main Flash window open with the "bad apple" movie clip.

Figure 9.5
The "bad apple" movie clip has 20 frames. Each frame shows the apple and a different consonant.

Both of these movie clips need to be set to Export this Symbol in the Symbol Linkage Properties dialog box. They should be assigned the appropriate identifier: "good apple" and "bad apple".

Writing the Code

The "actions" movie clip code is the same as the code used for the Apple Catch game. Only the functions will change.

The *initGame* function is the same except that I have increased the number of apples that will fall to 50.

```
function initGame() {
    // the range of falling apple clips
    firstApple = 1;
    lastApple = 0;

    // init the score
    score = 0;

    // set the number of apples to fall
    totalApples = 50;

    // init the speed and time delay
    timeSinceLastApple = 0;
    appleSpeed = 5;

    // create the fox so that it is on top of the apples
    attachMovie( "running fox", "fox", 999999 );
    fox._x = 275;
    fox._y = 300;
}
```

The *moveFox* function is identical to the Apple Catch game, so there is no use repeating the code here. The *dropNewApple* function is different, however, because it needs to decide which type of apple to drop, and then pick a random frame in that movie clip to display.

```
function dropNewApple() {
    // only drop if it has been long enough
    if (timeSinceLastApple > 20) {

        // only drop if there are more apples
        if  (lastApple < totalApples) {

            // only drop 10% of the time
            if (Math.random() < .1) {
```

```
                 // create next apple and set its locations
                 lastApple++;
                 if (Math.random() < .5) {
                     // 50% chance of a bad apple
                     attachMovie( "bad apple", "apple"+lastApple, lastApple );
                     _root["apple"+lastApple].type = "bad";
                 } else {
                     // 50% chance of a good apple
                     attachMovie( "good apple", "apple"+lastApple, lastApple );
                     _root["apple"+lastApple].type = "good";
                 }
                 f = int(Math.Random()*_root["apple"+lastApple]._totalFrames) + 1;
                 trace(f);
                 _root["apple"+lastApple].gotoAndStop(f);
                 _root["apple"+lastApple]._x = Math.random()*490+30;
                 _root["apple"+lastApple]._y = 0;

                 // reset time delay for next apple
                 timeSinceLastApple = 0;

                 // increase apple speed
                 if (appleSpeed < 10) appleSpeed += .5;
             }
         }
     }

     // even if no apple dropped, get closer to next drop
     timeSinceLastApple++;
 }
```

The *dropNewApple* function also sets a "type" variable for each movie clip. Although no scripts are attached to these movie clips, they can still be given values for variables to be associated with the movie clip. So the "type" for a vowel will be "good" and the "type" for a consonant will be "bad". In the *moveApples* function, this variable is checked when the player makes a catch. This is how a good catch is differentiated from a bad one.

```
function moveApples() {
    // loop through all existing apple clips
    for (i=firstApple;i<=lastApple;i++) {

        // get apple location
        x = _root["apple"+i]._x;
        y = _root["apple"+i]._y + appleSpeed;

        // see if apple reached ground
        if (y > 400) {
            removeApple(i);
```

```
        // see if apple hit basket
        } else if ((Math.abs(y-fox._y) < 10) and (Math.abs(x-fox._x) < 25)) {
            if (_root["apple"+i].type == "good") {
                // good apple, get a point
                score += 1;
            } else {
                // bad apple, lose a point
                score -= 1;

                // don't go below 0
                if (score < 0) score = 0;
            }
            removeApple(i);

        // continue to move apple
        } else {
            _root["apple"+i]._y = y;
        }
    }
}
```

The *removeApple* function is identical to the same function in the Apple Catch game.

Loose Ends

Like the Apple Catch game, there are "start" and "game over" frames on either side of the "play" frame. Remember the "score" text area and the other factors mentioned in the "Loose Ends" part of the previous section as well.

Other Possibilities

Hey, this is an educational game! Unfortunately, it is only useful for small children who have not learned the alphabet yet. However, you can change the contents of each frame of the good and bad apples to have more advanced content. You might have to enlarge the apples to fit longer pieces of information on them.

For older kids, you could have verbs and nouns on the apples. Or, you could have odd and even numbers, numbers divisible by three, or fractions that can be reduced. Still older kids can pick out countries in a certain continent, or trees versus other plants. You could come up with any topic that can be broken into correct and incorrect answers.

River Rafting Game

☉⊳Example file: Riverkayak.fla

The final section in this chapter will use the code from the previous two games to create a game that looks completely different than the other two. In this game, our hero fox will travel down a river in a kayak, avoiding obstacles and trying to make good time.

The transformation of the previous games into this one takes surprisingly little effort. However, players will never think of the games as the same. Look at Figure 9.6 to see just how different this game looks from the Apple Catch games.

Figure 9.6

The River Kayak Adventure game features a kayak in the center of the screen while rocks and tree branches rush upward toward it.

Project Goal

Part of the goal here is to create an illusion for the player. Although the kayak stays at the center of the screen as shown in Figure 9.6, the player should get the feeling that it is moving down the river. This will be accomplished by the objects moving up the screen.

Most of the code in this game will be borrowed from the two earlier games in this chapter. However, all, not just some, of the objects are to be avoided. Instead of counting objects hit as your "score", they will be counted as the number of spills. The game will end early if too many spills occur.

Approach

The first modification to the code is to make the objects move up instead of down. Then, any code that deals with collisions can be streamlined to account for the fact that all collisions are bad.

Much of the rest of the modifications are minor. The left- and right margins need to be moved so the rocks appear in the river. The speed of the game can go much faster and more rocks can be on the screen at one time.

Instead of having the speed of the game increase over time, it will decrease to 0 when a rock is hit. This will make the player feel the impact. The end of the game will also be delayed by this slowdown.

Preparing the Movie

Instead of the "apples" movie clips, we will need a "rocks" movie clip. In the example movie, Riverkayak.fla, the "rocks" movie clip has three frames. Each frame contains an animated graphic from another library element. Although each rock is in one frame of the movie clip, animation takes place in the graphic element. So if you try the example movie, you will see water running by each rock.

Instead of the "fox" movie clip featuring the fox with a basket ready to catch apples, it has a fox in a kayak. The first frame has the fox facing downstream with paddles out of the water. Then there is a "left" and "right" frame with the kayak turned and one paddle in the water. Figure 9.7 shows the fox turning right. After that, frame 4 starts a "spill" animation that will play when the kayak hits a rock.

Figure 9.7
The second frame of the fox movie clip shows the fox turning to the right.

The "rocks" and "fox" movie clips need to be linked, just like the "apples" and "fox" movie clips in the first game of this chapter, so that they are included with the movie.

Writing the Code

The script attached to the "actions" movie clip looks just like the one used in the first two games of this chapter. However, the names have been adjusted to apply to this game, rather than catching apples.

```
onClipEvent (load) {
    _root.initGame();
}

onClipEvent (enterFrame) {
    _root.moveFox();
    _root.newRock();
    _root.moveRocks();
}
```

The functions in the main timeline should look familiar to you at this point. Some sections of code are identical to the same functions earlier in this chapter. However, the variable names have been changed to make more sense for this game.

The "initGame" function starts the speed of the game at 0 this time. The location of the fox is placed right in the middle of the screen, instead of at the bottom.

```
function initGame() {
    // the range of rock clips
    firstRock = 1;
    lastRock = 0;

    // init the number of spills
    spills = 0;

    // set the number of rocks to pass
    totalRocks = 50;

    // init the speed and time delay
    timeSinceLastRock = 0;
    riverSpeed = 0;

    // create the fox so that it is on top of the rocks
    attachMovie( "kayaking fox", "fox", 999999 );
    fox._x = 275;
    fox._y = 200;
}
```

The "moveFox" function looks at the left- and right-arrow keys as before. In addition, it checks to see whether the kayak is performing a "spill" animation and ignores the keys if it is.

Instead of flipping the image like the Apple Catch game does, the code makes the "fox" go to frames labeled "left" or "right". The first frame is labeled "still" and shows the kayak going straight.

```
function moveFox() {
    if (fox._currentFrame > 4) {
```

```
        // if during a spill, don't look at keys
        dx = 0;
    } else if (Key.isDown(Key.RIGHT)) {
        // fox rows right
        dx = riverSpeed;
        fox.gotoAndStop("left");
    } else if (Key.isDown(Key.LEFT)) {
        // fox rows left
        dx = -riverSpeed;
        fox.gotoAndStop("right");
    } else {
        // no key
        dx = 0;
        fox.gotoAndStop("still");
    }

    // move the fox and limit that movement
    fox._x += dx;
    if (fox._x < 150) fox._x = 150;
    if (fox._x > 400) fox._x = 400;

    // go a little faster
    if (riverSpeed < 20) riverSpeed += .5;
}
```

The speed of the game is increased in the "moveFox" handler in this game to keep the kayak accelerating at a constant rate.

The "newRock" function is like the "dropNewApple" function of the previous game. However, it is simpler because it only has one movie clip to choose from.

```
function newRock() {
    // only add new one if it has been long enough
    if (timeSinceLastRock > 5) {

        // only start if there are more rocks
        if (lastRock < totalRocks) {

            // only add 10% of the time
            if (Math.random() < .1) {

                // create next rock and set its location
                lastRock++;
                attachMovie( "rocks", "rock"+lastRock, lastRock );
                _root["rock"+lastRock]._x = Math.random()*250+150;
                _root["rock"+lastRock]._y = 450;
```

```
            // decide which frame to show
            f = int(Math.Random()*_root["rock"+lastRock]._totalFrames) + 1;
            _root["rock"+lastRock].gotoAndStop(f);

            // reset time delay for next rock
            timeSinceLastRock = 0;

            // init whether rock was hit
            _root["rock"+i].hit = false;
        }
    }
}

    // even if no rock added, get closer to next rock
    timeSinceLastRock++;
}
```

Note that the variable "hit" is set to *false* for each new rock. This indicates that the kayak has never hit that rock. In the "moveRock" function, this is checked before a collision is allowed. When a collision happens, the "hit" variable of that movie clip is set to *true* so that it cannot be hit again as the boat passes over it.

Notice that the numbers for determining when a collision occurs are drastically different now that the fox has a kayak instead of a basket. The game looks for a collision within 60 pixels horizontally and 25 pixels vertically of the center. This approximates the shape of the kayak as shown in Figure 9.8.

Figure 9.8
The black box shows the area where a collision can occur. Because the collision occurs with the center of a rock, the edge of the rock can actually be much closer to the kayak than this box.

The number of hits is recorded in the "spills" variable. After the kayak has spilled six times, the game goes to a "lose" frame that declares the game over. Notice that this calls a new function, "removeAll", which will be explained later.

```
function moveRocks() {
    // loop through all existing rock clips
    for (i=firstRock;i<=lastRock;i++) {

        // get rock location
        x = _root["rock"+i]._x;
        y = _root["rock"+i]._y - riverSpeed;

        // see if rock reached past top
        if (y < -50) {
            removeRock(i);

        // to have a hit, rock must not have been hit before
        // and rock and boat are close enough
        } else if ((_root["rock"+i].hit == false) and (Math.abs(y-fox._y) < 60)
          and (Math.abs(x-fox._x) < 25)) {
            spills += 1;

            // note that rock was hit
            _root["rock"+i].hit = true;

            // turn boat over
            fox.gotoAndPlay("spill");

            // stop boat
            riverSpeed = 0;

            // is game over?
            if (spills > 5) {
                removeAll();
                gotoAndPlay("lose");
            }

        }
        // continue to move rock
        _root["rock"+i]._y = y;
    }
}
```

The "removeRock" function, like the "removeApple" function, will look to see whether this is the last rock. If so, the game goes to a frame labeled "win".

```
function removeRock(n) {
    // take away rock movie clip
    _root["rock"+n].removeMovieClip();
```

```
    // reset range of rocks to move
    firstRock = n+1;

    // see if this was the last rock
    if (n == totalRocks) {
        removeAll();
        gotoAndPlay("win");
    }
}
```

In the previous code, you see two occasions in which the game ends. In both cases, the "removeAll" function is called. This function removes all the remaining rocks, if any, and the fox movie clip. This is needed because otherwise they will stay on the screen even after the game is over.

```
function removeAll() {
    // take away all remaining rocks
    for (i=firstRock;i<=lastRock;i++) {
        _root["rock"+i].removeMovieClip();
    }
    fox.removeMovieClip();
}
```

Loose Ends

Instead of just one "game over" frame, this game features two. The first, labeled "lose" contains a message for players who hit too many rocks and did not complete the game. The second, "win", contains a message for players who made it past the rocks. The frames are essentially the same except for the message. They both have a "Play" button so the game can be restarted.

Other Possibilities

Because hitting a rock slows the player down, this game is an ideal candidate for a timer. You could mark the starting time of the game using the date object similar to the clock gadget in Chapter 6, "Toys and Gadgets." Then, you could see how long it takes the player to finish the course. Not only will hitting a rock affect the speed of the kayak, but you can alter the code so that the kayak only accelerates when the boat is pointed straight ahead. This adds even more challenge to the game.

Another possibility for a different game would be to flip it around again so that the objects are moving down and change the kayak to a car or bike and the river to a road. This would make a good driving game.

Aim and Shoot Games

- Move and Shoot the Balloons
- Aim and Shoot

Aim and shoot games are similar to catch and avoid games in two ways: The main character moves, and so do the other objects in the game. However, the new element introduced in this chapter is shooting. The character and objects never meet. Instead, the character shoots at the objects.

The first game you'll build in this chapter allows the player to move a character across the bottom of the screen and shoot directly up at objects overhead. In the second game, the character stands still, but is able to aim and shoot diagonally at the objects.

Move and Shoot the Balloons

⊕☞∜Example file: Balloonshoot.fla

In this first game, there will be three primary elements: the fox, the balloons, and the bullets. In this case, the bullets are just peas being shot from a straw. That will make it suitable for all audiences. Figure 10.1 shows the example game on the Web site.

Figure 10.1
The Balloon Shoot game features a fox shooting peas through a straw at balloons passing by.

Project Goal

The goal is to build a game in which the fox moves left and right and can shoot bullets directly up from his position. The balloons float in from the left and right at random speeds and altitudes. After a fixed number of balloons float by, the game is over. The score is determined by how many balloons have been popped. Play the example movie, Balloonshoot.fla, on the Web site to see how it plays.

Approach

The fox's movement is similar to all the games in the last chapter. We'll even animate the fox as he moves and flip the movie clip horizontally so that he is facing the right direction.

The balloons will be taken from a single movie clip that contains a light gray balloon. As well as assigning a random altitude, speed and direction, we will also assign a random color.

The bullets being shot from the fox's straw will be another movie clip. We'll use a button that reacts to the spacebar to determine when the player fires. The new movie clip will be created at the tip of the straw, and then move upward from that moment on. We'll also set a timer and check it to make sure that the player can fire only once per second.

A balloon will pop when a bullet gets too close to it. Instead of using *hitTest* to determine a collision, we'll use a mathematical formula to determine when the bullet is close to the center of the balloon.

Preparing the Movie

In the example movie, Balloonshoot.fla on the Web site, the fox is a movie clip with a "stand" frame and a "walk" animation sequence. It actually shows the fox walking to the left, as shown in Figure 10.2, but we'll use ActionScript to flip the fox to make him appear to walk to the right when needed. The position of the straw, however, should be at the same location in all frames, relative to the center point of the movie clip.

Figure 10.2
The fox walks to the left, but always keeps the straw pointed and ready to fire.

The balloon movie clip also has several frames. The first shows the normal balloon. The rest shows an animation of the balloon exploding. When the balloon is hit, it is told to play this short animation. Figure 10.3 shows the only frame of the animation for the example movie, but you might want to have a more elaborate explosion.

Figure 10.3
When a balloon is hit, this balloon explosion animation appears.

The balloon only uses shades of gray as coloring. When you create a new balloon movie clip in the code, you also color it in. This allows you to use one balloon movie clip, but have it appear to be different colors every time.

The bullet movie clip is a short line. Even though it is supposed to be a pea, a short vertical line helps give the illusion of upward movement.

Writing the Code

A small "actions" movie clip is positioned off the Stage and will control the action through calls to functions in the main timeline. It will initialize the game when it loads, and then call a series of functions every frame.

```
onClipEvent(load) {
    _root.initGame();
}

onClipEvent(enterFrame) {
    _root.newBalloon();
    _root.moveBalloons();
    _root.moveFox();
    _root.moveBullets();
}
```

The "initGame" function resets all the important variables used in the game.

```
function initGame() {
    // init balloon variables
    nextBalloonTime = 0;
    nextBalloon = 0;
    balloons = [];
    numBalloons = 10;

    // init bullet variables
    nextBulletTime = 0;
    nextBullet = 0;
    bullets = [];

    // init score
    score = 0;
}
```

For a new balloon to be created, it must pass three tests. The first test determines whether any more balloons are left in the game. The second test determines whether enough time has passed since the last balloon was created. The final test is actually a coin flip: a 50% chance that a new balloon will be created at this instant.

After all three tests have passed, the "newBalloon" function creates a new balloon that has a 50/50 chance of coming from the left or right side of the screen. The speed of the balloon is a random number from 3 to 5. This number is positive if the balloon is meant to float from the left to the right, and negative if it's meant to float from the right to the left.

The color of the new balloon movie clip is picked from a list of five colors. The *setTransform* command is used on a color object created from the new movie clip to set the color.

You keep track of the balloon movie clips by placing their names and speeds into an array called "balloons."

Finally, the "nextBalloon" variable and "nextBalloonTime" variable are set so they can be used by future calls to "newBalloon".

```
function newBalloon() {
    // more balloons?
    if (nextBalloon < numBalloons) {

        // time for next?
        if (getTimer() > nextBalloonTime) {

            // 50% chance of a new balloon
            if (Math.Random() < .5) {

                // create new balloon clip
                attachMovie("balloon", "balloon"+nextBalloon, nextBalloon);

                // choose which side to come from and random speed
                if (Math.Random() < .5) {
                    _root["balloon"+nextBalloon]._x = -30;
                    dx = int(Math.Random()*3)+3;
                } else {
                    _root["balloon"+nextBalloon]._x = 580;
                    dx = -int(Math.Random()*3)-3;
                }

                // choose height of balloon
                _root["balloon"+nextBalloon]._y = int(Math.Random()*100)+20;

                // choose color of balloon
                balloonColor = new Color("balloon"+nextBalloon);
                r = int(Math.Random()*5)+1;
                if (r == 1) {
                    balloonColor.setTransform({rb: 255});
                } else if (r == 2) {
                    balloonColor.setTransform({gb: 255});
```

```
        } else if (r == 3) {
            balloonColor.setTransform({bb: 255});
        } else if (r == 4) {
            balloonColor.setTransform({rb: 255, gb: 255});
        } else if (r == 5) {
            balloonColor.setTransform({rb: 255, bb: 255});
        }

        // add balloon to array
        balloons.push({clip: "balloon"+nextBalloon, d: dx});

        // set things up for next balloon
        nextBalloon++;
        nextBalloonTime = getTimer() + 2000;
      }
    }
  }
}
```

NOTE

A quick way to determine a 50% change is to use the code *(Math.Random() < .5)*. Because *Math.Random()* returns a value from 0 to 1.0, but never exactly 1.0, testing for it to be less than .5 gives you a 50% chance.

After the balloons have been created, it is up to the "moveBalloons" function to keep them going. This function loops through the balloons and moves each movie clip the appropriate amount. It checks to see whether the balloon has reached the other side and removes the movie clip if it has. It also removes the item from the "balloons" array.

TIP

Note that the *for* loop in the "moveBalloons" function counts backwards. It starts with the last movie clip in the "balloons" array and counts down to 0. This is done so that when a balloon is removed from the array, it does not change the positions of the other items in the array. For instance, imagine if item 3 of a 5-item array is removed. Then, item 4 becomes item 3 and item 5 becomes item 4. If you were counting up, you would skip the new item 3 and go right to the new item 4. However, if you count down, there is no such problem.

The "moveBalloons" function also checks to see whether all the balloons have been created in the first place, and that they have all since disappeared. This signals the end of the game.

```
function moveBalloons() {
    // loop through balloons in array
    for(i=balloons.length-1;i>=0;i--) {
```

```
    // get speed and clip
    dx = balloons[i].d;
    balloon = _root[balloons[i].clip];

    // move balloon
    balloon._x += dx;

    // balloon exit left
    if ((dx < 0) and (balloon._x < -20)) {
        balloon.removeMovieClip();
        balloons.splice(i,1);

    // balloon exit right
    } else if ((dx > 0) and (balloon._x > 570)) {
        balloon.removeMovieClip();
        balloons.splice(i,1);
    }
}

// see if all balloons gone
if ((nextBalloon >= numBalloons) and (balloons.length < 1)) {
    gotoAndStop("game over");
}
}
```

The "moveFox" function checks the left- and right-arrow keys and moves the fox 10 pixels left or right. Like the games in the previous chapter, it uses the _xscale property to flip the fox movie clip to face the right direction. It also sends the movie clip to its animated segment starting at frame 2 for walking, and to its standing-still segment, at frame 1 for standing.

```
function moveFox() {
    // move fox to left, no flip
    if (Key.isDown(Key.LEFT)) {
        dx = -10;
        fox._xscale = Math.abs(fox._xscale);

    // move fox to right, flip
    } else if (Key.isDown(Key.RIGHT)) {
        dx = 10;
        fox._xscale = -Math.abs(fox._xscale);

    // stop moving
    } else {
        dx = 0;
    }
```

```
    // move fox
    fox._x += dx;

    if ((dx == 0) and (fox._currentFrame != 1)) {
        // set fox to stand
        fox.gotoAndStop(1);
    } else if ((dx != 0) and (fox._currentFrame == 1)) {
        // set fox to move
        fox.gotoAndPlay(2);
    }
}
```

To shoot a bullet, the player hits the spacebar. This keypress is intercepted by a button and the "shootBullet" function is called. Check the "Loose Ends" section later to see the code for the button.

The "shootBullet" function checks the current time to make sure enough time has passed since the last bullet was fired. This prevents the player from just shooting a shower of bullets that will hit everything.

Like the balloons, the bullets are both a movie clip and an item in an array—in this case, the array "bullets". The array will be used by "moveBullets" to keep it going after being fired.

Notice in the following code that the bullet movie clip starts off at the location of the fox, but 2 pixels to the right and 55 pixels above. This corresponds to the exact position of the tip of the fox's straw in relation to the center of the fox.

```
function shootBullet() {
    // see if there has been enough time to reload
    if (getTimer() > nextBulletTime) {

        // create bullet clip
        attachMovie("bullet","bullet"+nextBullet,nextBullet+9999);

        // set location
        _root["bullet"+nextBullet]._x = fox._x+2;
        _root["bullet"+nextBullet]._y = fox._y-55;

        // add to array
        bullets.push(nextBullet);

        //get set for next bullet
        nextBullet++;
        nextBulletTime = getTimer()+1000;
    }
}
```

The "moveBullets" function works just like the "moveBalloons" function, except that it moves the bullets up instead of left or right. It checks to see whether the bullet has hit the top of the screen. It also checks to see whether the bullet has hit a balloon by calling "checkCollision". In either case, the bullet movie clip and array element are deleted.

```
function moveBullets() {
    // loop through all bullets
    for(i=bullets.length-1;i>=0;i--) {

        // get clip
        bullet = _root["bullet"+bullets[i]];

        // move clip
        bullet._y -= 10;

        // see if it reached top
        if (bullet._y < 0) {
            bullet.removeMovieClip();
            bullets.splice(i,1);

        // see if it hit a balloon
        } else {
            if (checkCollision(bullet)) {
                bullet.removeMovieClip();
                bullets.splice(i,1);
            }
        }
    }

}
```

The "checkCollision" function loops through all the balloons and determines whether any are close to this particular bullet. It uses a function called "distance" to get the distance from the center of the bullet to the center of the balloon. We'll look at that function next.

If the distance is less than 10 pixels, which is the approximate diameter of the balloon, then it is scored a hit. The balloon movie clip goes to frame 2, and a *true* is returned. This signals the "moveBullet" function shown previously to dispose of the bullet.

TIP

Why not use *hitTest* to determine when a bullet hits a balloon, rather than this "distance" function? Well, *hitTest* will return *true* if the bullet hits any part of the balloon. This includes the string hanging down from the balloon.

```
function checkCollision(bullet) {
    // loop through all balloons
    for(j=balloons.length-1;j>=0;j--) {
        balloon = _root[balloons[j].clip];

        // see if the bullet is close to the balloon
        if (distance(bullet,balloon) < 10) {

            // go to "pop" frame of balloon
            balloon.gotoAndPlay(2);

            // remove balloon from array
            balloons.splice(j,1);

            // add to score
            score += 1;

            // return true, since there was a collision
            return(true);
        }
    }

    // return false, since there was a collision
    return(false);
}
```

The distance function uses a mathematical formula to determine the exact distance, in pixels, between two movie clips. First, it determines the horizontal and vertical difference between the two clips' locations. This is stored in "dx" and "dy". Then, it takes the square root of the sum of the squares of these numbers. This is the mathematical formula used to determine distance.

```
function distance(clip1, clip2) {
    // find distance between two movie clips
    dx = clip1._x - clip2._x;
    dy = clip1._y - clip2._y;
    return (Math.sqrt(dx*dx+dy*dy));
}
```

Loose Ends

To get the spacebar key press, we'll use a button. In the example movie, you can see this button as a piece of text "button" just off the Stage to the upper left. This code is attached to it:

```
on (keyPress "<Space>") {
    _root.shootBullet();
}
```

According to the code, this button does not even react to a click. It doesn't matter if the button does anyway, because the button is off the Stage. However, the program does look for and capture the spacebar. Then it calls the "shootBullet" function.

TIP

The reason we use this button to capture the spacebar and not use a *Key.isDown* test in the "moveFox" function is not easy to see at first. The *Key.isDown* test only tests to see whether a key is pressed during a certain instant. In our game, this happens once per frame. However, if a player presses the spacebar quickly, he could press it and release it between *Key.isDown* tests. Then the bullet wouldn't fire because the program didn't ever see it pressed. Using a button to capture a keystroke, however, guarantees that the keystroke will be captured and used.

The example movie is set to run at 30 frames per second. I did this to make the animation smoother. If you want to change this, note that you will need to change the movement amounts for the fox, balloons, and bullets to match. Otherwise, the game will go faster or slower than you might have intended.

Other Possibilities

The example movie can be made a little more interesting in a number of ways. Instead of the colors being random, they can be linked to a certain number of points. For instance, red balloons can be worth 100 points, blue worth 50, and so on. Then, in turn, the colors can be linked to speeds and altitudes. Obviously, the higher and faster balloons should be worth more.

Next, you can move away from balloons altogether. This game is essentially similar to various anti-aircraft, "Sea Wolf," and alien invasion games. All you need to do is replace all the graphics.

Aim and Shoot

Example file: Aimandshoot.fla

What if, in the previous game, the character stood still instead of moving side-to-side? Then, in addition, he could aim his straw to point anywhere on the screen, not just straight up. Also, what if the bullets obeyed the law of gravity and arced as they flew, eventually falling back to the ground?

Example movie Aimandshoot.fla shows how the game plays with these changes. Figure 10.4 shows the game in action, and you can see that the fox is in the middle, but bullets have been fired off at an angle. Now, let's look at how this is done.

Figure 10.4
The "Aim and Shoot" game is similar to the "Balloon Shoot" game, but with aiming and gravity.

Project Goal

The goal is to take the previous game, remove one element and add two new ones. The element to be removed is the fox's left and right movement. In this game, the arrow keys will have no affect and the fox will stay in the center of the screen.

The two new elements are aiming and gravity. The player should be able to use the mouse to aim, and the straw will point in the right direction. Then, after the bullet leaves the straw, it will gradually fall back to Earth.

Approach

To make the straw point in the right direction, you first have to measure the horizontal and vertical distance from the cursor to the straw. Then, you have to calculate the angle from this measurement.

This angle can easily be used to rotate the straw movie clip to point in the right direction. However, you also have to use this angle to determine where the bullet starts and how many vertical and horizontal pixels it moves each frame.

Adding gravity is a little easier. When an object such as a bullet starts moving, gravity has no initial effect. However, each frame that goes by adds a little bit to the speed at which the bullet is falling. Because the bullet will have a strong initial force upward, the bullet will keep moving upward, but at a slower and slower speed as gravity overcomes the initial push. Then, inevitably, the bullet will begin to come down, faster and faster.

This is called "acceleration due to gravity," and it is approximately 32 feet per second per second (9.8 meters per second per second) in the real world. In the game world, we can use whatever number seems to create the right feeling for the player.

Preparing the Movie

The biggest noncode difference between this game and the previous one is that the straw is a separate movie clip. This is done so that the straw can be rotated independently of the fox.

The fox movie clip is also different because it doesn't need the walking animation. The fox is really no more than a piece of background in this game, although it appears on top of the straw.

Writing the Code

Several of the functions for this game are identical to the "Balloon Shoot" game, so there is no need to show those here. They are the "initGame", "newBalloon", "moveBalloons", "checkCollision", and "distance" functions.

One of the new functions will be "aimStraw". This function replaces the "moveFox" function. It is called from the "actions" movie clip, which now uses the following code:

```
onClipEvent(load) {
    _root.initGame();
}

onClipEvent(enterFrame) {
    _root.newBalloon();
    _root.moveBalloons();
    _root.aimStraw();
    _root.moveBullets();
}
```

The "aimStraw" function needs to calculate the angle in which the player is aiming, and then set the straw movie clip's rotation. It will also store the angle in a variable called "strawRadians", which will be used by the "shootBullet" function.

To calculate an angle from two points, you first find the horizontal and vertical difference between the two points. In this function, they are stored in "dx" and "dy". Then you run these two numbers through the *Math.atan2* function to return the angle in radians.

TIP

Angles can be measured in radians or degrees. A radian is a measure in which 6.28 radians (two times pi) makes one complete circle. In degrees, this is 360 degrees for a full circle. Flash uses radians in mathematical functions such as *Math.sin* and *Math.cos*, and degrees for movie clip properties is *_rotation*. Therefore, it is necessary at times to convert between these two types of measurements.

NOTE

The *Math.atan2* function is a great tool for game programmers. An arctangent is a function that converts the slope of a line into an angle. Because you can get the slope of a line from two points, an arctangent can then be used to convert two points to an angle. However, arctangents do not take into account which point is the anchor and which is the pointer in determining an angle. Therefore, it is easy to get angles that are actually the opposite of what you wanted. To fix this, you would have to write several *if* statements to take care of various cases. However, the *Math.atan2* function lets Flash handle all those special cases. It just takes the horizontal and vertical difference and returns the angle, plain and simple.

```
function aimStraw() {
    // find x and y differences
    dx = _xmouse - straw._x;
    dy = _ymouse - straw._y;

    // calculate angle
    strawRadians = Math.atan2(dy,dx);

    // convert to degrees and set rotation
    strawDegrees = 360*strawRadians/(2*Math.PI);
    straw._rotation = strawDegrees;
}
```

Now, when a bullet is shot, more information than just its movie clip needs to be recorded in the "bullets" array. For each frame movement, we also need to know the angle at which the bullet was fired.

We'll also add an item called "down" to each bullet object in the "bullets" array for the cumulative effect of gravity on the bullet. It will start at 0.

To make the bullet start at the tip of the straw, set the x and y location of the bullet to the straw's location, plus 20 pixels. Distribute these 20 pixels between x and y by using *Math.sin* and *Math.cos* to separate the horizontal and vertical components of the angle.

NOTE

Math.sin and *Math.cos* can be used to take an angle and determine its horizontal and vertical component. To visualize this, imagine a circle with the center at 0,0, the top-most point at 0,−1 and the rightmost point at 1,0. Run any angle through *Math.sin* and you will get the y-coordinate of the point on the circle that is at that angle. The *Math.cos* function gives you the x-coordinate. So, *Math.sin(0)* is −1 and *Math.cos(0)* is 0, corresponding to 0,−1.

More importantly than understanding this, it is important that you understand that movement can be broken down into two things: speed and angle. Measurements for computer screens are always in horizontal and vertical distances, not diagonal ones. *Math.sin* and *Math.cos* allow you to convert speed and angle into horizontal and vertical distances.

```
function shootBullet() {
    // see if there has been enough time to reload
    if (getTimer() > nextBulletTime) {

        // create bullet clip
        attachMovie("bullet","bullet"+nextBullet,nextBullet+9999);
        bullet = _root["bullet"+nextBullet];

        // set location
        bullet._x = straw._x + Math.cos(strawRadians)*20;
        bullet._y = straw._y + Math.sin(strawRadians)*20;

        // add to array
        // clip = movie clip name
        // angle = angle of initial force
        // down = effect of gravity so far
        bullets.push({clip: bullet, angle: strawRadians, down: 0});

        //get set for next bullet
        nextBullet++;
        nextBulletTime = getTimer()+1000;
    }
}
```

The "moveBullets" function will now use the "angle" and "down" properties of each bullet to move them the appropriate amount. In addition, the "down" property will be increased to show the continuing affect of gravity.

Because what goes up must come down, we check for the bullet to hit the bottom of the Stage before we remove it from the array and destroy the movie clip.

```
function moveBullets() {
    // loop through all bullets
    for(i=bullets.length-1;i>=0;i--) {

        // get clip
        bullet = bullets[i].clip;

        // move clip according to initial force
        bullet._x += Math.cos(bullets[i].angle) * 10;
        bullet._y += Math.sin(bullets[i].angle) * 10;

        // add gravity effect
        bullet._y += bullets[i].down;

        // gravity acceleration
        bullets[i].down += .2;
```

```
        // see if it reached bottom
        if (bullet._y > 400) {
            bullet.removeMovieClip();
            bullets.splice(i,1);

        // see if it hit a balloon
        } else {
            if (checkCollision(bullet)) {
                bullet.removeMovieClip();
                bullets.splice(i,1);
            }
        }
    }
}
```

Loose Ends

Because the bullets in this game move in all different directions, I changed the bullet movie clip so that it resembles a small dot rather than a short line.

Other Possibilities

Like the previous game in this chapter, you can add many complexities, such as more points for faster and higher balloons. The idea of making this into an anti-aircraft war game works well, because anti-aircraft guns are usually stationary, but can fire at different angles.

Ball and Paddle Games

- Wall Ball
- Paddle Ball
- Paddle Bricks

The next genre of games that we will examine dates back to the first video game: "Pong." This simple game started the arcade revolution in the 70s.

These games all involve a simple ball that bounces off walls and a paddle that the player controls. The player tries to not let the ball get past the paddle.

The first game we will build has a single paddle and a ball. The second game will feature a second, computer-controlled paddle and an artificially intelligent opponent. The final game in this chapter will have the player trying to hit blocks with the ball, like the classic arcade game "Breakout."

Wall Ball

▷⟨Example file: Wallball.fla

The first game is called Wall Ball. It features a single, player-controlled paddle and three walls that the ball can bounce off of. The fourth wall is open. The player's task is to not let the ball get past the paddle and through the open wall. Figure 11.1 shows this simple game.

Figure 11.1
The Wall Ball game features a ball, a paddle, and three walls.

Project Goal

The goal is to build a game where a moving ball reflects off of walls and a paddle. The paddle should follow the vertical location of the mouse. When the ball gets past the paddle and reaches the edge of the screen, the game should end. Also, when the ball hits the paddle, it should increase in speed slightly.

Approach

The most complex part of this game is getting the ball to accurately reflect off the walls. Many programmers over-simplify this, not taking into account the width of the ball and its speed. As a result, the ball can appear to reflect at a point beyond the wall.

We'll look for the situation in which the ball has moved beyond the wall. Then we'll determine how far beyond the wall the ball is. Because the ball will be moving at several pixels per frame, it can easily overshoot the wall by several pixels.

After you know how far past the wall the ball is, you can change its direction, and then place the ball at the appropriate distance from the correct side of the wall. Figure 11.2 shows a diagram of how this works.

Figure 11.2   *The diagram explains how the ball is repositioned after a collision with a wall.*

Collisions with the paddle are treated just like collisions with a wall. The only difference is that you must make sure the vertical position of the paddle is such that the ball will hit it.

When a ball passes the horizontal location of the paddle, but the paddle is not there, you set a variable flag so that you know the paddle was missed. This way, you won't give the player a second chance to hit the ball as it continues on its journey to the edge of the screen.

Preparing the Movie

The only graphics needed for this game are the ball, the paddle, and the walls. The wall graphics are actually not even used by the code, because the actual game boundaries are in the code as number constants.

Writing the Code

You only need three functions for this game. Check out the example movie, Wallball.fla. All three of these will be called from an "actions" movie clip:

```
onClipEvent(load) {
    _root.initGame();
}

onClipEvent(enterFrame) {
    _root.moveBall();
    _root.movePaddle();
}
```

The functions are stored in the main timeline. The first one, "initGame", stores the location of the ball into "x" and "y". It starts "dx" and "dy", which are the horizontal and vertical speeds of the ball, at 5 for each. Then, the function sets a bunch of constants that determine the positions of each wall.

This function also gets the radius of the ball, a value that will be useful in the "moveBall" function. The "passedPaddle" variable is a flag that is set to *true* after the player misses. You should also take this opportunity to turn off the cursor, because it would be a distraction to the player.

```
function initGame() {
    // get start position of the ball
    x = ball._x;
    y = ball._y;

    // set initial speed
    dx = 5;
    dy = 5;

    // set constants
    rightWall = 550;
    leftWall = 0;
    topWall = 0;
    bottomWall = 400;
    ballRadius = ball._width/2;
    passedPaddle = false;

    // hide cursor
    Mouse.hide();
}
```

The "movePaddle" function is the workhorse of this game. It starts by changing "x" and "y" to "dx" and "dy" to get the new location of the ball ①. Then, it checks to see whether the ball has gone past the right wall ②. It adds the radius of the ball to the location of the ball to get the exact position of the right edge of the ball. If the ball has passed the wall, the "movePaddle" function calculates by how much and stores that in "overshoot". The location of the ball is then moved back by twice "overshoot". The direction of the ball is changed by multiplying "dx" by –1. This will effectively change the sign of "dx". So if it was 5 before hitting the wall, it becomes –5.

Next, the code checks to see whether the ball has passed the bottom wall ③. This is similar to the previous segment, except that "y" and "dy" are used instead of "x" and "dx".

When the code checks the top wall, some of the calculations are a little different ④. To determine the location of the top edge of the ball, the radius of the ball is subtracted from the location of the ball. Then, "overshoot" is calculated by subtracting the location of the top edge of the ball from the wall's location.

To detect whether the ball has hit the paddle, the code first calculates the location of the right edge of the paddle ⑤. Then, if the ball is far enough to the left, it calculates the top and bottom of the paddle and determines whether the ball and paddle intersect ⑥.

If the ball hits the paddle, it behaves like any other wall However, it also increases the speed of the ball by 5% ⑦. If the ball misses the wall, the only action taken at this point is to set "passedPaddle" to *true*.

If "passedPaddle" is *true* and the ball is where the left wall should be, the game is over ⑧. The cursor is set back to normal, and the movie jumps to the "game over" frame.

The "moveBall" function ends by setting the location of the ball movie clip to "x" and "y".

NOTE

The operator "*=" works like "+=", except that it multiplies the original variable by the specified amount. So if "a" is 5, the line "a *= 3" will change "a" to 15. Likewise, if you use "a *= –1", then "a" will become –5. Using "*= –1" is a quick way to change the sign of a number.

```
    function moveBall() {
①      // change x and y
        x += dx;
        y += dy;

②      // check right wall
        if (x+ballRadius > rightWall) {
            overshoot = (x+ballRadius) - rightWall;
            x -= overshoot*2;
            dx *= -1;
        }

③      // check bottom
        if (y+ballRadius > bottomWall) {
```

```
        overshoot = (y+ballRadius) - bottomWall;
        y -= overshoot*2;
        dy *= -1;
    }
```

④➤
```
    // check top
    if (y-ballRadius < topWall) {
        overshoot = topWall - (y-ballRadius);
        y += overshoot*2;
        dy *= -1;
    }
```

⑤➤
```
    // is it where it should hit the paddle?
    paddleRight = paddle._x+(paddle._width/2);
    if ((x-ballRadius < paddleRight) and !passedPaddle) {
```

⑥➤
```
        // is the paddle there?
        paddleTop = paddle._y-(paddle._height/2);
        paddleBottom = paddle._y+(paddle._height/2);
        if ((y > paddleTop) and (y < paddleBottom)) {

            // hit paddle
            overshoot = paddleRight - (x-ballRadius);
            x += overshoot*2;
            dx *= -1;
```

⑦➤
```
            // speed up
            dx *= 1.05;
            dy *= 1.05;
        } else {

            // missed paddle, don't check again
            passedPaddle = true;
        }
    }
```

⑧➤
```
    // check left wall
    if ((x-ballRadius < leftWall) and passedPaddle) {
        Mouse.show();
        gotoAndPlay("game over");
    }

    // set ball location
    ball._x = x;
    ball._y = y;
}
```

Although the "moveBall" function is long and complex, the "movePaddle" function couldn't be any shorter. All it needs to do is set the vertical location of the paddle to the vertical location of the cursor.

```
function movePaddle() {
    // align paddle with cursor
    paddle._y = _ymouse;
}
```

Loose Ends

Make sure the ball movie clip instance is given the name "ball" and the paddle movie clip instance is given the name "paddle". Also, if the walls are not exactly where they are in the example movie, then be sure to set the constants in the "initGame" function to match them.

The main game frame also needs a *stop* on it so that the main timeline stops, although the "actions" movie clip will continue to loop and call functions.

Other Possibilities

One improvement that can be made to this game is to give the player a certain number of balls that they can loose. Then, instead of the game ending as soon as the first ball is lost, it can continue.

You can do this by setting a variable, such as "ballNum", to 3 or something at the start of the game. Then, instead of going to a "game over" frame, you can go to a "ball lost" frame if "ballNum" is greater than 0. The player can press a button and play again, but with a "ballNum" of one less.

Paddle Ball

⬤▷✕Example file: Paddleball.fla

Although the previous game is fun, it lacks a serious challenge. There is no real way to "win" the game. Instead, you play for as long as you can until you lose.

A more interesting game would allow the player to control one paddle, while the computer controls the other. The player tries not to let a ball get past and hopes the computer misses.

Figure 11.3 shows what the example movie, Paddleball.fla, looks like. The player controls the left paddle and the computer controls the right paddle.

Figure 11.3
In Paddle Ball, the player volleys back and forth with the computer.

Project Goal

The goal for this game is to create an artificially intelligent opponent for the player to compete against. The left paddle will be controlled by the player, whereas the right paddle will use logic to try to mimic what a human opponent might do.

The ball will bounce off of the top and bottom of the screen, but it is up to the human player and the computer player to make sure it does not leave the screen from the sides.

When a ball gets past either player, the game will pause until the player hits a "serve" button. Then the ball will launch itself from the middle of the screen. The game will keep score and end when either player gets seven points.

Approach

There are many ways to make the artificial intelligence for this game. One would be to have the paddle follow the ball. This would be too perfect, however, because it would be impossible for the computer to miss.

A better way would be to have the computer's paddle move slowly toward the position of the ball. If the ball is moving too fast, the computer might not be able to make it to the correct position fast enough. Also, the paddle will move only when the ball is moving toward the computer's side.

TIP

Artificial intelligence sounds mysterious and complex. For games, however, it isn't so important that the opponent be smart. The computer opponent merely needs to facilitate fun game play. In many cases, like in this game, it would be easy to make an opponent that is flawless. However, that would make an impossible-to-win game that is no fun. The challenge is to be able to make an opponent that presents enough of a challenge so that game is not easy, but not so much of a challenge that you can't win.

Keeping score just requires a couple of variables. However, pausing the game between serves can be tricky, so the game will have two frames: one in which the program waits for the player to press the "serve" button, and one in which the game action takes place. This second frame starts by setting a random initial direction for the ball.

Preparing the Movie

The movie is basically the same as the previous one. Instead of three frames, you'll need four: a "start game" frame, a "start level" frame, a "play" frame, and a "game over" frame. The "start level" frame will be seen before every ball is served. The "game over" frame will only be seen after the last ball has been lost.

There needs to be one paddle movie clip named "paddle" like in the previous game, and one named "computerPaddle". This second paddle is controlled by your ActionScript. Because the computer paddle will be on the right, the right wall needs to be removed. The top and bottom walls should stay.

Writing the Code

Starting with the previous movie, you need to make some changes to the existing functions, and add an important new function. Here is the "actions" movie clip script, which adds a call to this new function, "moveComputerPaddle":

```
onClipEvent(load) {
    _root.startLevel();
}

onClipEvent(enterFrame) {
    _root.moveBall();
    _root.movePaddle();
    _root.moveComputerPaddle();
}
```

Instead of a "startGame" function, this game will have a "startLevel" function that does all the same things as the previous "startGame" function, but also sets the ball moving in a random direction. It does this by sending the ball up 50% of the time, down 50% of the time, as well as left 50% of the time and right 50% of the time. This gives you four possible diagonal directions.

```
function startLevel() {

    // get start position of the ball
    x = ball._x;
    y = ball._y;

    // set initial speed, one of four random diagonals
    dx = 5;
    dy = 5;
```

```
        if (Math.random() < .5) dx *= -1;
        if (Math.random() < .5) dy *= -1;

        // hide cursor
        Mouse.hide();

        // set constants

        rightWall = 550;
        leftWall = 0
        topWall = 0;
        bottomWall = 400;
        ballRadius = ball._width/2;
        passedPaddle = false;
    }
```

The "moveBall" function now includes code to detect when the ball has passed the computer's paddle on the right ⑩ . This is similar to the code that handles the player's paddle on the left ⑨ , which is the same as in the previous game.

When the ball is lost on either the left side ⑪ or the right side ⑫ , the game is usually back to the "start level" frame. However, if there are no more balls left, it is sent to the "game over" frame. Depending on who lost the ball, a point is awarded to either "computerScore" or "playerScore."

```
    function moveBall() {
        // change x and y
        x += dx;
        y += dy;

        // check bottom
        if (y+ballRadius > bottomWall) {
            overshoot = (y+ballRadius) - bottomWall;
            y -= overShoot*2;
            dy *= -1;
        }

        // check top
        if (y-ballRadius < topWall) {
            overshoot = topWall - (y-ballRadius);
            y += overShoot*2;
            dy *= -1;
        }

        // is it where it should hit the paddle?
        paddleRight = paddle._x+(paddle._width/2);
        if ((x-ballRadius < paddleRight) and !passedPaddle) {
```

⑨→

```
    // is the paddle there?
    paddleTop = paddle._y-(paddle._height/2);
    paddleBottom = paddle._y+(paddle._height/2);
    if ((y > paddleTop) and (y < paddleBottom)) {

        // hit paddle
        overshoot =  paddleRight - (x-ballRadius);
        x += overShoot*2;
        dx *= -1;

        // speed up
        dx *= 1.05;
        dy *= 1.05;
    } else {

        // missed paddle, don't check again
        passedPaddle = true;
    }
}
```

(10)→
```
// is it where it should hit the computer's paddle?
paddleLeft = computerPaddle._x-(computerPaddle._width/2);
if ((x+ballRadius > paddleLeft) and !passedPaddle) {

    // is the paddle there?
    paddleTop = computerPaddle._y-(computerPaddle._height/2);
    paddleBottom = computerPaddle._y+(computerPaddle._height/2);
    if ((y > paddleTop) and (y < paddleBottom)) {

        // hit paddle
        overshoot =  (x+ballRadius) - paddleLeft;
        x -= overShoot*2;
        dx *= -1;

        // speed up
        dx *= 1.05;
        dy *= 1.05;
    } else {

        // missed paddle, don't check again
        passedPaddle = true;
    }
}
```

(11)→
```
// check left wall
if ((x-ballRadius < leftWall) and passedPaddle) {
```

```
        Mouse.show();
        computerScore++;
        if (numBalls == 0) {
            gotoAndPlay("game over");
        } else {
            numBalls--;
            gotoAndPlay("start level");
        }
    }
```

⑫➤
```
    // check right wall
    if ((x+ballRadius > rightWall) and passedPaddle) {
        Mouse.show();
        playerScore++;
        if (numBalls == 0) {
            gotoAndPlay("game over");
        } else {
            numBalls--;
            gotoAndPlay("start level");
        }
    }

    // set ball location
    ball._x = x;
    ball._y = y;
}
```

The "movePaddle" function is identical to the one in the previous game. However, you need to add the "moveComputerPaddle" function that controls the right paddle. This function only moves the paddle if the ball is headed to the right. Then, it moves the paddle up if the ball is above the height of the paddle, and down if it is below.

The speed at which it moves is set at the start of the function. The higher you make this value, the longer the paddle will be able to keep up with the ball.

```
function moveComputerPaddle() {
    // set speed of paddle
    moveAmount = 8;

    // see if ball is moving in this direction
    if (dx > 0) {

        // move paddle up
        if (y < computerPaddle._y-moveAmount) {
            computerPaddle._y -= moveAmount;
```

```
        // move paddle down
        } else if (y > computerPaddle._y+moveAmount) {
            computerPaddle._y += moveAmount;
        }
    }
}
```

One additional piece of code that you need for this movie is something in the "start game" frame to initialize the number of balls and the score. This can't be put into the "startLevel" function because they should only be set at the start of the game, not before each ball is served.

```
numBalls = 7;
computerScore = 0;
playerScore = 0;
stop();
```

Loose Ends

You will also need to create the "playerScore" and "computerScore" text areas and place them on the Stage. They have been placed in all but the "start game" frame so that they are visible between serves and at the end of the game.

Other Possibilities

It is easy to change the number of balls by just changing the one value in the "start game" frame. However, you can also change other things about the game to make it longer or more difficult. You can increase the speed of the computer's paddle by changing one value in the "moveComputerPaddle" function.

You can also make the computer smarter. For instance, you can write code to predict the destination of the ball and have the computer paddle move there rather than just follow the ball. The ball will bounce off the top or bottom wall only once while crossing the screen, so this prediction can be done with just a bit of simple math if you are up for it.

Paddle Bricks

Example file: Paddlebricks.fla

The next game uses the three primary elements of the previous two games—a ball, a paddle, and walls—to build a game far more advanced. This is another classic arcade game, first called "Breakout," and then cloned under various names.

Figure 11.4 shows the example movie. In addition to a ball and paddle, you can see five rows of bricks at the top of the screen. The object of the game is to bounce the ball off these bricks, which makes them disappear. Get rid of all the bricks and the next level is even faster.

Figure 11.4
The "Paddle Bricks" game features rows of bricks that the player must hit with the ball.

Project Goal

The goal is to build a classic paddle and brick arcade game. The paddle moves horizontally along with the mouse. The ball bounces off the top and sides, but is lost if it gets past the paddle on the bottom.

When a brick is hit by the ball, the ball bounces back, but the brick disappears. After all the bricks have been removed, the level ends. The next level has the same bricks, but a faster ball. If the player looses three balls, the game is over. Check out the movie, Paddlebricks.fla, to see how the game plays. You'll find it on the Web site.

Another change from the previous ball and paddle games is that the direction of the ball is affected by where the ball hits the paddle. If the ball strikes the left side of the paddle, the ball goes left, if it hits the right side, it goes right. The angle is determined by how far from the center of the paddle the impact occurs.

Approach

The code to detect whether the ball hits the paddle or the walls is similar to the previous two games. One difference is to allow the ball to bounce back from the paddle at any point, not just the top side of the paddle. This makes it a little easier to hit the ball.

When the ball intersects a brick, it reverses the vertical direction. The brick is repositioned off the screen.

Instead of using *hitTest* to determine when the ball hits a brick, we will examine all four sides of the ball against all four sides of the brick. If the ball and brick overlap at all, it's counted as a hit. If we had used *hitTest*, then we could only have detected when the center of the ball was inside the rectangle of the brick. That's not accurate enough for this game.

When the ball hits the paddle, we calculate the distance from the center of the ball to the center of the paddle. The paddle is 50 pixels long, so the distance can be a little more than 25 pixels, either positive or negative. Divide this number by 4 to get a value between about −7 and 7. This is used as the new value of "dx", which will be the horizontal speed.

This means that the player can direct the ball. If the player hits the ball on the left corner, for instance, they can send it sharply to the left. If they hit the middle, it should go straight up.

Preparing the Movie

This movie requires five frames, more than any other game so far. The first frame is the "start game" frame. It only appears at the start of a brand new game. Pressing the "Play" button takes the player directly to the "play" frame and the game starts.

The second frame is the "start level" frame. It is shown when the player starts level 2, or any level after that. The "Play" button here also takes the player to the "play" frame in which the new level will start.

The third frame is the "start ball" frame. This frame is shown when the player loses a ball and needs to be served another one. Figure 11.5 shows the main timeline for the example movie. You can see that the bricks exist on both frames three and four, which is the "play" frame. This allows the brick movie clips to remain in place while the movie travels from the "play" frame to the "start ball" frame. Otherwise, the bricks would be reset to their original positions.

Figure 11.5

The main timeline for the Paddle Bricks game shows the five frames needed for the game.

The last frame is the "game over" frame. Pressing the "Play" button on this frame takes you back to the "start game" frame where some important variables will be reset.

Besides the frame arrangement, the bricks for frames three and four need to be created. In the example movie, these are 48 pixels wide by 8 pixels high. They are spaced 50×10 pixels in the example movie, which makes 11 bricks across by 5 down for a total of 55 bricks.

TIP

To avoid having to name 55 bricks on the Stage, consider starting with no bricks on the Stage at all, and using *attachMovie* to add each brick with code. Although this technique is not used here, you can see it in action in the Pegs game in Chapter 14, "Brain Puzzles."

Unfortunately, each brick must be individually named for the code to recognize it. They are named "a1" to "a55" in the example movie. The ball clip is named "ball" and the paddle clip is named "paddle".

Writing the Code

Before the game frame is reached, two important variables need to be set in the "start game" frame of the movie. These represent the initial vertical speed of the ball, and the number of balls to be served:

```
dy = 3;
numBalls = 3;
stop();
```

When the "play" frame is reached, the usual "actions" movie clip is used to trigger functions on a regular basis. In this game, all the wall and paddle collision detection has been placed in the "moveBall" function, but a separate function—"checkCollisions"—was made for the bricks.

```
onClipEvent(load) {
    _root.startBall();
}

onClipEvent(enterFrame) {
    _root.moveBall();
    _root.movePaddle();
    _root.checkCollisions();
}
```

When the "play" frame begins, the ball is served. The location of the ball is determined by where it happens to be sitting on the Stage. The horizontal speed of the ball is always 3 to the right. The vertical speed is set in the first frame when "dy" was given a value of 3. However, this will be changed before the next level.

In addition to the ball settings, take this opportunity to set some values that will never change during the course of play.

```
function startBall() {
    // get starting point of ball
    x = ball._x;
    y = ball._y;

    // set starting x speed
    dx = 3;

    // hide cursor
    Mouse.hide();
```

```
      // set constants
      rightWall = 550;
      leftWall = 0
      topWall = 0;
      bottomWall = 400;
      ballRadius = ball._width/2;
      paddleTop = paddle._y-paddle._height/2;
      paddleBottom = paddle._y+paddle._height/2;
}
```

The next function controls the paddle by aligning it horizontally with the mouse:

```
// paddle follows cursor
function movePaddle() {
      paddle._x = _xmouse;
}
```

You will recognize the next function because it looks a lot like the "moveBall" function in the other games of this chapter. There are some differences, however.

To determine whether the ball hits the paddle, the code checks to see whether the sides of the ball and the sides of the paddle show the two overlapping at all ⑬. Then, when there is a hit, the horizontal speed of the ball is determined based on where the ball hit the paddle ⑭. In addition, the code to determine when the ball has been missed is simpler because it just checks to see whether the ball has passed the bottom ⑮.

```
function moveBall() {
      // change x and y
      x += dx;
      y += dy;

      // check right
      if (x+ballRadius > rightWall) {
          overshoot = (x+ballRadius) - rightWall;
          x -= overShoot*2;
          dx *= -1;
      }

      // check left
      if (x-ballRadius < leftWall) {
          overshoot = leftWall - (x-ballRadius);
          x += overShoot*2;
          dx *= -1;
      }

      // check top
      if (y-ballRadius < topWall) {
          overshoot = topWall - (y-ballRadius);
          y += overShoot*2;
```

```
        dy *= -1;
    }
```

⑬➤
```
    // is it where it should hit the paddle?
    if ((y+ballRadius > paddleTop) and (y-ballRadius < paddleBottom)) {

        // is the paddle there?
        paddleLeft = paddle._x-(paddle._width/2);
        paddleRight = paddle._x+(paddle._width/2);
        if ((x+ballRadius > paddleLeft) and (x-ballRadius < paddleRight)) {

            // hit paddle
            overshoot =  paddleTop - (y+ballRadius);
            y += overShoot*2;
            dy *= -1;
```

⑭➤
```
            // set horizontal speed of ball
            // depending on where the paddle
            // and ball connected
            dx = (ball._x - paddle._x)/4;

        } else {

            // missed paddle, don't check again
            passedPaddle = true;
        }
    }

    // check bottom
```

⑮➤
```
    if (y > bottomWall){
        Mouse.show();
        if (numBalls == 0) {

            // no more balls, game over
            gotoAndPlay("game over");
        } else {

            // one less ball
            numBalls--;
            gotoAndPlay("start ball");
        }
    }

    // set ball
    ball._x = x;
    ball._y = y;
}
```

To determine whether the ball has hit a brick, the code loops through all 55 bricks. A brick at the horizontal location –1000 has already been hit, so those are ignored. Otherwise, the "brickHit" function is called to see whether they overlap. If they do, the brick is removed and the ball bounces.

Notice the variable "leveldone". It starts off as *true*, but is changed to *false* as soon as a brick is encountered that is in play and is not being hit by the ball. If the "leveldone" variable remains *true* after all balls have been hit, then the player has succeeded in removing all the bricks. The game now goes to the "start level" frame, but not before the vertical speed of the ball, "dy", has been increased.

TIP

Notice that you must check to see whether the vertical speed of the ball is greater than 7, and set it back to 7 if it is. This is because the bricks are all 8 pixels high. A speed of 8 or higher could mean that the ball skips right over bricks without hitting them. Fortunately, a speed of 7 is fast enough that even a good player should not be able to keep up for long.

```
function checkCollisions() {
    // get sides of ball
    ballTop = ball._y - ball._height/2;
    ballBottom = ball._y + ball._height/2;
    ballLeft = ball._x - ball._width/2;
    ballRight = ball._x + ball._width/2;

    // assume level is done
    leveldone = true;

    // loop through bricks to see if any were hit
    for(i=1;i<=55;i++) {
        brick = _root["a"+i];

        // see if brick is still around
        if (brick._x <> -1000) {
            if (brickHit(brick)) {

                // brick hit, so take away
                brick._x = -1000;

                // reverse direction of ball
                dy *= -1;

            } else {

                // brick stays, so level is not over
                leveldone = false;
```

```
                }
            }
        }

        // see if all bricks gone
        if (leveldone) {

            // start new level
            Mouse.show();
            gotoAndPlay("start level");

            // increase vertical speed
            dy += 1;
            if (dy > 7) dy = 7;
        }
    }
```

The "hitBrick" function checks all four sides of the ball against all four sides of the brick to see whether there is any overlap. It returns a *true* or *false*.

TIP

Notice that the "hitBrick" function contains four nested *if* statements. You might wonder why not use a string of four tests with *and* between each one. The reason is speed. With four nested *if* statements, Flash can find one of these conditions to be *false* and never have to check the others. This will significantly reduce the amount of work that Flash has to do, and increase the speed of the game. With *and* operators, Flash would have to check all four conditions, even if the first one is *false* to begin with.

```
function brickHit(brick) {
    // perform tests on all four sides
    if (ballTop <= brick._y + brick._height/2) {
        if (ballBottom >= brick._y - brick._height/2) {
            if (ballRight >= brick._x - brick._width/2) {
                if (ballLeft <= brick._x + brick._width/2) {

                    // all four tests true, so brick is hit
                    return(true);
                }
            }
        }
    }

    // brick not hit
    return(false);
}
```

Loose Ends

A lot of elements need to be set perfectly for the code to work. Check out the example movie, Paddlebricks.fla to see a working version of this game in action. To make your own version, you have to remember to name all the movie clips and place *stop* commands in each frame. You'll also need to remember the little pieces of code in the buttons and the first frame.

The rows of bricks were colored in using the "Tint" effect to make the game more visually interesting. It has nothing at all to do with the functionality of the game.

Other Possibilities

To make this a real game, you should add scoring. I didn't want to further complicate the code with this in the example here. Just add a "score" text area and link it to the "score" variable. Then, add a point every time the player gets a brick.

You might also want to add text areas to tell the player what level they are on and how many balls they have left. Sound effects would be a nice and easy addition too.

Quizzes and Word Puzzles

- Flash Quiz
- Flash Trivia
- Hangman

Let's get away from arcade games for a while and look at a series of games that involves words, not actions. There are two different types of word games that we will look at in this chapter. This first is a type of game that asks questions and then determines whether the player answered correctly. The second type of game makes the player figure out a word or phrase by guessing one letter at a time.

Flash Quiz

Example file: Flashquiz.fla

The first two games you will build in this chapter involve questions and answers. The first is a quiz game in which 10 questions are presented, each with 4 possible answers. After the player selects an answer for each, he sees how he has done.

Figure 12.1 shows the main game frame. The question is near the top, and the four possible answers are below it. The user must click the buttons to the left of each answer.

Figure 12.1
The main game frame shows a question and four answers.

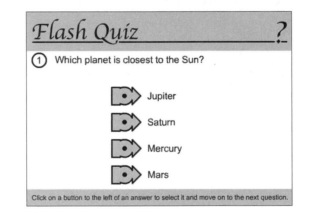

Project Goal

The goal for this game is to read a set of questions from an external text file. Then, the game displays the questions one by one for the player to answer. Four possible answers are shown. A sound that plays when the player chooses her answer signifies whether she got it right or wrong.

When all 10 questions have been asked, the game is over. A final score is displayed. Go to the example movie Flashquiz.fla on the Web site and play a few rounds to get the idea of how it works.

Approach

The first task is to get the questions and answers from a text file. You can use *loadVariables* for this; it will grab a local text file and take the questions and answers from there.

Unfortunately, *loadVariables* can't handle arrays or objects, which is what you need to store a set of questions and answers efficiently. However, you can read in a single piece of text and use *split* to break it into parts to store in an array. This is how you can get 10 questions, 4 answers for each question, and the number of the correct answer, all from one block of text.

After the questions are in an array, the rest is simple. The text from each question and the answers are placed in the appropriate text areas. The number of the correct answer is stored in a variable. Then, the program waits for the player to press a button.

Each button calls a function, telling it which answer it represents. If the right button is pressed, a good sound plays and the number of questions correctly answered is incremented. Either way, the next question is asked.

When all 10 questions have been asked, the game advances to a "game over" frame where the final score is displayed.

The only extra feature of this game is a neat special effect that causes the text to fly in from the right when each question is first asked.

Preparing the Movie

A lot of things need to be set up before the coding can begin. The first frame, shown in Figure 12.2, shows the "loading" frame. Because the questions will be loaded from an external text file, the movie has to wait to make sure that the questions are all there before it can proceed.

Figure 12.2
The "loading" frame stays on the screen until the questions have been loaded.

After the questions have been loaded, some ActionScript moves the game along to the second frame, labeled "start game". This frame features some instructions and a button, as shown in Figure 12.3.

Figure 12.3
The "start game"
frame waits until
the user is ready for
the first question.

The game frame itself, shown earlier in Figure 12.1, is the most complex. It features a text area for the question, four text areas for the answers, and even a small text area with the question number. There are also four buttons, one to the left of each answer.

The five main text areas are not all they seem in Figure 12.1. Each is actually a text area named "text" inside a movie clip. These five movie clips are called "question" and "answer0" to "answer3". This was done instead of using plain text areas so the clips can be moved on the Stage to create a certain effect to be discussed later.

Writing the Code

There isn't much code in this game, but it is scattered in a few places. The first frame has code attached to a movie clip and code attached to the frame.

The "Loading…" text in Figure 12.2 is actually inside a movie clip because I needed a movie clip, any movie clip, to attach the following code to. It starts by requesting the questions from a text file, and then waits until the data has been loaded. Then, it sends the data to a function in the main timeline. This is needed because when a *loadVariables* command is used attached to a movie clip, the variables are loaded into that movie clip. To get that information to the main timeline, you pass it up to a function on the root level. The same is true for the assignment of the variable "topic" on the root level.

NOTE

The *loadVariables* command attempts to grab a text file from a URL. It then reads in the text file as if it were variable assignments. For instance, a text file that contained "myVariable=Hello" would set the variable "myVariable" to "Hello". The variable is set when the text file has been read in. Because things do not load instantly on the Web, this might happen several seconds after the *loadVariables* command has been issued.

```
onClipEvent(load) {
    // get the questions
    this.loadVariables("flashquiz.txt", 0);
}


onClipEvent(data) {
    // set the topic text
    _root.topic = topic;

    // put the questions into an array
    _root.initQuestions(questions);

    // start the game
    _root.gotoAndPlay("start game");
}
```

NOTE

The *onClipEvent(data)* function gets called when a *loadVariables* request is complete. You can use it to run commands that need to wait for the *loadVariables* command to complete.

The "initQuestions" function is located in the main timeline on the first frame. It takes a long string of text and converts it into an array with questions, answers, and the number of the correct answer for each question.

Here is what the first part of the Flashquiz.txt file looks like. The first line assigns the text "The Planets" to the variable "topic". This assignment ends with the "&" character. Then, it starts setting the variable "questions". This text is several lines long. Each line is a single question. Each question is broken into three parts: the question text, the answers, and the number of the correct answer. A colon is used to divide these three elements. Furthermore, a semicolon is used to divide the four answers.

```
topic=The Planets&questions=Which planet is closest to the
Sun?:Jupiter;Saturn;Mercury;Mars:2:
Which planet is tilted on its axis the most?:Earth;Venus;Mars;Uranus:3:
Which planet is the largest?:Jupiter;Earth;Neptune;Pluto:0:
Which planet has exactly two moons?:Venus;Mars;Saturn;Uranus:1:
```

TIP

An extra colon was used at the end of each line so that when the line is broken into parts by the code, any extra characters at the end of the line will be placed in a fourth, unused, part. What extra elements would there be? Well, if you use some Windows text editors, an extra invisible character is placed at the end of every line of text. If you let this extra character be a part of the number of the correct answer, it will prevent Flash from converting that number to something it can use. Thus, the extra colon places this extra character harmlessly in an unused fourth element of each line.

CAUTION

Be careful not to place an unwanted blank line at the end of the text file. It is easy to press Return or Enter at the end of the last question to create this line. If a blank line is added to the end of the text file, the code will use that as an eleventh question.

This text is broken into array elements by using the *split* command several times. First it is used to separate questions from each other. Then, it is used to separate the parts of the questions. Finally, it is used to separate the answers. The result is a nested array with all the information you need:

```
function initQuestions(questions) {
    // break into questions
    qArray = questions.split(String.fromCharCode(13));

    // break each question into question, answers, and right answer
    for(i=0;i<qArray.length;i++) {
        qArray[i] = qArray[i].split(":");

        // break the answers apart
        qArray[i][1] = qArray[i][1].split(";");
    }
}
```

CAUTION

I used *String.fromCharCode(13)* to get the carriage return character which is used to break up the lines of a text file. Why didn't I use the ActionScript Constant *newline*? Becase *newline* is different between the Mac and Windows version of Flash. On the Mac, it returns character number 13, but on Windows it returns character number 10.

NOTE

The *split* function takes a string and breaks it into an array of strings. The one parameter it takes is the character used to divide the items. In the previous example, both a colon and then a semicolon is used to split strings into arrays.

When the game goes to the "play" frame, the ActionScript in the main timeline immediately calls "initGame". This sets the "questionNum" and "numRight" to 0. It calls "displayQuestion" to show the first question.

```
function initGame() {
    // set variables
    questionNum = 0;
    numRight = 0;

    // ask the first question
    displayQuestion();
}
```

The "displayQuestion" function determines whether the game is over, displays the final score if necessary, and jumps to the "game over" frame if the game is over. Otherwise, it takes the question and each answer and places them in the text areas inside the appropriate movie clips. It places the number of the correct answer in "correctAnswer".

```
function displayQuestion() {
    // see if all the questions have been asked
    if (questionNum >= qArray.length) {

        // show final score and end the game
        finalScore = numRight + " out of " + qArray.length;
        gotoAndPlay("game over");

    } else {

        // place the question and answers on the screen
        question.text = qArray[questionNum][0];
        answer0.text = qArray[questionNum][1][0];
        answer1.text = qArray[questionNum][1][1];
        answer2.text = qArray[questionNum][1][2];
        answer3.text = qArray[questionNum][1][3];

        // show the question number
        questionNumDisplay = questionNum+1;

        // remember which one is right
        correctAnswer = int(qArray[questionNum][2]);

        // make the text slide in
        animateIn();
    }
}
```

NOTE

When you have an array inside another array, you can refer to a specific item by using multiple bracket sets. For instance, "myArray[3][8]" refers to the eighth item in the third array in the "myArray" variable. "myArray" is made up of four or more arrays and the third one has at least nine items.

The "animateIn" function is just a special effect, and does not really affect game play. It sets the position of each text movie clip off the Stage to the right. It then sets a variable called "xstop" for each of these movie clips to the x position that the movie clip should be at. Code assigned to each of these clips then acts to move the clips to the left until they line up with "xstop".

```
function animateIn() {
    // set the location of each piece of text
    // and set where each movie clip should stop
    question.xstop = 300;
    question._x = 800;

    answer0.xstop = 400;
    answer0._x = 1000;

    answer1.xstop = 400;
    answer1._x = 1200;

    answer2.xstop = 400;
    answer2._x = 1400;

    answer3.xstop = 400;
    answer3._x = 1600;
}
```

When the user clicks one of the four buttons, the button calls "selectAnswer" with the number of the answer, from 0 to 3. If this matches "correctAnswer", a good sound is played, and "numRight" is increased. If not, a bad sound is played. Either way, the "questionNum" is incremented and the next question is displayed.

```
function selectAnswer(n) {
    // add to count if correct
    if (n == correctAnswer) {
        triggerSound("right");
        numRight++;
    } else {
        triggerSound("wrong");
    }

    // ask next question
```

```
        questionNum++;
        displayQuestion();
    }
```

"triggerSound" is a simple function that comes in handy in a number of game situations.
It just plays a sound with the proper link name.

```
function triggerSound(soundName) {
        // simply play a sound
        soundfx.stop();
        soundfx = new Sound();
        soundfx.attachSound(soundName);
        soundfx.start();
    }
```

That's it for the main timeline script. However, there are two important small scripts
assigned to other elements on the Stage. The first is the script assigned to each text
movie clip. It checks to see whether the clip's position is to the right of "xstop" and
moves it more to the left if it is. The result is that the movie clip keeps moving left until
it hits "xstop". Therefore, when the position of the clip is set off screen to the right by
the "animateIn" function, the question will slide in from the right.

```
onClipEvent(enterFrame) {
    if (_x != xstop) _x -= 20;
}
```

Each button also has a short script attached to it. It calls the "selectAnswer" function
with a number from 0 to 3. So the first button has this script:

```
on (release) {
    selectAnswer(0);
}
```

Other buttons will use a 1, 2, or a 3 in place of the 0.

Loose Ends

You'll need two sounds, one linked with the name "right" and one with the name
"wrong". You'll also need a "continue" button of some sort, like the one shown in
Figure 12.3 earlier. Check out the Flashquiz.fla movie on the Web site if you have any
questions about how this all fits together.

Other Possibilities

Although the goal of this program is to present 10 questions to the player, nothing in
the code restricts the game to 10 questions. You can ask more or less by changing the
Flashquiz.txt file.

Also, in addition to showing the player that he got "8 out of 10" right, you can give the player a ranking. So "8 out of 10" might qualify the player as a "You know your planets!", although only 2 out of 10 might get him the message "Go back to school."

Flash Trivia

Example file: **Flashtrivia.fla**

Now that you have a working quiz game, you can build on that to create a trivia game. There are really only a few differences between the quiz game and the trivia game. You'll add more advanced scoring, giving players a chance to score more points if they are quick, and also allowing them to guess more than once while losing points for each wrong guess.

Another feature is randomness. The answers will be scrambled so they won't always appear in the same order for everyone. This will make it easier to build the question list, because the first answer in the data file will always be the correct one, but it will not usually be presented at the first answer that the player sees.

Figure 12.4 shows the main play frame of the example movie, Flashtrivia.fla.

Figure 12.4

The trivia game looks a lot like the quiz game, but scoring takes time into account.

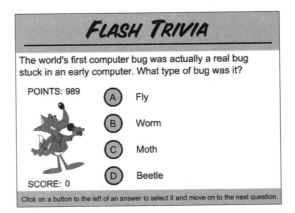

Project Goal

The goal for this movie is to create a basic trivia game that builds build on the previous game. Instead of the answers always being shown in the same order, they will be shown in a random order each time.

When a question first appears, it will be worth 1,000 potential points. As the player tries to determine the correct answer, the number of potential points rapidly decreases. If the player makes an incorrect guess, she will lose even more potential points. When the player finally gets the right answer, the number of potential points remaining will be added to her score.

Approach

Like the previous movie, the questions and answers will be loaded from an external text file. However, this text file will be a little different. In the previous game, the answers were presented in a set order, and an additional item pointed out which answer was the correct one. This time, the correct answer will always be first, followed by three incorrect answers. You can do this because the answers will be shuffled anyway. Here are a few lines from the "flashtrivia.txt" file:

```
questions=The world's first computer bug was actually a real bug stuck in an
early computer. What type of bug was it?:Moth;Beetle;Fly;Worm:
Which is the world's largest Island?:Greenland;Iceland;Australia;New Zealand:
Besides humans, what other animal also has individual fingerprints?:Koala
Bears;Apes;Snakes;Frogs:
```

CAUTION

Just like with the previous project, be careful not to place an unwanted blank line at the end of the text file. It is easy to press Return or Enter at the end of the last question to create this line. If a blank line is added to the end of the text file, the code will use that as an eleventh question.

Before each question is asked, the four answers are randomly shuffled into a new array. The correct answer can appear in any of the four spots. Its value is stored in a variable to use for comparison later.

We'll use the same animation as in the previous game, but we will speed it up a little. The question appears right away, with no animation, but the answers fly in quickly from the right. The number of potential points only starts to decrease after all four answers are in place.

When a player picks a wrong answer, not only are points deducted from the number of potential points, but the answer he selected also disappears.

Preparing the Movie

This movie has four frames. The first loads the questions and answers and places them in an array. The second frame explains the game to the player.

The action takes place in the third frame. This frame shows the question, four answers, and a button next to each answer. It also shows the number of potential points and the score, which are both dynamic text areas, the first linked to the variable "potentialPoints" and the second linked to the variable "score".

Remember that the four answers are actually movie clips with text areas inside them. The text areas are all set to represent a variable called "text". The four movie clips, however, are named "answer0" to "answer3".

The last frame of the game is the "game over" frame. This shows the final score and allows the player to press a button to play again.

Writing the Code

The first piece of code is attached to the "loading" movie clip on frame 1. It is basically the same code used in the previous game to load the questions from the text file. When the questions arrive, it calls "initQuestions", which is in the main timeline.

```
onClipEvent(load) {
    // get the questions
    this.loadVariables("flashtrivia.txt", 0);
}


onClipEvent(data) {
    // put the questions into an array
    _root.initQuestions(questions);

    // start the game
    _root.gotoAndPlay("start game");
}
```

The "initQuestions" function breaks the string into questions with two parts. The first part is the question, and the second part is the answers. Then it breaks the answers into individual answers. This is all stored in the "qArray" array.

```
function initQuestions(questions) {
    // break into questions
    qArray = questions.split(String.fromCharCode(13));

    // break each question into question and answers
    for(i=0;i<qArray.length;i++) {
        qArray[i] = qArray[i].split(":");

        // break the answers apart
        qArray[i][1] = qArray[i][1].split(";");
    }

}
```

Most of the code is in the "play" frame. This is where the questions get asked and the player has to react. When the frame begins, the "initGame" function sets the score to 0 and displays the first question.

```
function initGame() {
    // set variables
    questionNum = 0;
    score = 0;
```

```
      // ask the first question
      displayQuestion();
  }
```

The "displayQuestion" function takes the next question and places the question and answer text in the proper text areas. It also sets the number of potential points for this question to 1,000.

```
  function displayQuestion() {
      // see if all the questions have been asked
      if (questionNum >= qArray.length) {

          // show final score and end the game
          gotoAndPlay("game over");

      } else {
          // rearrange
          answers = shuffleArray(qArray[questionNum][1].slice(0));

          // place the question and answers on the screen
          question.text = qArray[questionNum][0];
          answer0.text = answers[0];
          answer1.text = answers[1];
          answer2.text = answers[2];
          answer3.text = answers[3];

          // show the question number
          questionNumDisplay = questionNum+1;

          // remember which one is right
          correctAnswer = qArray[questionNum][1][0];

          // make the text slide in
          animateIn();

          // start potential points at 1000
          potentialPoints = 1000;
      }
  }
```

The "scoreCount" function is called once per frame by the "actions" movie clip. It subtracts one point from the number of potential points, making sure that it never drops below 0.

```
  // every frame that goes by subtracts one point
  function scoreCount() {
```

```
    // make sure that last answer has arrived
    if (answer3._x == 400) {

        // subtract point
        potentialPoints -= 1;
        if (potentialPoints < 0) potentialPoints = 0;
    }
}
```

The "shuffleArray" function is used by "displayQuestion" to re-order the answers randomly. It works by creating a new array and then adding one element at a time from the old array to the new array.

```
// take array1 and shuffle into array 2
function shuffleArray(array1) {
    // create new, empty array
    array2 = new Array();

    // loop through array
    do {
        // select a random item
        r = int(Math.random()*array1.length);
        // add item to new array
        array2.push(array1[r]);
        // remove item from old array
        array1.splice(r,1);
    } while (array1.length > 0);

    // send back the new array
    return(array2);
}
```

The "animateIn" function sets the location of the four answers off the Stage to the right. It also notes that each of these movie clips should stop moving left when it gets to the horizontal location 400. A script attached to each movie clip moves the clip quickly to the left until that happens.

```
function animateIn() {
    // set the location of each answer
    // and set where each should stop
    answer0.xstop = 400;
    answer0._x = 800;

    answer1.xstop = 400;
    answer1._x = 1000;
```

```
    answer2.xstop = 400;
    answer2._x = 1200;

    answer3.xstop = 400;
    answer3._x = 1400;
}
```

When the player clicks a button, the answer she selected is compared to the
"correctAnswer" variable, which was assigned in "displayQuestion". If she got it right,
she gets the potential points, and the next question is displayed. If not, then 200 points
are deducted from the number of potential points, and the answer is removed from the
screen.

```
function selectAnswer(n) {
    // correct
    if (answers[n] == correctAnswer) {
        triggerSound("right");

        // add score
        score += potentialPoints;

        // ask next question
        questionNum++;
        displayQuestion();

    } else {
        // wrong
        triggerSound("wrong");

        // subtract from potential points
        potentialPoints -= 200;
        if (potentialPoints < 0) potentialPoints = 0;

        // remove the answer
        _root["answer"+n].text = "";
    }
}
```

The "triggerSound" utility function is the same one used earlier in this chapter. It simplifies adding quick sounds to the rest of the code.

```
function triggerSound(soundName) {
    // simply play a sound
    soundfx.stop();
    soundfx = new Sound();
    soundfx.attachSound(soundName);
    soundfx.start();
}
```

The other pieces of code on the "play" frame include the bit of code on the "actions" movie clip that calls "scoreCount".

```
onClipEvent(enterFrame) {
    _root.scoreCount();
}
```

The code found on each of the four answer movie clips is also used (here is the code for one of the clips). Notice that it moves the movie clip twice as fast as in the quiz game.

```
onClipEvent(enterFrame) {
    if (_x != xstop) _x -= 40;
}
```

Each of the four buttons includes a script that triggers "selectAnswer". Not only do these buttons react to mouse clicks, but each button is assigned a keyboard key as well. For instance, the first button, which you can see is labeled "A" in Figure 12.4 (shown previously), also reacts to the key "A".

```
on (release, keyPress "A") {
    selectAnswer(0);
}
```

Loose Ends

Browse through each element in the example movie Flashtrivia.fla on the Web site. There are many named text areas, including the question, the four answers, the potential points, and the score. Each button is the same movie clip, but a static letter has been placed on top of it. These letters don't do anything except remind the user that he can press a key on the keyboard instead of clicking the button itself.

Other Possibilities

Like the quiz game, you can place as many questions in the text file as you want. If you know server-side CGI programming, you could even write a server program to generate the Flashtrivia.txt information from a database of questions.

You can easily change the number of potential points that a question starts with, and change the number of points deducted for a wrong answer.

Hangman

⊕▷⊲**Example file: Hangman.fla**

This next game should be familiar to all. The classic pencil-and-paper game, Hangman, asks the player to guess which letters are used in a phrase. If the letter she guesses is in the phrase, that letter is revealed in every position where it is located. If the letter is not in the phrase at all, a piece of a drawing of a man getting hanged is added. If the drawing is complete before the phrase has been guessed, the player loses.

Project Goal

This goal here is to recreate the classic Hangman game in Flash. The player can use the keyboard to make guesses. Flash takes care of showing the letters and drawing the hanging man, or in this case, the fox.

Figure 12.5 shows the main game frame with the fox fully drawn and some letters showing. In this case, the game has just been lost.

Figure 12.5
This Hangman game has been lost.

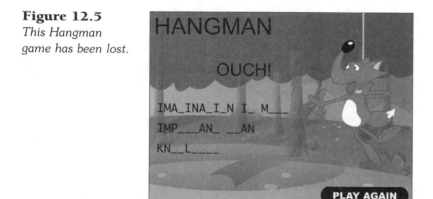

Approach

This game requires a lot of string manipulation. The phrase to be guessed is a string. From that, you build a string that uses underscore characters in place of letters. This will be what the player sees.

When the player makes a guess, that letter is compared to every letter in the original phrase. If the letter matches one in the phrase, that letter is shown in that position on the screen.

If the player guesses wrong, the fox movie clip is advanced to the next frame, which adds a part of the fox. If this is the last frame of the fox movie clip, the game is over.

Preparing the Movie

The main element is the text area on the screen. The text area starts with all underscores and spaces, which are replaced gradually with letters as letters are correctly guessed.

The text area has to be set up as "Dynamic Text" and linked to the variable "display". Figure 12.6 shows the Text Options panel for this text area. You can see that you also need the Word Wrap option turned on.

Figure 12.6
The Text Options panel for the Hangman text area is shown here.

The display text uses the "Monaco" font, which is a monospaced font found on every Mac. If you are building your movie in Windows, you might have to use another monospaced font such as "Courier New" instead.

> **TIP**
>
> Monospaced font is necessary for this game so that the words wrap around from line to line exactly the same as game play continues. If the letters were different widths, the addition of new letters that were smaller or larger than the underscore would force Flash to rewrap the text.

This game also needs an "actions" movie clip that accepts keyboard input and passes it on to the main timeline script.

Writing the Code

The main parts of the code lie in the main timeline. There are only three functions. The first sets up the phrase at the start of the game.

The first function loops through all the letters in the phrase and creates a "display" string that contains underscores in place of letters. This is what the player sees at the start of the game.

```
function initGame() {
    // get phrase
    phrase = "Imagination is more important than knowledge";

    // build display
    display = "";
    for(i=0;i<phrase.length;i++) {
        // place spaces in the right spots
        if (phrase.charAt(i) == " ") {
            display = display + " ";
```

```
        } else {
            // place underscores in place of letters
            display = display + "_";
        }
    }
}
```

NOTE

The *charAt* function returns the character at a position in a string. Like most functions in ActionScript, the first character is at position 0.

Each time the player presses a key, the "actions" movie clip sends the character code for that letter to the "makeGuess" function. The first thing this function does is convert the code to a letter.

NOTE

The *fromCharCode* function takes a number, such as 65, and converts it to a character, such as "A". All characters have a corresponding code. Numbers 65 to 90 refer to all the capital letters. Numbers 97 to 122 refer to all the lowercase letters. Character 32 is a space. You can find a complete list of characters and codes in the Flash 5 documentation.

The "letter" variable is tested by the utility function "isAlpha" to see whether it is a letter. This means that other keys, such as the spacebar or a number, are ignored. We'll look at the "isAlpha" function later.

Then, the function loops through each letter of the phrase looking for matches. While it is doing this, the function is rebuilding the "display" variable. Every match found is placed in "display", as well as every letter that was there before.

The variable "gotOne" is set to *false* before all this happens. If any match is found, "gotOne" is set to *true*. If it remains *false* at the end of the loop, the player guessed wrong, and the fox movie clip is advanced to the next frame.

NOTE

The *toUpperCase()* function takes any string and converts all lowercase letters in it to capitals. This function is useful in situations like this in which you want the letters to match even if one is uppercase and the other is lowercase.

```
function makeGuess(code) {
    // get the character that corresponds to the key pressed
    letter = String.fromCharCode(code);
```

```
    // check to see if it is a letter
    if (isAlpha(letter)) {

        // assume that the letter will not be found
        gotOne = false;

        // start building new display
        newDisplay = "";
        for(i=0;i<phrase.length;i++) {

            // see if letters match
            if (phrase.charAt(i).toUpperCase() == letter.toUpperCase()) {

                // place letter in display text
                newDisplay = newDisplay + letter.toUpperCase();

                // note that at least one match has been found
                gotOne = true;

            } else {

                // not found, so display same character
                newDisplay = newDisplay + display.charAt(i) ;
            }
        }

        // show new display
        display = newDisplay;

        // if no match found, then add more to fox
        if (!gotOne) {
            fox.nextFrame();

            // see if the fox is done
            if (fox._currentFrame == 8) {
                gotoAndPlay("lose");
            }

        } else if (display == phrase.toUpperCase()) {
            // the display matches the original, game over
            gotoAndPlay("win");
        }
    }
}
```

The "isAlpha" function is a good utility function that takes any character string and tests
to see whether the first character is a letter. It uses *charCodeAt* to get the code of the

first letter. Because lowercase letters are 32 higher than uppercase, we will subtract 32 from any code greater than 90, to be able to look for uppercase and lowercase letters with one test.

NOTE

The *charCodeAt* function returns the code of any character in a string. The one argument it takes is the position of the character. So you can use it to look at the first character with *charCodeAt(0)*.

```
// utility to test whether a character is in A-Z
function isAlpha(letter) {
    // get character code
    n = letter.charCodeAt(0);

    // convert lowercase to uppercase
    if (n > 90) n -= 32;

    // see if it is in A-Z
    return ((n >= 65) and (n <= 90));
}
```

The other piece of code needed here is attached to the "actions" movie clip. It takes any keypress and sends it along to the "makeGuess" function.

NOTE

The *Key.getAscii()* function returns the character code of the key pressed. It should be used inside an *onClipEvent(keyUp)* function attached to a movie clip.

```
onClipEvent (keyUp) {
    _root.makeGuess(Key.getAscii());
}
```

Loose Ends

The final movie needs a "win" and "lose" frame to jump to when the game is over. The example movie, Hangman.fla, keeps these frames simple, but you can insert animation for each of these. For instance, the "win" animation can show the fox being set free, while the "lose" animation can show something more gruesome.

Other Possibilities

The phrase in this example is hard-coded into the "initGame" function. However, you can use what you learned about loading external text from the two other games in this chapter to make it easier to change the phrase. You could even include a list of phrases that will be shown one after the other.

If you want to include punctuation in the game, you can modify the code to look for other things besides spaces that will be automatically displayed at the start of the game. In fact, you could use *isAlpha* to test to see whether it is a letter, and display it at the start of the game if not.

Picture Puzzles

- Jigsaw Puzzle
- Sliding Puzzle
- Matching Game

Games that use images as the central playing pieces are very versatile. The images can be anything from any topic. Therefore, you can use them on just about any kind of Web site.

In this chapter, we'll look at three different types of picture puzzles. The first is a simple jigsaw puzzle, in which the player assembles pieces of a picture. The second game asks the player to slide square puzzle pieces along a grid until he or she has put the picture together. In the last game, the player turns over puzzle pieces two at a time to try to find matches.

Jigsaw Puzzle
⊕▷⊀Example file: Jigsawpuzzle.fla

Jigsaw puzzles consist of a number of similar-sized pieces that interlock to create a complete picture. They are usually made of cardboard and require the player to use a large surface area, such as a dining room table, to solve them. Something like this does not translate well into a computer game because a typical computer screen is pretty small in comparison.

However, you can easily make a similar game that will provide light entertainment on a Web site. Figure 13.1 shows the example movie, Jigsawpuzzle.fla. It consists of 24 puzzle pieces and an empty grid where they are to be placed.

Figure 13.1
This jigsaw puzzle game is mostly completed.

Project Goal
The goal for this game is to be a simple, yet usable, jigsaw puzzle game. The player will be able to drag the pieces from the edge of the Stage onto the grid. When the correct piece is placed near the correct spot, it will lock into place.

Approach

We'll be able to accomplish this goal with a short movie clip script attached to an "actions" movie clip off the Stage. When the user clicks the Stage, this script determines which piece is under the cursor. It then enables standard Flash dragging for this piece.

When the mouse button is lifted, the code determines whether the piece is now near its correct spot. If the piece is there, then it locks the piece to that exact spot.

We'll start with all the piece movie clips at 75% alpha to make them slightly lighter. Then, when the player sets a piece in its spot, it will change to 100% alpha. This will provide some feedback to the player that the piece is now at rest. We'll also check to make sure that a piece is not at 100% when the user clicks to drag, so that any pieces already properly place can't be dragged again.

You'll know whether a piece is in the right spot because all the pieces will be made so that their centers are at the center of the entire picture. For instance, the piece for the upper-left corner will have a center far to the right and below the piece, as shown in Figure 13.2.

Figure 13.2

The center of this piece corresponds to the center of the image.

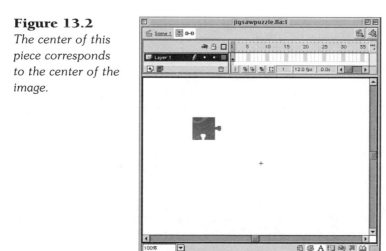

Now, imagine every piece built like this. The center point remains at the center of the picture no matter where in the picture the piece falls. If you are unsure of what I mean, stop and take a look at the example movie, Jigsawpuzzle.fla, right now. Examine several of the puzzle-piece movie clips and you will see how this center point remains constant.

This simplifies the code a great deal. Each piece now needs to be in exactly the same location as the puzzle outline to fit properly. So instead of figuring out what the location of each piece should be, they are all exactly the same.

Preparing the Movie

So how did I make the 24 puzzle pieces in this game? That, indeed, was the hardest part. However, there is no magic trick to it; it just took a lot of hard work. For the benefit of those who must know, I'll try to explain. This is not the only way to make puzzle pieces from a Flash graphic, however; I'm sure there are others, some possibly easier.

First, I started with the image, which was a bunch of ungrouped lines and fills on a single layer. I converted all the lines to fills, so I had just filled areas making up the entire picture.

Then, I assembled the puzzle frame. This was a collection of lines that looks like the outline shown earlier in Figure 13.1. I drew only a few parts of it along Flash's grid, and then copied and pasted it enough times to make the whole outline.

Next, I filled each area of the grid with red. I then selected all these filled areas except the one representing the puzzle piece in the upper-left corner. I copied these filled areas and then pasted them on top of my picture. I then selected and removed the entire red area, which left just that one puzzle piece.

Because many these actions destroyed previous steps, I kept copies of the outline and the picture in other layers. I was then able to redo half of these steps to get the next piece. I did that 24 times to get all 24 pieces.

When this was all done and I had 24 movie clips. I still had to use the grid to realign them so that the center point was where I wanted. It took me about 20 minutes to complete the process after I figured it out. However, you might be able to come up with an even faster method.

After I had all the pieces, I placed each movie clip on the Stage and gave it an instance name to match its movie clip name. The 24 pieces are named "0-0" to "5-3" to match the horizontal and vertical position of the piece. However, I placed each piece randomly around the edge of the Stage. I also set each movie clip to use the "alpha" effect at 75%. Then I placed a movie clip of the outline of the puzzle in the center and named it "outline".

Writing the Code

All the code is attached to a simple "actions" movie clip just off the Stage. It starts with an *onClipEvent(mouseDown)*, which will react to the user clicking somewhere on the Stage.

This code just loops through each of the puzzle pieces and finds out whether one is under the cursor. It also makes sure that this piece is not at 100% alpha, which would indicate that it has already been placed.

If a piece is found, Flash is told to drag that piece with the *startDrag* command. The nested loops are then abandoned.

NOTE

The *startDrag* command is a basic action that allows the user to drag a single movie clip. It isn't as versatile as drag methods used earlier in this book, but it works in this simple case. A *stopDrag* command returns the piece to normal.

```
onClipEvent(mouseDown) {
    // get mouse location
    mx = _root._xmouse;
    my = _root._ymouse;

    // loop through pieces looking for hit
    for(x=0;x<6;x++) {
        for(y=0;y<4;y++) {
            piece = _root[x+"-"+y];

            // see if the piece is under the cursor
            // and if it has not yet been placed
            if (piece.hitTest(mx,my) and (piece._alpha < 100)) {
                // this is the piece clicked
                piece.startDrag();

                // break out of all loops
                x = 6;
                y = 4;
                break;
            }
        }
    }
}
```

When the player lifts up the mouse button, the piece is set down. The code checks the distance of the center of the piece from the center of the outline. If they are closer than 10 pixels, the piece is moved to the exact position where it belongs. The alpha effect is then set to 100% for the player to see and for the code to recognize that the piece can no longer be dragged.

```
onClipEvent(mouseUp) {
    // stop piece from moving
    stopDrag();

    // get distance from center of piece
    // to center of outline

    dx = _root.outline._x - piece._x;
    dy = _root.outline._y - piece._y;
    dist = Math.sqrt(dx*dx+dy*dy);
```

```
    // if close enough, then set it in place
    if (dist < 10 ) {
        piece._x = _root.outline._x;
        piece._y = _root.outline._y;

        // set to full color
        piece._alpha = 100;
    }
}
```

Other Possibilities

This game is about as simple as jigsaw puzzle programs can get. There are a few small changes that can be made without much trouble. For instance, you could store the original position of each piece when dragging starts, and then have it snap back to that position if the player does not place it in the right spot.

You could also write a function that checks to see whether all the pieces have been placed. Then, you could go to another frame that contains some sort of payoff. You could also go further than the 24 large pieces here and have more, smaller pieces.

Each piece could be randomly rotated 90, 180, or 270 degrees. The player could press the spacebar to rotate the pieces around as they drag. A piece will only fit in place if it's rotated properly.

Of course, there are more difficult variations, such as puzzles that don't have a fixed outline. The player could combine any two or more pieces anywhere on the screen until they have assembled the whole picture. However, this sort of game would take much more programming. Instead, let's move on to another type of picture puzzle.

Sliding Puzzle

Example file: Slidingpuzzle.fla

Although jigsaw puzzles can make an incomplete transition to the computer screen, sliding puzzles work better as computer games than they do as physical games. Sliding puzzles usually consist of 15 square puzzle pieces that slide around on a grid made for 16 pieces. The empty space provides an extra area needed for sliding pieces around.

Figure 13.3 shows our game, a 15-piece sliding puzzle of the fox. You can play it in the example movie, Slidingpuzzle.fla. Any of the 4 pieces adjacent to the empty space can be clicked to slide that piece into the empty space. The object of the game is to arrange the picture properly, with the empty space at the bottom right.

Figure 13.3
The sliding puzzle game features 15 pieces and 1 empty slot.

Project Goal

The goal of this project is to create a simple, easy-to-play sliding puzzle game. The only player interaction will be clicking a single piece at a time. If a piece is adjacent to the empty spot, it will move there.

An important part of this game is the setup. The Flash movie will feature the puzzle pieces all in the right spots. To create more of a challenge, the program will start by making 100 random moves. This will sufficiently shuffle the pieces, making the puzzle challenging but solvable.

Approach

Most of the code in this game is used to shuffle the pieces at the start. First, a piece is picked at random. Next, the four spaces around it are examined to see whether any of them are the empty space. If one is, then the piece is moved there. If not, another piece is selected until one is found that is adjacent to the empty space. This process is repeated 100 times.

When the shuffle is over, it's up to the player to move the pieces. When the player clicks a piece, the piece is examined to see whether an empty space is adjacent. If so, the piece is moved there.

Preparing the Movie

You can use any method you like to create the pieces. I selected squares from a graphic to get the 15 pieces. Unlike the jigsaw puzzle pieces, they don't need any special positioning. The center of each movie clip can be the center of each piece. This makes these pieces easy to create.

After you have all the pieces, place them on the Stage as they would be when the puzzle has been solved. I made the puzzle pieces 54×54 pixels. This means that they need to be spaced 54 pixels apart both horizontally and vertically. Because Flash is not always precise when you manually place movie clips, even with the grid turned on, we'll use ActionScript to align all the pieces exactly before starting the game.

For now, it's just important to get the pieces close to their starting spots and name them. I gave them the names "tile1" to "tile15" so that the code can find them.

Writing the Code

Most of the code is on the main timeline. It starts by aligning the pieces at exactly 54 pixel distances. Then, it loops 100 times, making 100 random moves.

```
function initGame () {
    // set the horizontal and vertical distance
    // between tiles
    tileDist = 54;

    // set all tiles in exactly the right spot
    for (x=1;x<=4;x++) {
        for (y=0;y<=3;y++) {
            tile = x+y*4;
            _root["tile"+tile]._x = x*tileDist;
            _root["tile"+tile]._y = y*tileDist+tileDist;
        }
    }

    // make 100 random but valid moves
    for(tilenum=0;tilenum<100;tilenum++) {
        do {
            // pick a random tile
            tile = "tile"+(random(15)+1);
            // see if there is an empty space near it
            emptySpace = findEmpty(tile);
        // keep looping until a tile is found that
        // has an empty space near it
        } while ( emptySpace == "none" );

        // move this tile to the empty space
        moveTile(tile,findEmpty(tile));
    }
}
```

When a random tile is selected, the "findEmpty" function is used to determine whether any of the four adjacent spots are the empty one. Note that the code needs to make sure that the space is not beyond the edge of the playing area before testing for a piece.

```
// given a tile, see if the empty space is near it
function findEmpty (tile) {
    // get location of tile
    tilex = _root[tile]._x;
    tiley = _root[tile]._y;
```

```
    // see if there is a tile to the left
    if (tilex > tileDist) {
        if (!tileThere(tilex-tileDist, tiley)) {
            return("left");
        }
    }

    // see if there is a tile to the right
    if (tilex < tileDist*4) {
        if (!tileThere(tilex+tileDist, tiley)) {
            return("right");
        }
    }

    // see if there is a tile above
    if (tiley > tileDist) {
        if (!tileThere(tilex, tiley-tileDist)) {
            return("above");
        }
    }

    // see if there is a tile below
    if (tiley < tileDist*4) {
        if (!tileThere(tilex, tiley+tileDist)) {
            return("below");
        }
    }

    // tiles are in all directions
    return("none");
}
```

NOTE

Placing an exclamation point in front of a condition reverses it. That is, it turns a *true* into a *false* and a *false* into a *true*. It is known as a "not" operation. For instance, in the previous code, instead of checking for "tileThere", the code is checking for "not tileThere".

The "findEmpty" function uses "tileThere" to see whether any piece is at a certain location. The function calls "tileThere" for the location to the left, right, above, and below.

```
// check to see if there is a tile at a certain location
function tileThere (thisx, thisy) {
    // loop through tiles
    for (i=1;i<=15;i++) {
```

```
    // see if x matches
    if (_root["tile"+i]._x == thisx) {
        // se if y matches
        if (_root["tile"+i]._y == thisy) {
            return true;
        }
    }
}

// no tile there
return false;
}
```

After a move has been decided on, the "moveTile" function is used to make the move. This same function will be used to allow the player to make moves as well.

```
// move a tile in a certain direction
function moveTile (tile, direction) {
    if (direction == "above") {
        _root[tile]._y -= tileDist;
    } else if (direction == "below") {
        _root[tile]._y += tileDist;
    } else if (direction == "left") {
        _root[tile]._x -= tileDist;
    } else if (direction == "right") {
        _root[tile]._x += tileDist;
    }
}
```

After the player is in control, the "tileUnderMouse" utility function is used to determine which piece has been clicked on.

```
// utility function to see which tile the
// player clicked on
function tileUnderMouse () {
    for (i=1; i<=15; i++) {
        if (_root["Tile"+i].hitTest(_xmouse, _ymouse)) {
            return (i);
        }
    }
}
```

The main timeline script ends by calling "initGame" and kicking off the shuffle.

```
initGame();
stop();
```

The player interacts with the puzzle through a small "actions" movie clip just off the Stage. The movie clip grabs mouse clicks, figures out what was clicked, and makes the move.

```
onClipEvent(mouseDown) {
    // get tile clicked
    tileClicked = _root.tileUnderMouse();

    // see if there is an empty space nearby
    emptySpace = _root.findEmpty("tile"+tileClicked);

    // move the piece to the empty space
    _root.moveTile("tile"+tileClicked,emptySpace);
}
```

Loose Ends

The code relies on the fact that the puzzle pieces are exactly 54 pixels apart, and the playing area is a 4×4 grid. If you want to change any of this, you will need to check the code carefully and make changes.

Other Possibilities

One desirable addition to this game would be for it to recognize when the puzzle is complete and go to some sort of payoff frame. You could do this by recording the original position of the pieces in an array and comparing the positions of the piece with these after each move. When the positions all match, the puzzle has been solved.

Matching Game

Example file: Matching.fla

This next game is probably the most common computer game on the Web. I've seen it in Shockwave, Flash, Java, JavaScript, and even as plain HTML with a CGI backend. It is simple to build, addictive to play, and easy to customize for any site or situation.

A matching game, or memory game as it is sometimes called, involves a grid of cards, all facedown. There are two of every type of card. The player gets to turn two cards faceup at a time. If they match, the cards are removed. If not, they both are turned back over. The player tries to remember where each card is to make it easier to find matches.

Figure 13.4 shows a screenshot of the game on the Web site named Matching.fla with a 36-card grid, in which 4 cards have been removed so far and 2 cards have just been turned over. Those 2 cards do not match, so they are set back to facedown as soon as the player selects another card.

Figure 13.4
The object of the matching game is to remove all the cards and reveal the picture behind.

Figure 13.4
The object of the matching game is to remove all the cards and reveal the picture behind.

Project Goal

The goal of this project is to create a simple yet versatile matching game. The player will be able to pick one card, then a second card. Each card will turn over to reveal its picture when clicked. If the cards match, they will both be removed. If not, they will both turn back over when the user selects another card.

Approach

There are actually only two library elements for this entire game. The first is a movie clip that contains a frame representing the cards facedown. All the rest of the frames show each picture. Because there will be 18 different pictures, the movie clip will have a total of 19 frames. If you want the clip to show the back of a card, send it to frame 1. If you want the clip to show a picture, send it to a frame from 2 to 19.

The second library element will be a button that is inside cards movie clip. It will be used to react to user clicks.

The game will start off by creating the 36 movie clips, arranged in a grid on the Stage. Each movie clip will be facedown, but will remember what picture it is supposed to show when faceup. There will be two clips with each picture, making 18 pairs of cards.

When the player selects the first card, the card shows its picture. Then, when the player selects the second card, it also turns over and compares itself to the other card. If they match, both are removed. If not, nothing happens until the next player clicks. When that occurs, the two old cards turn back over, and a new card is revealed.

Preparing the Movie

In the example movie, Matching.fla, you will see the "Cards" movie clip. The timeline of this movie clip shows 19 frames. Figure 13.5 shows this timeline. The first frame represents the card facedown, and thus has no picture on it. The other 18 frames each have their own, different picture.

Figure 13.5

The timeline of the "Cards" movie clip shows 19 frames, the first with no picture and the other 18 with different pictures.

The card button is just a rectangle the same size as the cards. The card button is placed in the third layer of the "Cards" movie clip, as you can see in Figure 13.5. This places it under the background. The button will not be seen, but it will react to mouse clicks just the same.

The "Cards" movie clip also includes a background. The first frame, representing the back of a card, has a gray background. The other frames, all of which have a picture to show, have white backgrounds.

Writing the Code

Almost all the code for this game is in the main timeline. The movie starts off by calling the "initGame" function. This function creates a list of 18 pairs of cards, picks random cards from this first list, and then places them in the second list to shuffle the deck.

Next, it creates 36 cards, all along a 6×6 grid. Each movie clip automatically starts facedown, but a custom property of the movie clip, "picture", is set to the number of the picture it should represent.

```
initGame();
stop();

function initGame() {
    // make sorted list of cards
    cardsListOrdered = [];
    for(i=1;i<=18;i++) {
        cardsListOrdered.push(i,i);
    }

    // shuffle list
    cardsListSorted = [];
    while (cardsListOrdered.length > 0) {
        r = int(Math.random()*cardsListOrdered.length);
        cardsListSorted.push(cardsListOrdered[r]);
        cardsListOrdered.splice(r,1);
```

```
    }

    // create card clips and assign their location and picture
    x = 0;
    y = 0;
    for(i=0;i<36;i++) {
        attachMovie("Card","Card"+i,i);
        _root["Card"+i].picture = cardsListSorted[i];
        _root["Card"+i]._x = x*60+200;
        _root["Card"+i]._y = y*60+50;

        // move to next card spot
        x++;
        if (x > 5) {
            x = 0;
            y++;
        }
    }

    firstclip = 0;
}
```

NOTE

Notice that the *push* command can be used to add more than one item to an array at a time. For instance, "myArray.push(7,12)" will add a 7 and then a 12 to the array "myArray".

The "initGame" function ends by setting "firstclip" to 0. This is the variable that will hold a reference to the first card clicks. When a movie clip is clicked, the button inside the movie clip will react to the click by sending a message up to the main timeline through the "clickCard" function that will include a reference to the movie clip.

The "clickCard" function can take one of three actions. If "firstclip" is 0, then it sets "firstclip" to the movie clip that was clicked, and turns that card over by telling it to go to the frame that has the appropriate picture on it.

If "firstclip" is set to a movie clip reference, then one card is already showing. In that case, the program turns a second card over, sets "secondclip" to that movie clip, and compares the two movie clips. If they match, both clips are immediately removed.

A third condition, which is actually checked before the other two options, occurs if the player clicks the same card twice. In this case, "clip" will equal "firstclip". The card is simply turned back over and "firstclip" is set to 0.

Before any of these three conditions are checked for, the "clickCard" function checks to see whether two cards are already turned over. If so, that means the player just completed selecting two cards and did not get a match. Before the next card is turned over, these two cards are set to facedown.

```
function clickCard(clip) {
    // see if two card are showing
    if (secondclip != 0) {

        // turn those two cards back over
        firstclip.gotoAndStop(1);
        secondclip.gotoAndStop(1);
        firstClip = 0;
        secondClip = 0;
    }

    // see if same card was clicked
    if (firstclip == clip) {

        // turn card back over
        firstclip.gotoAndStop(1);
        firstClip = 0;

    // see if no cards are showing
    } else if (firstclip == 0) {

        // turn first card over
        clip.gotoAndStop(clip.picture+1);
        firstclip = clip;

    // must be one card showing
    } else {

        // turn second card over
        clip.gotoAndStop(clip.picture+1);
        secondClip = clip;

        // see if two cards match
        if (firstclip.picture == secondClip.picture) {

            // remove both cards
            firstClip.removeMovieClip();
            secondClip.removeMovieClip();
            firstClip = 0;
            secondClip = 0;
```

```
            }
        }
    }
```

That's all there is to the game. The button inside the "Cards" movie clip has just one line of code in it that sends the message that the movie clip was clicked on back to the main timeline.

```
on (press) {
    // send click info to main timeline
    _root.clickCard(this);
}
```

Loose Ends

Remember to place a *stop()* command in the first frame of the "Cards" movie clip. Otherwise, all the cards will start by animating through all the pictures.

Other Possibilities

This game can easily be customized by adding a background image to appear behind the cards. The pictures on the cards can match the theme of that picture. You can pick almost any theme. You can also add a picture to the first frame of the "Cards" movie clip to represent the back of the cards.

Although the example here has 36 cards, you can easily expand or shrink that number. Just remember to adjust the grid size as well as the array lengths at the start of the game. If the number of cards won't fit into a square grid, you will have to adjust the code, or write new code, to determine the layout of the cards.

Another possibility is to have four of each card, rather than two. This will make it easier to find the first match.

If you want to have the game recognize when all the cards have been removed, you can include a counter that increments every time a match is found. In the case of the example movie, when the counter hits 18, the game is over. You can then go to a "you win" frame.

Brain Puzzles

- Memory Game
- Deduction
- Pegs

The sliding puzzle and the matching game from the last chapter are both thinking puzzles. The player is not timed, but is given every opportunity to examine the problem at hand and solve the puzzle. Let's look at some more of these brain puzzles.

This chapter shows you three classics. In the first game, the player is asked to memorize a sequence and repeat it. In the next game, the player must deduce the items in a short sequence given hints after each guess. Then, in the last game, the player jumps pegs to eliminate them until he has only one peg left.

Memory Game

⊕▷ Example file: Memory.fla

The memory game is sometimes called "Simon" after a popular electronic toy that allows you to play the game. The game described here, like that toy, has four different elements that play in a random sequence. You can see it in the example movie, Memory.fla. An element is a colored light that lights up and a sound that plays at the same time. In this game, the elements are represented on the screen by four birds sitting on a branch (see Figure 14.1).

Figure 14.1

The memory game features four birds that chirp in a random sequence.

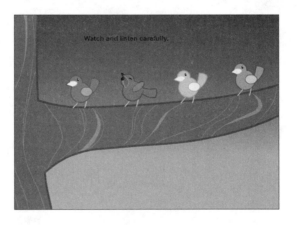

Watch and listen carefully.

The game has two main phases. The first phase is when the birds chirp in a sequence. The second phase is when the user tries to recreate that sequence in the same order. Then the phases repeat, adding a new chirp to the sequence. Pretty soon, the sequence gets so long that the player cannot recreate it and the game is over.

Approach

The sequence of chirps is stored in an array. Every turn, a new, random number from 1 to 4 is added to the array. The number determines which bird chirps at that part of the sequence.

The first part of the game consists of the birds singing. That frame is controlled by an "actions" movie clip, which moves through the numbers in the sequence and tells the birds when to chirp.

The next part of the game waits for the player to click the birds. When the player does, this part of the game checks to see whether the right bird was clicked. It follows the player through the sequence of chirps, waiting for the player to mess up. If the player doesn't mess up, it adds a new chirp to the sequence and starts over again.

Preparing the Movie

This movie has six frames. You can see them all in Figure 14.2. The two key frames are frames 3 and 4, the "play" and "repeat" frames. The "play" frame is where the birds chirp automatically, and the "repeat" frame is where the player clicks the birds.

Figure 14.2

The six frames of the memory game are "start", "wait", "play", "repeat", "correct", and "wrong".

Each bird has three parts. The first part is a movie clip with the bird. The first frame has the bird as a still image. The second frame and the rest of the movie clip are an animation of the bird opening its mouth to chirp. The movie starts with each bird stopped on the first frame.

The second part of each bird is a button. The same button is used for each bird, but different code is attached to it. The button is behind each bird and invisible.

TIP

If you look closely at the "Bird Button" library element in the example movie, you will see that the "Up", "Over", and "Down" frames of the button are blank, but the "Hit" frame contains the shape of the bird. This means that no image will be displayed for the button on the Stage, but the valid hit area of the button will match the shape in the "Hit" frame of the button. This is a different technique for making an invisible button than simply creating a button and setting its alpha effect to 0.

The third part of each bird is a simple animation that shows a note flying out of the bird's mouth. This is a single movie clip used once for each bird. Each instance of this note animation and each bird is named to match. For instance, the first bird and note are named "bird1" and "note1". The note animation has a blank first frame, where it is stopped. The second frame has a short animation that loops back to the first frame. We'll trigger the note to fly out of the bird's mouth at the appropriate time.

If you examine the "bird" animations, you will see that a sound is included with each one. This sound automatically plays when the bird animates. Each sound is slightly different.

The different parts of the birds appear in different frames. The bird movie clips themselves appear in all six frames. However, the buttons only appear in the "repeat" frame because that is the only place where the player should be able to click the birds. The note animations only appear on frames 3–6 because they aren't needed in frames 1 and 2.

The movie also has specific instructions on each frame about what the user should be doing. A "scoreDisplay" text area is in the upper-right corner of all frames except the first.

Writing the Code

The code for this movie is divided into two parts. The first part is a bunch of functions placed in the first frame of the movie. The second part is in a "playback actions" movie clip that controls the playback of the chirps in the "play" frame. Many other places also have short pieces of code.

The functions used in this movie can all be found in the first frame of the main timeline. They are used to set up the game, react to user clicks, and help play back the chirps.

Calling "initGame" to set up all the variables is the first thing that happens in this game. This happens when the game first runs, and when the game is over, the player chooses to play again and the game gets sent back to frame 1.

The "initGame" function clears the "notes" array and then calls "addNextNote" to place a random number in that array. It also sets the score display to 0.

```
initGame();
stop();

function initGame(n) {
    // start notes array
    notes = new Array();
    scoreDisplay = "Score: 0";

    // add first note
    addNewNote();
}
```

The "addNextNote" function picks a number frame 1 to 4 and places it in the "notes" array.

```
function addNewNote() {
    // pick a number from 1 to 4
    r = int(Math.Random()*4+1);
```

```
    // add number to list
    notes.push(r);
}
```

The other functions in the main timeline deal with different stages of the game. This next function, "startRepeat" is called when the player is done hearing the birds chirp, and it's now the player's turn to click the birds to make them chirp.

The variable "repeatNum" is used to keep track of which note the player should be clicking. It starts at 0 and counts along as the player clicks each bird.

```
function startRepeat() {
    // mark which note the user should play next
    repeatNum = 0;

    // go to the frame where buttons are active
    gotoAndPlay("repeat");
}
```

The "clickBird" function is called from the buttons hidden behind the birds. It sends along the number of the note clicked. The first thing the function does with the number is to trigger the bird animation and the matching note animation. Then it compares the note against the next note in the list of notes. If they match, the player got it right. The "repeatNum" variable increments. If this is the last note, the game jumps to the "correct" frame. If not, it waits for another note. If the note does not match, then the game jumps to the "wrong" frame and the game is over.

```
function clickBird(note) {
    // make the bird play the note
    _root["bird"+note].gotoAndPlay(2);

    // also trigger the note animation
    _root["note"+note].gotoAndPlay(2);

    // see if it was the right note
    if (note == notes[repeatNum]) {

        // expect the next note
        repeatNum++;

        // if no more notes, then he got it right
        if (repeatNum > notes.length-1) {
            scoreDisplay = "Score: " + notes.length;
            gotoAndPlay("correct");
        }
    } else {
```

```
        // he got one wrong
        gotoAndPlay("wrong");
    }
}
```

The "play" frame plays back each note in the sequence through a script attached to a "playback actions" movie clip. The script here starts off by setting two variables. The "noteNum" variable keeps track of which note to play next, and the "nextTime" variable keeps track of when to play the next note.

```
onClipEvent(load) {
    // start with note 0
    noteNum = 0;
    nextTime = 0;
}
```

In each step of the movie that passes while the movie sits on the "play" frame, the current time is compared to the value of "nextTime". If the current time is greater, the next note plays.

The bird and note animation are triggered just like they will be when the player clicks them. Then, the "noteNum" and "nextTime" are changed to prepare for the next note. The "nextTime" is increased by 1000, so the next note will play 1 second later.

When all the notes have been played, the game calls the "startRepeat" function previously discussed. This will send the game to the "repeat" frame to await the player's attempt at recreating the sequence.

```
onClipEvent(enterFrame) {
    // if it is time to play the next note
    if (getTimer() > nextTime) {

        // get the note
        note = _root.notes[noteNum];

        // make the bird sing and note animate
        _root["bird"+note].gotoAndPlay(2);
        _root["note"+note].gotoAndPlay(2);

        // wait 1 second until next note
        nextTime = getTimer() + 1000;
        noteNum++;

        // if no more notes, then continue to next step
        if (noteNum > _root.notes.length) {
            _root.startRepeat();
        }
    }
}
```

Each button on the Stage in the "repeat" frame must call "clickBird" when clicked. Each of the four scripts is slightly different, because they must send a different number to "clickBird". Here is the script for the first one:

```
on (press) {
    clickBird(1);
}
```

Loose Ends

All six of the frames in this movie should have a *stop()* command placed on them. In frames 2 to 6, that is the only command on those frames.

There are also buttons on the "wait", "correct", and "wrong" frames. The "wait" frame has a button that takes the game to the "play" frame where the sequence is played. The "correct" frame button takes the player back to the "play" frame. However, it must also call "addNewNote" to add a note to the sequence.

```
on (press) {
    addNewNote();
    gotoAndPlay("play");
}
```

The button on the "wrong" frame sends the game back to the "start" frame where the game is reinitialized so another game can begin.

Also, remember to include a text area that is linked to the variable "scoreDisplay", so players will know how well they have done.

Other Possibilities

You can customize this game to fit all sorts of different themes by changing the background and the four elements. You can also have more or fewer than four elements to change the difficulty level of the game.

Deduction

Example file: Deduction.fla

This next game is played completely by using logic. You might have seen it as a computer game before, or you might recognize it as the two-player, store-bought game called "Mastermind."

The object of the game is to guess a random sequence of five colors. The player starts off with a wild guess. Then, the computer responds by telling the player how he did. The player gets the number of colors correctly placed, and the number of colors that are correct, but in the wrong spot. Based on this information, the player makes another guess. This continues for a set number of turns or until the player gets the sequence right.

Figure 14.3 shows the deduction game as it looks in the example movie Deduction.fla. The playing area is a log and the colors are rocks. The player can choose any of five colored rocks, or no rock at all, to fill a space. The computer responds with a white rock for every correct color, and a black rock for every right color in the wrong spot.

Figure 14.3
The deduction game allows the player to build a sequence of rocks and then grades the results with white and black rocks.

Project Goal

The goal of this movie is to create the simple game called Deduction. The player gets 10 chances to guess the right sequence. The player is given feedback after every guess.

Approach

The game starts by creating a random sequence of five colors. This sequence is kept a secret by the computer until the end of the game.

Each turn starts by presenting five new empty spaces for the player to set. In addition to these five spaces, a "Done" button appears to the right. Figure 14.4 shows what the game looks like when the player starts.

Figure 14.4
The game starts by presenting five empty spaces and a "Done" button.

The player can click any of the five spaces to change its color. The spaces actually rotate through one of six possibilities: five colors and an empty space.

After the player has set the five spaces to her satisfaction, then she can press the "done" button to have it graded. A white stone represents a correctly placed color, and a black stone represents a color that is correct if used elsewhere.

The next five empty spaces are then shown below the previous row, along with a new "done" button. Figure 14.5 shows what the game play looks like after several moves.

Figure 14.5

The deduction game looks like this after several moves.

Preparing the Movie

The "rock" movie clip contains eight frames. The first frame shows an empty space. Frames 2–6 show the five colors that the player has to choose from. Frames 7 and 8 show the white and black stones, and are labeled "white" and "black" so the code can refer to them easily.

Only the background and instructions need to be placed on the Stage. The rocks and "done" button are created by the code. You will need to set the "linkage" property of the "rock" to "rock". I also create a small button to go inside each rock. The "done" button is easily created, but because we want to manipulate its existence and location, we need to place it inside a movie clip and set the linkage on that as well.

Writing the Code

The code for the game is all in the first frame of the main timeline. It starts by setting a whole bunch of constants. These numbers determine the location of various elements on the Stage as the script creates them. Instead of having these constants spread through-out the code, I have gathered them at the start of the program so they will be easy to find and change.

The solution sequence is created from five random numbers and stored in "solution". The "row" variable is used to store the turn number. The "createRow" function is called to start the game.

```
initGame();
stop();

function initGame() {
    // define locations and spacing
    // of the elements
    topRowLoc = 60;
    leftColLoc = 280;
    rightColLoc = 390;
    horizSpace = 21;
    vertSpace = 23;
    solutionx = 336;
    solutiony = 320;

    // create a random solution
    solution = new Array();
    for(i=0;i<5;i++) {
        solution.push(int(Math.Random()*5));
    }

    // init variables
    rows = new Array();
    row = 0;

    // set up first row
    createRow();
}
```

At the start of every turn, "createRow" makes five new movie clips and sets their location. In addition, a new "done" movie clip is set to be just to the right of that. The result looks like Figure 14.4 (shown previously).

```
function createRow() {
    // create a new row of 5 empty spaces
    for(i=0;i<5;i++) {
        attachMovie("rock","rock"+row+"-"+i,row*10+i);
        clip = _root["rock"+row+"-"+i];
        clip._x = leftColLoc + i*horizSpace;
        clip._y = topRowLoc + row*vertSpace;
        clip.active = true;
    }

    // create the "done" button
    attachMovie("done","done",1000);
    _root.done._x = rightColLoc+20;
    _root.done._y = topRowLoc + row*vertSpace;
}
```

When the player clicks the "done" button, "doneGuess" is called. "doneGuess" starts by making the five buttons in the current row inactive. In "createRow", a custom property of each movie clip called "active" was set to *true*. Now, this property is set to *false* ①. The code attached to each button uses this value to determine whether it can be clicked or not.

The array "temp" is used to store the number of each color that appears in the sequence ②. For instance, if there are two of color 1, one of color 4, and two of color 5, the array is "[2,0,0,1,2]".

The next loop checks to see how many colors match the solution perfectly ③. As matches are found, the numbers in the "temp" array are reduced. This means that the values in "temp" now represent all the colors still left to be matched.

The next loop checks each of the unmatched colors in the player's sequence and determines which of those are in "temp" ④. By counting these, you can get the number of colors that are useful, but in the wrong spots.

The next two loops create white and black rocks to represent the number of colors that are right, and the number of colors that are right, but in the wrong spots ⑤.

The "done" button is removed so that it does not remain in each column ⑥. A new "done" button will be created when the next turn begins.

Finally, the function ends by checking to see whether all five colors are right ⑦. If so, the movie jumps to the "win" frame. If not, the code checks to see whether this was the 10th turn. If it was, the movie jumps to the "lose" frame. If not, "createRow" is called to start the next turn.

```
function doneGuess() {
    numRightSpot = 0;
    numRightColor = 0;

①  // make all five button inactive
    for (i=0;i<5;i++) {
        _root["rock"+row+"-"+i].active = false;
    }

②  // determine how many of each color there are
    temp = [0,0,0,0,0];
    for (i=0;i<5;i++) {
        temp[solution[i]]++;
    }

③  // see how many are right
    for (i=0;i<5;i++) {
        color = _root["rock"+row+"-"+i]._currentFrame - 2;
        if (color == solution[i]) {
```

```
            numRightSpot++;
            temp[color]--;
        }
    }
```

(4)━►
```
    // see how many are right color, but wrong spot
    for (i=0;i<5;i++) {
        color = _root["rock"+row+"-"+i]._currentFrame - 2;
        if (color != solution[i]) {
            if (temp[color] > 0) {
                numRightColor++;
                temp[color]--;
            }
        }
    }
```

(5)━►
```
    // create white rocks
    level = row*10+5;
    x = rightColLoc;
    for(i=0;i<numRightSpot;i++) {
        attachMovie("rock","white rock"+level,level);
        clip = _root["white rock"+level];
        clip.gotoAndStop("white");
        clip._x = x;
        clip._y = topRowLoc + row*vertSpace;
        level++
        x+=horizSpace;
    }

    // create black rocks
    for(i=0;i<numRightColor;i++) {
        attachMovie("rock","black rock"+level,level);
        clip = _root["black rock"+level];
        clip.gotoAndStop("black");
        clip._x = x;
        clip._y = topRowLoc + row*vertSpace;
        level++
        x+=horizSpace;
    }
```

(6)━►
```
    // remove "done" button
    done.removeMovieClip();
```

(7)━►
```
    // see if the player wins
    if (numRightSpot == 5) {
        gotoAndPlay("win");
```

```
    } else {
        row++;

        // see if the player loses
        if (row >= 10) {
            showSolution();
            gotoAndPlay("lose");
        } else {
            createRow();
        }
    }
}
```

When the player loses the game, the "showSolution" function creates five new movie clip instances and uses them to display the actual solution. In the example movie, this is placed at the bottom of the playing area.

```
function showSolution() {
    // place solution at bottom of screen
    for(i=0;i<5;i++) {
        attachMovie("rock","solution"+i,1001+i);
        clip = _root["solution"+i];
        clip._x = solutionx + i*horizSpace;
        clip._y = solutiony;
        clip.gotoAndStop(solution[i]+2);
    }
}
```

Figure 14.6 shows a game that has been lost. The "showSolution" function has placed the actual solution at the bottom of the screen.

Figure 14.6
This game has been lost, and the code has placed the actual solution at the bottom.

The only piece of code that remains is the little bit that is attached to the button in every "rock" movie clip. Its job is to advance the color by one, looping back to the first frame, an empty space, if clicked enough times. This code also checks the "active" property to make sure this is the current row.

```
on (press) {
    if (active) {
        f = _currentFrame+1;
        if (f > 6) f = 1;
        gotoAndStop(f);
    }
}
```

Loose Ends

Remember to label the last two frames of the "rock" movie clip "black" and "white". Also, remember to include the "done" button insider a "done" movie clip, which is then linked as "done". Unfortunately, this is necessary because buttons by themselves cannot be created dynamically by ActionScript. Think of the "done" movie clip as a wrapper around the "done" button.

Other Possibilities

The important thing to remember if you modify this game is that the constants at the beginning of the code need to be adjusted to match any change to your background. If you keep that in mind, you can do just about anything with this game.

To change the difficulty of the game, try increasing the number of guesses allowed. You can also increase or decrease the number of colors and spaces.

Pegs

Example file: Pegs.fla

The classic game of pegs has probably been around for thousands of years. Recent versions are made of cheap plastic, or as Web-based games like this one.

The game consists of a grid of peg holes, like the one in Figure 14.7. Pegs are in every hole except one. The player has to take a peg and jump another peg, landing in an empty hole. The peg that was jumped is then removed. Play continues until no more moves are possible.

Figure 14.7
This is the most common of many pegboard configurations. You can make up your own as well.

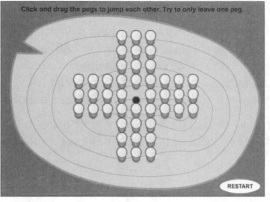

A good player can "win" the game by getting down to a single peg. A quick game, without much thought put into the moves, can leave 8 or 12 pegs.

Project Goal

The goal of this project is to make a "pegs" game using the most common configuration, shown previously in Figure 14.7. The player clicks and drags to move pegs. An invalid move is not allowed, and a valid move automatically removes the piece jumped.

Approach

This entire game takes place in a single frame and starts without a single game element on the Stage.

The holes and pegs are separate movie clips. Both are placed on the Stage by the code, which allows you to avoid the tedious task of placing each movie clip and naming it. Instead, the code does the work.

When the player drags a peg to a new hole, a lot of code is needed to determine whether the move is valid. First, the move has to be to an empty hole, two spaces away from the current hole. Then the hole that was jumped must have a peg in it. If these conditions are met, the move is allowed. The jumped peg is removed from the board.

Preparing the Movie

Only a "peg" and "hole" movie clip are needed. The "peg" movie clip also has a button placed inside it that sends a message to the main timeline when the button is clicked and when it is released.

Because neither movie clip is on the Stage before the movie runs, they both have to be linked. The code refers to them with the names "peg" and "hole".

Writing the Code

Almost all the code is in the only frame of the main timeline. The code starts off by creating the "hole" and "peg" movie clip instances and arranging them on the Stage. It uses an *if* statement that you can see commented in the following code to rule out any holes that are not on the grid shown earlier in Figure 14.7. The code also checks to make sure that pegs are added to every hole, except the one in the center.

The function ends by storing the total number of holes in the variable "maxHole". This will be useful in future functions that need to loop through each movie clip to check for certain conditions.

```
initGame();
stop();

function initGame() {
    // location constants
    holeSpace = 30;
    puzzleLeft = 160;
    puzzleTop = 80;

    // loop through and create pegs
    i = 0;
    for(y=0;y<9;y++) {
        for(x=0;x<9;x++) {

            // check to see if peg should not be created
            // this will create the + pattern
            if (((y < 3) or (y > 5)) and ((x < 3) or (x > 5))) continue;

            // add new hole and place it
            attachMovie("hole","hole"+i,i);
            _root["hole"+i]._x = x*holeSpace + puzzleLeft;
            _root["hole"+i]._y = y*holeSpace + puzzleTop;

            // do not add peg to center hole
            if ((x != 4) or (y != 4)) {

                // add new peg and place it
                attachMovie("peg","peg"+i,100+i);
                _root["peg"+i]._x = x*holeSpace + puzzleLeft;
                _root["peg"+i]._y = y*holeSpace + puzzleTop;
            }

            i++;
        }
    }
}
```

```
    // remember how many holes/pegs
    maxHole = i;
}
```

When the player clicks a peg, she is actually clicking a button inside that movie clip. Both the "press" and "release" action are passed on to the functions in the main timeline. The "dragPeg" function is called by the "press" action. The "dragPeg" function records the position of the peg in "pegx" and "pegy" and then allows the peg to be dragged. It also uses *swapDepths* to bring the peg in front of all others.

```
function dragPeg(peg) {
    // remember the original location
    pegx = peg._x;
    pegy = peg._y;

    // move this peg on top of all others
    peg.swapDepths(2000);

    // allow Flash to drag the movie clip
    startDrag(peg, true);
}
```

The "dropPeg" function is called when the player releases the mouse button while dragging. It starts by releasing the movie clip from being dragged ⑧. Then "dropPeg" loops through all the holes to see whether any are under the mouse location ⑨.

If the mouse is over a hole, the next step is to determine whether the hole is currently empty ⑩. Next, the code looks in all four directions to see which of the four possible holes it could be. It uses "dx" and "dy" to define the relative location of the hole ⑪ For instance, if the player jumped to the right, then "dx" is set to 1, "dy" to 0. If the player jumped up, then "dx" is 0, "dy" is −1. If the hole that the player jumped to is not one that is two spaces to the right, left, above, or below the starting hole, then both "dx" and "dy" are 0 ⑫.

Even if the player moved two spaces to an empty hole, the move is only valid if she jumped another peg. This next section of code checks for that middle peg ⑬. If the code finds a middle peg there, it removes the peg and sets the peg doing the jumping to its new location.

If any of these conditions fail, the move is not a valid one. The "placed" variable remains *false* and is detected at the end of the function ⑭. The peg is then moved back to its starting position.

```
  function dropPeg(peg) {
⑧→    // release control of peg clip
      stopDrag();
```

```
            // assume this is not a valid move
            placed = false;
            overHole = false;

            // find which hole, if any, the peg was released over
            for(i=0;i<maxHole;i++) {
                hole = _root["hole"+i];
                if (hole.hitTest(_xmouse,_ymouse)) {
                    overHole = true;
                    break;
                }
            }

            // see if the hole is empty
            if (!pegThere(hole._x,hole._y)) {

                // find out difference between starting location
                // and destination
                dx = 0;
                dy = 0;
                if ((pegx == hole._x) and (pegy-holeSpace*2 == hole._y)) {
                    // above
                    dy = -1;
                } else if ((pegx == hole._x) and (pegy+holeSpace*2 == hole._y)) {
                    // below
                    dy = 1;
                } else if ((pegy == hole._y) and (pegx-holeSpace*2 == hole._x)) {
                    // left
                    dx = -1;
                } else if ((pegy == hole._y) and (pegx+holeSpace*2 == hole._x)) {
                    // right
                    dx = 1;
                }

                // dx and dy will both be 0 unless the destination
                // was a valid distance away
                if ((dx != 0) or (dy != 0)) {

                    // find the peg in the middle
                    midThere = false;
                    for(i=0;i<maxHole;i++) {
                        mid = _root["peg"+i];
                        if ((mid._x == pegx + dx*holeSpace) and (mid._y == pegy +
                        ➥dy*holeSpace)) {

                            // since there is a peg in the middle,
                            // this move is valid
```

```
                        // set the new location of the peg
                        peg._x = hole._x;
                        peg._y = hole._y;

                        // remove the middle peg
                        mid.removeMovieClip();

                        // remember that the move was successful
                        placed = true;
                        break;
                    }
                }
            }
        }
```

⑭→
```
        // check to see if the move was successful and
        // reset the peg location if not
        if (!placed) {
            peg._x = pegx;
            peg._y = pegy;
        }
    }
```

"dropPeg" uses the "pegThere" utility function to take a location and return *true* if a "peg" movie clip is found at exactly that location.

```
function pegThere(x,y) {
    // loop through all pegs to see if any is in this location
    for(i=0;i<maxHole;i++) {
        peg = _root["peg"+i];
        if ((peg._x == x) and (peg._y == y)) {
            return true;
        }
    }
    return false;
}
```

During the game, a "Restart Game" button is always at the bottom of the screen. This allows the player to restart when she runs out of moves, or when she realizes that she has started the game off badly. The button needs to do more than just call "initGame". It first needs to clear out any remaining "peg" clips and all the "hole" clips.

```
function restartGame() {
    // remove all movie clips
    for(i=0;i<maxHole;i++) {
        _root["peg"+i].removeMovieClip();
        _root["hole"+i].removeMovieClip();
    }
```

```
     // start new game
     initGame();
 }
```

The code attached to the button inside the "peg" movie clip is simple. All it does is pass on the press and release to other functions.

```
on (press) {
     _root.dragPeg(this);
 }

on (release) {
     _root.dropPeg(this);
 }
```

Other Possibilities

The main way in which you can vary this game is to create other game boards. I've seen pages of combinations in old game books like the ones you find in the "Games" section of a large bookstore. Many grids involve diagonal jumps instead of horizontal and vertical ones. This requires some reworking of the code.

Another variation would be to have a single peg that is a different color from all the rest. The extra-hard challenge to the player to leave only that specific peg.

Casino and Card Games

- Slot Machine
- Video Poker
- Simple Blackjack

Gambling games have always been a popular genre of computer games. The Web is full of casino and card games in Flash, Shockwave, or Java. Most are just for fun, but some allow you to bet real money.

In this chapter, you'll look at three just-for-fun casino games. The first is a pure game of chance, a slot machine. Next, you'll see how to make a video poker game. Then, you'll look at a game that requires a little more skill for the player, blackjack.

TIP

It's a good idea to warn developers about the difference between a just-for-fun casino game and a real one. Real casino games that involve real money or prizes require complex security programming to make sure the player can't cheat by hacking at the data on his computer or the data sent over the network. A developer who accepts a project to build a real casino game should be an expert in computer and network security, not just a Flash expert. Even if you are an expert at both, proceed with great caution in accepting such a project: It will be difficult and probably cause you many headaches.

Slot Machine

⊕▷ᵡExample file: Slotmachine.fla

A slot machine is a simple type of game, but with a somewhat complex interface. The player just clicks the slot machine's lever to pull it, and then waits for the result. The slot machine does the rest of the work.

Figure 15.1 shows the example movie slot machine. The lever to the right is the only part that the player interacts with. The three windows each present a different item when the slot machine is done.

Figure 15.1
A simple slot machine with a lever and three windows.

Project Goal

Although some slot machines have many strange and interesting ways to bet and win, this one is simple. The player clicks to pull the lever. Then, the wheels in the three windows appear to spin. One by one, they will stop on a random item.

When all three wheels stop, the three items showing determine the outcome of the turn. The amount won is equivalent to the amounts shown at the bottom of the machine in Figure 15.1.

Approach

The only difficult part in this game is the spinning. One way to do it would be to have different items move from bottom to top through the window. The problem with this approach is that they would have to move very fast to appear to be spinning as fast as real slot machine wheels spin. Flash just can't animate things at that speed on most computers.

Instead, you can use a blurry spin animation. This animation is a few frames of blurred color in a movie clip. Figure 15.2 shows a few of these frames.

Figure 15.2

These frames of animation create the effect of a spinning wheel when played rapidly.

Each of the three windows will have a copy of the "spin" movie clip. When it's time for the wheels to spin, all three of these movie clips will be told to play, and told precisely how many times to loop. They will be given different amounts so that the wheels stop spinning at different times.

Check out the example movie Slotmachine.fla to see how the wheels spin and stop at different times.

Preparing the Movie

There are three key library elements in this movie. All the rest are just background elements. The first element is the lever. The first frame has a button on it that the player can click. The rest of this movie clip is an animation of the level being pulled.

The "spin" movie clip starts with a blank frame where the "spin" movie clip will wait until the player pulls the lever. The frame is transparent so that the "symbols" movie clip can show through.

The rest of the frames in the "spin" movie clip contain the blur animation shown earlier in Figure 15.2. Behind these images is an opaque white field that covers the "symbols" clip while the wheels are spinning.

The "symbols" movie clip contains seven frames, each with a different symbol on it. In the example movie, the symbols include an acorn, apple, leaf, log, moon, sun, and fox.

Writing the Code

Most of the code for this game creates functions in the main timeline. However, let's start by looking at all the pieces of code found in the movie clips.

In the example movie, if you move the lever from its current spot, you will see a button under it. Attached to this button is a simple script that calls the "pull" function in the main timeline:

```
on (release) {
    pull();
}
```

The "spin" movie clip has two short scripts in it. A plain stop() command appears on the first frame. A script that reduces a counter called "numTimes" by one appears on the last frame. If this counter is 0, it returns the movie clip to the first frame and notifies a function in the main timeline. Otherwise, it causes the movie clip to loop back to frame 2.

```
numTimes--;
if (numTimes <= 0) {
    gotoAndStop(1);
    _root.spinDone(_name);
} else {
    gotoAndPlay(2);
}
```

Much of the code in the main timeline deals with determining how much money, if any, the player won on the spin.

The code starts, however, by setting each of the three symbols to a random frame, and giving the player $100 in cash:

```
initGame();
stop();

function initGame() {
    // start three symbols out randomly
    for(i=1;i<4;i++) {
        _root["symbol"+i].gotoAndStop(randomSymbol());
    }

    // start cash at $100
    cash = 100;
    showCash();
}
```

Instead of displaying the player's cash as a plain number, the next function places a dollar sign, followed by the "cash" variable into "displayCash". This variable is linked to a text area on the Stage.

```
// display cash with $
function showCash() {
    cashDisplay = "$"+cash;
}
```

When the player clicks on the lever button, several things happen. First, $1 is subtracted from the player's cash. Next, the "arm" movie clip is sent to frame 2 so it can animate the lever going down. Then, all three "spin" movie clips begin animating. Each clip starts with a different "numTimes" setting—8, 6, and 4—to make the first animation loop 8 times, the second 6, and the third 4.

The result of each spin is also determined at this time. The "symbol" movie clips are set, although they are hidden behind the opaque "spin" animations until they are done.

```
// pull the handle
function pull() {

    // deduct $1 per pull
    cash--;
    showCash();

    // play arm animation
    _root["arm"].gotoAndPlay(2);

    // tell spin animations to go
    for(i=1;i<4;i++) {
        // tell spin animations how many times
        _root["spin"+i].numTimes = 8-i*2;
        _root["spin"+i].gotoAndPlay(2);
    }

    // pick a random result for each symbol
    for(i=1;i<4;i++) {
        _root["symbol"+i].gotoAndStop(randomSymbol());
    }
}
```

The way a random symbol is picked is not simple. If each of the seven symbols had an even chance of appearing, then each matching outcome would have the same chance of happening. In other words, three acorns would appear as often as three foxes. This would mean that having different payouts for different matching sets wouldn't make sense.

TIP

Actual slot machines have a surprisingly complex method for picking the symbols that end up in the windows. These methods involve complex mathematical formulas so that the casino can control exactly how much of a chance the player has of winning.

Instead, each symbol needs to have a different chance of appearing. A log symbol, for instance, appears 29% of the time. A fox symbol, on the other hand, appears only 6% of the time.

The way this is done is by placing the relative chance of a symbol appearing into a list. Then, a random number is picked. If this random number falls within the percentage chance of the first symbol, then the first symbol is picked. If not, then the code proceeds to the next number in the list. This is done until a symbol is picked. Walk yourself through the following code to see how it works:

```
// choose a random symbol based on probability calculations
function randomSymbol() {
    // get chances of each symbol appearing
    chances = [29,21,16,12,9,7,6];

    // determine total count of chances
    totalChances = 0;
    for(j=0;j<chances.length;j++) {
        totalChances += chances[j];
    }

    // pick a random number
    r = int(Math.random()*totalChances);

    // determine which symbol the number represents
    for(j=0;j<chances.length;j++) {
        if (r < chances[j]) {
            return(j+1);
        } else {
            r -= chances[j];
        }
    }
}
```

When a "spin" movie clip is done animating, it calls the "spinDone" function with the name of the movie clip instance. Movie clip "spin1" is singled out as the last animation in the sequence. When this one is done, the "calcWin" function is called to determine the winnings.

```
// called by each spin animation
function spinDone(name) {
```

```
    // see if this is the last symbol to stop spinning
    if (name == "spin1") {

        // calculate winnings
        win = calcWin();
        cash += win;
        showCash();
    }
}
```

The "calcWin" function determines whether all three symbols match. It also counts the number of acorns in the sequence. If all three match, then the amount won is determined by which symbol it is. If there is no match, the player can still win a little with one or two acorns present.

```
// determine how much the player won
function calcWin() {

    // how many acorns
    numAcorns = 0;
    for(i=1;i<4;i++) {
        if (_root["symbol"+i]._currentFrame == 2) numAcorns++;
    }

    // is it three matching symbols?
    firstSymbol = _root["symbol1"]._currentFrame;
    threeOfAKind = true;
    for(i=2;i<4;i++) {
        if (_root["symbol"+i]._currentFrame != firstSymbol) threeOfAKind = false;
    }

    // determine payout of three matches
    if (threeOfAKind) {
        if (firstSymbol == 1) {
            win = 20;
        } else if (firstSymbol == 2) {
            win = 10;
        } else if (firstSymbol == 3) {
            win = 30;
        } else if (firstSymbol == 4) {
            win = 50;
        } else if (firstSymbol == 5) {
            win = 80;
        } else if (firstSymbol == 6) {
            win = 100;
        } else if (firstSymbol == 7) {
            win = 1000;
```

```
        }

    // two acorns
    } else if (numAcorns == 2) {
        win = 2;

    // one acorn
    } else if (numAcorns == 1) {
        win = 1;

    // nothing
    } else {
        win = 0;
    }

    return(win);
}
```

Loose Ends

If you look at the example movie, you will see that the slot machine background is actually in the foreground. The three windows are holes in this image where the symbols and spin animations show through.

You might also want to decide what to do when the player reaches $0. You can check for this condition and then branch to another frame when it happens. You can tell the player that the game is over, or that they have been given another $100 to play with.

Other Possibilities

More complex slot machines could include multiple symbols in a window. Some machines show three symbols, stacked vertically, and the player can win my matching symbols across three horizontal lines and two diagonal lines between the windows. Sometimes the player can choose to insert from one to five coins to enable potential wins along different lines.

Because this Flash movie is not for gambling, but just for fun, it is more important to see the potential for changing the graphics to match different Web site themes. For instance, you could have candy symbols for a kid's site. The appearance of the machine and the type of symbols chosen can make a slot machine movie a good addition to many Web sites.

Video Poker

⊕▷Example file: Videopoker.fla

In casinos, the video poker machines are right next to the slot machines. They are essentially the same thing: You insert a coin and take a chance that you might win. The only difference is that you get to interact with the machine in the middle of the game to affect the outcome.

Make no mistake: The house always wins. However, because the player gets to replace some cards in the middle of the game, video poker makes the player feel like he has a better chance. This will also make it more difficult for us to build.

Project Goal

Video poker is played in three steps. The first step is the game waiting for the player to ask cards to be dealt. Then, the player looks at the five cards and accesses them. The second step is when the player decides which cards to keep and which to discard. The last step is when new cards have been dealt and the final value of the hand is decided. This immediately leads back into the first step.

The game needs to present the player with a set of five cards randomly chosen from a shuffled deck. Figure 15.3 shows the screen with five cards.

Figure 15.3
The video poker game shows the player five cards.

Then the player can choose to replace any or all the cards. After that is done, the program must examine the final five cards and determine what they are worth.

Approach

The first thing the program needs is a shuffled deck of cards. This will be an array of strings such as "h7", which represents the seven of hearts. The four suits are represented by "c", "d", "h", and "s". An ace is a 1, as in "c1" for the ace of clubs, and the jack, queen, and king are "11", "12", and "13".

Creating an ordered deck of cards is easy; however, a random deck is another matter. To create a shuffled deck, you start with an ordered array and then pick random items from it, one by one, and place them in a new array.

The first five cards from the array are then displayed on the screen. A button is placed under each card. One click changes the card to the image of the back of a card. A second click returns the card in case the player changes her mind.

After the player is satisfied with her choices, she hits the "Draw" button. Then, any cards tagged for replacement are replaced by the next cards in the shuffled deck.

The trickiest bit of programming comes at the end of the game. An array of the five final cards must be evaluated for its poker value. Here is a list of possible values:

- **Low pair**—A pair of cards, 10 or lower.
- **High pair**—A pair of jacks, queens, kings, or aces.
- **Three-of-a-kind**—Any three cards of the same value.
- **Straight**—Five cards with consecutive values like 8, 9, 10, jack, and queen. An ace can be either before a 2 or after a king.
- **Flush**—Five cards of the same suit.
- **Full house**—A pair and three-of-a-kind.
- **Four-of-a-kind**—Four cards of the same value.
- **Straight flush**—Five cards with consecutive values, all the same suit.
- **Royal flush**—A straight flush with a 10, jack, queen, king, and ace.

To determine whether the final hand meets any of the previously listed criteria, you have to analyze the array of cards in several ways.

After the hand's value has been determined, the final step is to match that value to a win amount and give the player the cash.

Preparing the Movie

The main library element in this game is the deck of cards, which is a 54-frame movie clip. The first frame shows the blank outline of a card. The second frame shows the back of any card. Frames 3 to 54 each show a different card in the deck. Each frame is named with the same name the code uses to identify cards. For instance, "c1" is the ace of clubs and "h11" is the jack of hearts.

If you look at the example movie, Videopoker.fla, you will see that the "deck" movie clip is complimented by a whole library folder filled with graphics. This makes it easier to reuse elements from card to card.

The movie is set up with five instances of the "deck" movie clip. They are named "card0" to "card4". The first frame only needs a "deal" button, as does the third frame.

The middle frame should have a "draw" button instead, as well as a "hold/replace" button under each card.

Writing the Code

The first frame of the main timeline contains most of the code. It starts by setting the player's "cash" to 100.

```
startGame();
stop();

// init cash
function startGame() {
    cash = 100;
}
```

Like the slot machine, use a function to display the player's cash with a "$" before it:

```
// display cash with $
function showCash() {
    cashDisplay = "$"+cash;
}
```

A hand starts with the player paying $1. Each hand is dealt from a fresh new deck of 52 cards. The "firstDraw" function picks the first five cards and the "showCards" function sets the movie clips on the Stage to those cards.

```
// start a hand
function startDeal() {
    // deduct from cash
    cash--;
    showCash();

    // shuffle and deal
    createDeck();
    firstDraw();
    showCards();
}
```

Creating a completely random deck involves two steps. The first is to create an ordered deck. This is done by looping through all the suits and values and adding a card to an array for each combination.

Next, the program takes random cards from this ordered deck and places them in another array. When that array is full and the previous array is empty, you have a shuffled deck.

```
// create a shuffled deck
function createDeck() {
```

```
// creat an ordered deck
suits = ["c","d","s","h"];
temp = new Array();
for(suit=0;suit<4;suit++) {
    for(num=1;num<14;num++) {
        temp.push(suits[suit]+num);
    }
}

// pick random cards until deck has been shuffled
deck = new Array();
while (temp.length > 0) {
    r = int(Math.random()*temp.length);
    deck.push(temp[r]);
    temp.splice(r,1);
}
}
```

The "firstDraw" function takes five cards from the deck and pushes them into the "cards" array. It also initializes a small array called "hold", which remembers which cards the player wants to keep.

```
// deal first five cards
function firstDraw() {
    cards = new Array();
    for(i=0;i<5;i++) {
        cards.push(deck.pop());
    }

    // set hold array to all held
    hold = [true,true,true,true,true];

    showCards();
}
```

To translate the array of cards in the player's hand to something that the player can see, the "showCards" handler sets the frame for each of the five movie clip instances on the Stage to match the strings in the "hand" array:

```
// set card movie clips to the player's hand
function showCards() {
    for(i=0;i<5;i++) {
        _root["card"+i].gotoAndStop(cards[i]);
    }
}
```

After all the cards have been shown to the player, he must decide what to do next. The "Hold/Draw" button under each card calls the "holdDraw" function with a number from

0 to 4. The first time a button is clicked, the code changes the movie clip instance to show the back of a card. If the player clicks it again, it replaces the card. The player can toggle back and forth as many times as he wants before clicking the "Draw" button.

The "hold" array will have a true in any position to represent that the player wants to keep the card, and a false if the player wants to replace it:

```
// toggle a card between hold and draw
function holdDraw(cardNum) {

    // card being held, turn it over
    if (hold[cardNum]) {
        _root["card"+cardNum].gotoAndStop("back");
        hold[cardNum] = false;

    // card turned over, hold it instead
    } else {
        _root["card"+cardNum].gotoAndStop(cards[cardNum]);
        hold[cardNum] = true;
    }

}
```

When the player clicks the "Draw" button, the "secondDraw" function replaces any cards that are marked by a false in the "hold" array. The function calls "showCards" to display the changes.

The code then immediately uses the function "handValue" to determine what the player has. This value is passed into "winnings" to determine how much cash, if any, should be added to the player's "cash". Also, the variable "resultsDisplay" is used to display both of these values on the screen.

```
// replace cards not held and decide on winnings
function secondDraw() {

    // replace cards not held
    for(i=0;i<5;i++) {
        if (!hold[i]) {
            cards[i] = deck.pop();
        }
    }
    showCards();

    // figure out what player has
    handVal = handValue(cards);

    // determine the amount they won
    winAmt = winnings(handVal);
    resultsDisplay = handVal + ": " + winAmt;
```

```
// add winnings
cash += winAmt;
showCash();

gotoAndPlay("done");
}
```

Before you get into the critical "handValue" function, you need to create a utility function called "compareHands". The function "handValue" needs to sort the cards in the player's hand so that lowest values are first. Flash doesn't know anything in particular about a deck of playing cards, so you have to teach it.

The "compareHands" function takes two cards and compares them. It isolates characters 1 and 2 from each card, which means that it ignores character 0. This means that "c7" becomes 7 and "c13" becomes 13.

It then returns one of three responses: -1 means card a is before card b, 0 means card a is the same value as card b, and 1 means card a comes after card b.

This function is required by the sort command that will be used in the "handValue" function. If sort didn't have this specialized function, it would attempt to sort the "hand" array in alphabetical order, which would place all clubs in front of all diamonds because one starts with a "c" and the other a "d". Instead, you want the cards to be sorted in numerical order.

```
// this function is used by the sort command to
// decide which cards come first
function compareHands(a,b) {

    // get number value of cards
    numa = Number(a.substr(1,2));
    numb = Number(b.substr(1,2));

    // return -1, 0, or 1 depending on comparison
    if (numa < numb) return(-1);
    if (numa == numb) return (0);
    if (numa > numb) return (1);
}
```

The "handValue" function which is coming up next starts by making a copy of the "cards" array and storing it in the "hand" array. It then sorts this array using the "compareHands" function ① .

For instance, if the player's hand is ["h4", "d5", "c2", "s3", "h6"], then the array after the sort will be ["c2", "s3", "h4", "d5", "h6"]. This makes it easier for the code to determine whether the array has a set of cards that are in consecutive order, called a "straight."

A "straight" is determined by looking at each card and seeing if it is one value higher than the card before it ②. If this condition holds throughout the array, then it is a straight.

This technique won't find one type of straight: when a straight starts with a 10, goes up to a king and then wraps back around to an ace. This is a special type of straight recognized in poker and you can perform a simple test to determine whether it has occurred ③.

TIP

Some people think that straights can wrap around the end of a deck, with the ace acting as the first and last card. For instance: a queen, king, ace, two, and three. This is not a valid poker straight, but merely an odd variation used in some friendly amateur games. An ace can be used as the first card of the straight (ace, two, three, four, five), or the last card of a straight (ten, jack, queen, king, ace), but not both for wrap-around sequences. The rules of poker are detailed in many sources, such as the popular "Hoyle's" series of books.

Next, you check to see whether all the cards have the same suit ④. This is done by comparing all cards, except the first one, with the first card. If all cards match the suit of the first card, then they must all match.

The next step is to make an array called "counts" and store the number of cards of each value in it ⑤. This array will have 14 values, each representing the number of cards in the hand of that value. The first item in the array is not used because there is no card of "0" value.

For example, if a hand has an ace, two threes, a four, and a jack, the array would be [0,1,0,2,1,0,0,0,0,0,0,1,0,0].

Finally, the code can start the task of determining what type of hand the player has. The "counts" array is looped through and any 2, 3, or 4 is noted ⑥. A single appearance of a 2 means that the player has a pair. A single appearance of a 3 means the player has three-of-a-kind. A single appearance of a 4 means the player has four-of-a-kind. It is also possible to find a second appearance of a 2, or both a 2 and a 3 in the hand. The first is two-pair, and the second is a full house.

Next, a test is made to determine whether there are any pairs that are jacks or higher ⑦. Video poker typically only rewards pairs that are jacks or higher and gives nothing for pairs that are 10 or lower.

Another test checks to see whether the player has an ace in the hand ⑧. This will be used in case the player has a straight flush. If the player has a straight flush and one card is an ace, then it means the player has the highest sort of straight flush: a royal flush.

Now the function has a whole series of true or false values: "straight", "flush", "hasAce", "fourOfAKind", "threeOfAKind", "twoPair", "pair", "fullHouse", and "jackOrHigher". By using these true or false values, the actual value of the hand can be determined and returned as a string ⑨ .

```
// determine what the player has
function handValue() {

    // make a copy of the player's cards and sort them
    hand = cards.slice();
    hand.sort(compareHands);

    // make arrays with suits and numbers for easy access
    suits = new Array();
    nums = new Array();
    for(i=0;i<5;i++) {
        suits.push(hand[i].substr(0,1));
        nums.push(Number(hand[i].substr(1,2)));
    }

    // see if they are in perfect order
    straight = true;
    for(i=0;i<4;i++) {
        if (nums[i] + 1 != nums[i+1]) straight = false;
    }

    // look for 10, J, Q, K and Ace
    if ((nums[0] == 1) and (nums[1] == 10) and (nums[2] == 11)
        and (nums[3] == 12) and (nums[4] == 13))  straight = true;

    // see if they are all the same suit
    flush = true;
    for(i=1;i<5;i++) {
        if (suits[i] != suits[0]) flush = false;
    }

    // make array of how much of each number is in hand
    counts = new Array();
    for(i=0;i<14;i++) {
        counts.push(0);
    }
    for(i=0;i<5;i++) {
        counts[nums[i]]++;
    }

    // use counts array to find matches
    pair = false;
```

① hand.sort(compareHands);

② // see if they are in perfect order

③ // look for 10, J, Q, K and Ace

④ // see if they are all the same suit

⑤ // make array of how much of each number is in hand

⑥ // use counts array to find matches

```
    twoPair = false;
    threeOfAKind = false;
    fourOfAKind = false;
    for(i=1;i<14;i++) {
        // pair found
        if (counts[i] == 2) {
            // second pair found
            if (pair) {
                twoPair = true;
            // first pair found
            } else {
                pair = true;
            }
        // three-of-a-kind
        } else if (counts[i] == 3) {
            threeOfAKind = true;
        // four-of-a-kind
        } else if (counts[i] == 4) {
            fourOfAKind = true;
        }
    }
```

⑦→
```
    // see if any matches are jacks or higher
    jackOrHigher = false;
    for(i=1;i<14;i++) {
        if (((i == 1) or (i > 10)) and (counts[i] >= 2)) {
            jackOrHigher = true;
        }
    }
```

⑧→
```
    // see if high card is an ace
    hasAce = false;
    if (counts[1] > 0) hasAce = true;
```

⑨→
```
    // return the type of hand the player has
    if (straight and flush and hasAce) {
        return("Royal Flush");
    } else if (straight and flush) {
        return("Straight Flush");
    } else if (fourOfAKind) {
        return("Four-Of-A-Kind");
    } else if (pair and threeOfAKind) {
        return("Full House");
    } else if (flush) {
        return("Flush");
    } else if (straight) {
        return("Straight");
```

```
    } else if (threeOfAKind) {
        return("Three-Of-A-Kind");
    } else if (twoPair) {
        return("Two Pair");
    } else if (pair and jackOrHigher) {
        return("High Pair");
    } else if (pair) {
        return("Low Pair");
    } else {
        return("Nothing");
    }
}
```

The only function left is the "winnings" function, which takes a string generated by "handValue" and finds the appropriate amount won:

```
// take the type of hand and return the amount won
function winnings(handVal) {
    if (handVal == "Royal Flush") return(800);
    if (handVal == "Straight Flush") return(50);
    if (handVal == "Four-Of-A-Kind") return(25);
    if (handVal == "Full House") return(8);
    if (handVal == "Flush") return(5);
    if (handVal == "Straight") return(4);
    if (handVal == "Three-Of-A-Kind") return(3);
    if (handVal == "Two Pair") return(2);
    if (handVal == "High Pair") return(1);
    if (handVal == "Low Pair") return(0);
    if (handVal == "Nothing") return(0);
}
```

Loose Ends

Each "hold/draw" button contains a slightly different piece of code. The first one looks like this:

```
on (press) {
    holdDraw(0);
}
```

The "0" tells the "holdDraw" function that the request is about card 0. The other four buttons have the number 1 to 4 there instead.

Although the first frame of the movie immediately calls "startGame", as you can see from the code in the "Writing the Code" section, the second frame must call "startDeal". Check out the example movie to see it yourself.

Other Possibilities

I picked the amounts specified in "winnings" using common sense. However, you might want to pick different numbers depending on how much you want the game to favor the house or the player.

You will also want to handle the case where the player runs out of money. Send them to a "game over" frame, for instance.

Another variation on this game would be to allow the player to bet from $1 to $5 per turn. This allows the player to bet less when they feel unlucky and more at other times.

Simple Blackjack

🌐▷⦂**Example file: Blackjack.fla**

Blackjack is another popular casino card game that translates well to the computer screen. After all, the dealer in blackjack follows a precise set of rules. Therefore, you can write a program to imitate the dealer's behavior.

Project Goal

The goal here is not to create a full-featured blackjack game, but rather a basic one. There are several rules in blackjack that are rarely used, such as doubling down, insurance, and splitting. Although these are seldom used by the player, they complicate the code to the point of making it super-advanced. So instead of dealing with those rules and making this section of the book useful to only a few, those rules have been omitted so this section is easier to understand.

Figure 15.4 shows the example movie in action. You can see that the player has drawn five cards for a total of 18. The dealer drew three cards to get 21.

Figure 15.4
The Flash Blackjack game shows a hand just completed where the dealer beat the player 21 to 18.

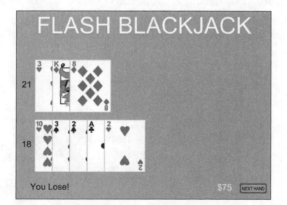

This simple blackjack game deals two cards to the player and dealer. The dealer's first card is facedown until the player is through drawing. The player can draw until he gets 21 or more. Then, the computer draws for the dealer until the dealer has at least 17.

If the player gets 21 in his first two cards, he immediately wins the bet, plus 50%. If the dealer gets 21, the hand ends immediately. After that, whoever gets the higher amount without passing 21, wins.

The player also can control how much he bets, from $5 to $25 in increments of $5.

Approach

Like the video poker game, there is a "deck" array that stores a shuffled deck of cards. The difference here is that there are actually six decks of cards shuffled into the same "deck" array. In blackjack, this is called a "shoe".

Both the player and the dealer have an array representing the cards in their hands. You'll have to make a special consideration for the dealer's first card, because it shouldn't be shown until the player is finished drawing.

Unlike video poker, determining the value of a hand is simple in blackjack. The only twist is than an ace can be worth 1 or 11. However, because two aces worth 11 would total 22, there is no point in ever making a second ace worth 11. So, all you need to do is to recognize that a hand has an ace in it, count it as 1, and then add 10 to the hand if that 10 won't put the hand over 21. So a hand with a 3, 9, and an ace equals 13, because making the ace worth 11 makes the hand worth 23.

Preparing the Movie

Unlike video poker, there can be anywhere from 2 to 11 cards in a hand. So for each hand, 11 movie clip instances are placed named "player0" to "player10" and "dealer0" to "dealer10". Instead of having a blank card outline for the first frame of the "deck" movie clip, nothing is placed in that frame. Therefore, when you place them on the Stage, all you see is Flash's default movie clip marker. You can see all 22 of them in Figure 15.5.

Figure 15.5
All the cards appear as little circles, Flash's movie clip marker for when there is nothing else visible for that movie clip.

This movie has a complex timeline. Each labeled marker in the timeline represents a different point in the game. Figure 15.6 shows this complex timeline and you can see most of the labels.

Figure 15.6

The complex timeline of the blackjack game has a labeled frame for each step. Frame 4's label is the only one obscured. It reads "shuffle."

As the game progresses, so does the playback head along the timeline. Each keyframe calls a different function in our code. The code itself appears in the first keyframe.

Because of the nature of Flash timelines, it is important to take a look at the example movie, Blackjack.fla, on the Web site to see for yourself where all the keyframes are and what code they call.

Writing the Code

The first frame called "initGame", but there is no stop() command right after it. This is because the timeline should continue and move right to the "shuffle" frame.

```
initGame();
```

The "initGame" function sets up the player's "cash".

```
function initGame() {
    cash = 100;
    showCash();
}
```

The "createDeck" function is similar to the one used in video poker, but it actually adds each card six times to create a show of six decks.

One of the drawbacks of the six decks is that it can take some time to shuffle in Flash. Therefore, the "shuffle" frame appears just one frame before the keyframe where the "createDeck" function is called. This insures that the word "shuffle" appears in the screen before the code starts working on the assignment. Therefore, the player doesn't have to wonder if her computer froze.

```
// create a shuffled deck
function createDeck() {
    // create an ordered deck
    suits = ["c","d","s","h"];
    temp = new Array();
```

```
for(i=0;i<6;i++) {
    for(suit=0;suit<4;suit++) {
        for(num=1;num<14;num++) {
            temp.push(suits[suit]+num);
        }
    }
}

// pick random cards until deck has been shuffled
deck = new Array();
while (temp.length > 0) {
    r = int(Math.random()*temp.length);
    deck.push(temp[r]);
    temp.splice(r,1);
}
}
```

The "initHand" function sets up the "playerHand" and "dealerHand" arrays. It also sets the flag "showDealerFirstCard" to false and sets the bet to the default $5.

```
// init hand arrays and bet
function initHand() {
    playerHand = new Array();
    dealerHand = new Array();
    showDealerFirstCard = false;

    bet = 5;
    showBet();
}
```

The "addToBet" function responds to the player clicking the "Add to bet" button. It adds $5 to the bet, but doesn't allow the player to go above $25.

```
// allow the player to increase her bet up to $25
function addToBet() {
    bet += 5;
    if (bet > 25) bet = 25;
    showBet();
}
```

When the player hits the "Deal" button, "makeBet" is called to transfer the bet amount out of the player's cash pool. The movie then flows forward through the four frames: "Deal1" to "Deal4".

```
// take the money away from the player
function makeBet() {
    cash -= bet;
    showCash();
}
```

Each of the four "Deal" frames calls "dealCard". Twice this function is called with "playerHand" and twice with "DealerHand". The function deals two cards to the player and two to the dealer. The function "showCards" is also called in each of these frames.

```
// take one card from the deck and give it to the player
function dealCard(hand) {
    hand.push(deck.pop());
}
```

The "showBet" and "showCash" functions display the current bet and the player's cash with a "$" in front of them. Remember to create the appropriate text areas for each of these.

```
// display cash with $
function showCash() {
    cashDisplay = "$"+cash;
}
```

```
// display bet with $
function showBet() {
    betDisplay = "$"+bet;
}
```

The "showCards" function loops through each of the cards in both the player's and dealer's hands and sets the movie clips on the Stage to represent them. It uses the flag "showDealerFirstCard" to determine whether the first card in the dealer's hand is shown or the back of a card is shown instead.

```
// show all cards in both hands
function showCards() {
    // only show the dealer's first card when player is done
    if (showDealerFirstCard) {
        _root["dealer0"].gotoAndStop(dealerHand[0]);
    } else {
        _root["dealer0"].gotoAndStop(2);
    }

    // show the rest of the dealer's cards
    for(i=1;i<dealerHand.length;i++) {
        _root["dealer"+i].gotoAndStop(dealerHand[i]);
    }

    // show all of the player's cards
    for(i=0;i<playerHand.length;i++) {
        _root["player"+i].gotoAndStop(playerHand[i]);
    }
```

```
    // show the numerical value of both hands
    playerValue = handValue(playerHand);
    dealerValue = handValue(dealerHand);
}
```

After the initial deal of two cards each, there is the chance that either player has black-jack. If the player does, then she immediately wins her bet, plus 50% more. If the dealer does, then the player loses right away.

```
// check to see if either has blackjack
function checkForBlackjack() {

    // if player has blackjack
    if ((playerHand.length == 2) and (playerValue == 21)) {
        // award 150% winnings
        cash += bet*2.5;
        showCash();
        result = "Blackjack!";
        gotoAndPlay("Done");

    // if dealer has blackjack, instant loss
    } else if ((dealerHand.length == 2) and (dealerHand == 21)) {
        result = "Dealer has blackjack!";
        gotoAndPlay("Done");
    }
}
```

After the initial four cards are dealt, the movie comes to a rest on the "Player" frame. This frame has a "Hit" and a "Stay" button. The player can use the "Hit" button to request another card. The "hit" function is called. If the new card puts the player at 21 or more, then the game automatically moves forward.

```
// player draws another card
function hit() {
    dealCard(playerHand);
    showCards();
    playerValue = handValue(playerHand);

    // if player gets 21 or busts, go to dealer
    if (playerValue >= 21) startDealer();
}
```

When the player is done drawing, the dealer gets to go. The "startDealer" function kicks off this stage of the game by setting the "showDealerFirstCard" to true and displaying it through an extra call to "showCards". Then, the game advances to the "Dealer" frame.

```
// show dealer's first card and let dealer draw
function startDealer() {
```

```
        showDealerFirstCard = true;
        showCards();
        gotoAndPlay("Dealer");
    }
```

The "Dealer" frame loops over and over, calling "dealerMove" each time. In each case, the dealer's hand is examined to see if it's worth 17 or more. The house rules for this game are that the dealer must hit on 16 or lower, stand on everything else. When the dealer stands, the "decideWinner" function is called.

```
// dealer draws if < 17
function dealerMove() {
    if (handValue(dealerHand) < 17) {
        dealCard(dealerHand);
        showCards();
        gotoAndPlay("Dealer");

    // dealer is done
    } else {
        decideWinner();
    }
}
```

The "handValue" function is used in many of the functions shown in the previous code to calculate the numerical value of a hand. The value of each card is added to the total, with aces representing 1. If an ace was found and the addition of 10 will not bust the hand, then 10 is added to the total.

```
// calculate hand value
function handValue(hand) {
    total = 0;
    ace = false;

    for(i=0;i<hand.length;i++) {
        // add value of card
        val = Number(hand[i].substr(1,2));

        // jack, queen, and king = 10
        if (val > 10) val = 10;
        total += val;

        // remember if an ace is found
        if (val == 1) ace = true;
    }

    // ace can = 11 if it doesn't bust player
    if ((ace) and (total <= 11)) total += 10;
```

```
    return(total);
}
```

The following function uses a series of conditions to determine who won. Not only is the "cash" adjusted if the player wins, but each case also sets the "result" variable, which is then displayed on the Stage in the "Done" frame.

```
// see who won, or if there is a tie
function decideWinner() {
    showCash();
    if (playerValue > 21) {
        result = "You Busted!";
    } else if (dealerValue > 21) {
        cash += bet*2;
        result = "Dealer Busts. You Win!";
    } else if (dealerValue > playerValue) {
        result = "You Lose!";
    } else if (dealerValue == playerValue) {
        cash += bet;
        result = "Tie!";
    } else if (dealerValue < playerValue) {
        cash += bet*2;
        result = "You Win!";
    }
    showCash();
    gotoAndPlay("Done");
}
```

The "Done" frame contains a "Next Hand" button that calls the following function. This function checks to make sure that there are more than 26 cards left in the deck. If not, another shuffle is performed. If there are enough cards left, then "initHand" is called and the game returns to the "Bet" frame.

Either way, the "resetCards" function is used to set all the "deck" movie clips on the Stage back to the first frame so that the cards don't persist on the screen.

```
// start next hand
function newDeal() {
    resetCards();

    // if deck has less than 26 cards, reshuffle
    if (deck.length < 26) {
        gotoAndPlay("shuffle");
    } else {
        initHand();
        gotoAndPlay("Bet");
    }
}
```

```
// remove cards from table
function resetCards() {
    for(i=0;i<dealerHand.length;i++) {
        _root["dealer"+i].gotoAndStop(1);
    }
    for(i=0;i<playerHand.length;i++) {
        _root["player"+i].gotoAndStop(1);
    }
}
```

Loose Ends

The main timeline for this movie is the most complex of any game in this book. Therefore, it is important to check out the example movie on the Web site to get a good sense of where everything goes.

You'll also need to create various text areas to display the value of each hand, the bet amount, the cash amount, and the result.

Other Possibilities

Although this game is a good one to learn a little ActionScripting from, it will disappoint avid blackjack players. Therefore, for the benefit of advanced ActionScript programmers, here's a bit about how to add some of the missing features to the game.

Doubling down is the easiest feature to add. All you need to do is create another button on the "Player" frame called "Double". When the player clicks it, he is dealt one new card, his bet is subtracted once again from his cash, and the play passes to the dealer. However, you have to make sure that the player has not already drawn any cards because doubling can only happen when the player has just his initial two cards.

Insurance is a little harder to do because it creates another branch in the flow of the game. Insurance happens when the dealer is showing an ace. In that case, the player can choose to take out insurance, which is basically a bet against the dealer having 21. If insurance is accepted, and the dealer has 21, then the hand immediately ends. In addition to the player losing his original bet, the player wins the insurance bet.

Splitting is a difficult addition to this game. If the player has two cards of equal value, such as two 9s, then she should be allowed to split the hand into two hands, each starting with a single 9. This means that you cannot store the player's hand in a single array, "playerHand", but you must make it an array of arrays. In most cases, this "playerHands" array contains a single array representing the only hand. If the player splits, then it will contain two arrays. The player might be able to split more than once, giving you three, four, or more arrays inside the "playerHands" array. Then, each hand must be played out. You can see how this complicates every part of the game. Even at the end of the game, the player could potentially win, lose, and tie some or all hands.

Arcade Games

- Space Combat
- Space Rocks
- Maze Chase
- Moon Lander

When most people think of computer games, they think of classic computer arcade games, such as Space Invaders, Asteroids, Pac-Man, Centipede, and Lunar Lander. In this chapter, you will create games in this genre.

The first game you'll build is a generic space combat game in which you shoot at objects coming at your ship. Then, you'll look at a similar game played from a different perspective called Space Rocks. Next, you'll build a maze chase game, and then finally a game called Moon Lander.

Space Combat

⊕▷Example file: Spacecombat.fla

Arcade games are sometimes also called "twitch" games because the only skill needed to do well is a fast reflex. This is very true of the first game, called Space Combat.

Figure 16.1 shows the example movie from the Web site, Spacecombat.fla. You can see that you are inside a spaceship with some nasty-looking asteroids coming your way.

Figure 16.1
The Space Combat game makes you the pilot of a spaceship trying to make it through an asteroid field.

Project Goal

This game allows the player to fire little bullets at the oncoming asteroids. If the bullets hit the asteroids, they explode harmlessly. However, if an asteroid makes it past the bullets, it might hit the player's ship, causing damage.

The game keeps track of the number of asteroids the player hits, as well as the number of asteroids that hit the player's ship. Some asteroids might pass above, below, or to the sides of the ship without causing any damage. The game ends after the player sustains 20 impacts.

Approach

The two active pieces of this game are the asteroids and the bullets. The asteroids originate from a spot near the center of the screen and move toward a spot in an area larger than the screen. If the asteroid winds up outside the screen area, it is assumed that it missed the ship. If it finishes inside the screen area, it hits the ship, causing damage. As the asteroid travels, its scale increases, creating the illusion of 3D space.

The bullets come from both the bottom-left and bottom-right corners of the screen. They travel toward a spot indicated by the position of the mouse at the time of the firing. When they reach that final spot, any asteroid at that location is destroyed.

Destroying an asteroid not only scores points, but prevents that asteroid from hitting the ship. Thus, the player should concentrate her fire on asteroids that look like they are coming toward the ship.

Preparing the Movie

There isn't too much to the library elements in this movie. The "foreground" is the top and the bottom pieces in Figure 16.1 that represent the interior of your ship. All the foreground elements, including the score and damage text near the bottom of the screen, are in the "foreground" movie clip. This way, you can easily move this single movie clip all the way in front of all the asteroids and bullets.

The asteroids are in a three-part movie clip called "rock". The first part is a static frame with an image of the rock as it appears to move closer to the ship. The second part consists of several frames of animation showing the rock exploding when it is hit by a bullet. This sequence is labeled "explode red". The final part is another sequence labeled "explode blue". Check the example movie on the Web site to see how this movie clip has been put together. Figure 16.2 shows this clip.

Figure 16.2

The Flash main window shows the "rock" movie clip. You can see part of the asteroid exploding.

There is also a "point" movie clip that is used to create the bullets, and a "cursor" movie clip that is used to replace the normal cursor with crosshairs.

The movie has three frames: "start", "play", and "game over". All the action takes place on the "play" frame.

Writing the Code

All the code is triggered by an action placed on a small "actions" movie clip just off the Stage and a "button" button just below it. The "actions" movie clip calls one function when the play begins, and four others every frame.

```
onClipEvent (load) {
    // set up game
    _root.initGame();
}

onClipEvent (enterFrame) {
    // move crosshairs
    _root.moveCursor();

    // move all bullets
    _root.moveBullets();

    // 10% chance of a new rock
    if (Math.random() < .1) _root.createRock();

    // move all rocks
    _root.moveRocks();
}
```

The "button" button captures the spacebar and uses that to call a function in the main timeline:

```
on (keyPress "<Space>") {
    // spacebar = fire bullets
    fire();
}
```

You'll find all the functions in the main timeline. The "initGame" function creates arrays to hold information about the asteroids and bullets. It moves the "foreground" and "cursor" movie clips to the front so that any rocks and bullets appear under them, which will make it appear as if they are outside the spaceship.

The "damage" and "hits" variables are reset. The "level" variable does not pertain to the level of play, but instead the current movie clip level used to create new clips. Each time a new movie clip is created to represent a bullet or an asteroid, a fresh new level starts.

The *Mouse.hide()* command is issued to make the normal computer mouse go away. You'll track the cursor with a movie clip instead.

```
function initGame() {
    // create arrays for bullets and rocks
    bullets = new Array();
    rocks = new Array();

    // move foreground crosshairs to front
    _root["foreground"].swapDepths(9999999)
    _root["cursor"].swapDepths(9999998)

    // set up game variables
    level = 0;
    damage = 0;
    hits = 0;


    // hide the mouse, use crosshairs instead
    Mouse.hide();
}
```

The "actions" movie clip calls the "moveCursor" function every frame. The function positions the "cursor" movie clip at the location of the cursor. The player uses this cursor to aim.

```
function moveCursor() {
    // move cursor to the mouse position
    cursor._x = _xmouse;
    cursor._y = _ymouse;
}
```

The "button" button passes on spacebar presses to the "fire" function. This records the location of the cursor, creates a pair of new "point" movie clips to represent the bullet, and adds items to the "bullets" array representing the starting points, ending points, distance traveled, and movie clip for each bullet.

```
function fire() {
    // get location of the mouse
    x = _xmouse;
    y = _ymouse;

    // add left bullet
    level++;
    attachMovie("point","bullet"+level,level);
    bullets.push({startx: 50, starty: 350, destx: x, desty: y, dist: 1.0, clip:
    ➥"bullet"+level});

    // add right bullet
    level++;
    attachMovie("point","bullet"+level,level);
```

```
bullets.push({startx: 500, starty: 350, destx: x, desty: y, dist: 1.0, clip:
➥"bullet"+level});
}
```

After a bullet has been fired, it is moved each and every frame by the "moveBullets" function. This function uses the "bullets" array to track each existing bullet. The "dist" property is decreased to 40% of its previous value each frame. The bullet is drawn at a location between its starting and ending points, determined by "dist". A value of 1.0 for "dist" would mean that it is drawn at its starting point, whereas a value of 0.0 would mean it is drawn at its ending point.

However, when the bullet reaches a "dist" of 0.01, it is considered close enough to the end of its journey. At that instant, the "checkForHit" function is called to determine whether it hit anything. Regardless, the bullet is removed from the movie and the array.

This game does not pretend to model a real 3D reality or real physics. Instead, it is creating an illusion that works as an arcade game.

```
function moveBullets() {

    // loop through all bullets
    for(i=bullets.length-1;i>=0;i--) {

        // increase distance traveled by 40%
        bullets[i].dist *= .4;

        // if bullet is too far away, remove it
        if (bullets[i].dist < .01) {
            checkForHit(bullets[i].destx,bullets[i].desty);
            _root[bullets[i].clip].removeMovieClip();
            bullets.splice(i,1);

        // reposition bullet closer to destination
        } else {
            bullets[i].x = bullets[i].dist*bullets[i].startx +
            ➥(1.0-bullets[i].dist)*bullets[i].destx;
            bullets[i].y = bullets[i].dist*bullets[i].starty +
            ➥(1.0-bullets[i].dist)*bullets[i].desty;
            _root[bullets[i].clip]._x = bullets[i].x;
            _root[bullets[i].clip]._y = bullets[i].y;
        }


    }
}
```

An asteroid is created in a similar way to a bullet. However, a random starting and ending spot is chosen. The starting point is 25 pixels horizontally and vertically away from the center of the screen. The ending point is 550 horizontal pixels away from the center and 400 vertical pixels. This is exactly twice the size of the Stage. The result means that the asteroid always starts near the center, but can finish anywhere from dead center to way off the screen.

```
function createRock() {
       // create a random origin for the rock
       startx = Math.random()*50+250;
       starty = Math.random()*50+175;

       // create a random destination for the rock
       destx = Math.random()*1100-275;
       desty = Math.random()*800-200;

       // add the rock movie clip
       level++;
       attachMovie("rock","rock"+level,level++);
       rocks.push({startx: startx, starty: starty, destx: destx, desty: desty, dist: .01,
       ➥clip: "rock"+level});
}
```

Like the "moveBullets" function, "moveRocks" uses the "dist" property of each asteroid to move it. However, this time it is getting closer to the screen, so "dist" starts at 0.01 and increases by 10% each frame. Not only is the location set according to the "dist" property, but the _xscale and _yscale is also set, which makes the asteroid appear to get larger as it approaches the ship.

If the asteroid makes it to a "dist" greater than 1.0, then it has reached the ship. If the asteroid is still on the Stage, then it has hit the ship. The asteroid explodes and "damage" is increased. If "damage" is greater than or equal to 20, then the game is over.

```
function moveRocks() {

       // loop through all rocks
       for(i=rocks.length-1;i>=0;i--) {

              // decrease distance by 10%
              rocks[i].dist *= 1.1;

              // see if rock is close enough to hit or pass ship
              if (rocks[i].dist > 1.0) {

                     // see if it hit ship
                     if (rocks[i].destx > 0 and rocks[i].destx < 550 and rocks[i].desty > 0
                     ➥and rocks[i].desty < 400) {

                            // explode and add to damage
                            _root[rocks[i].clip].gotoAndPlay("explode blue");
                            damage++;
                            foreground.displayDamage = damage;
```

```
            // see if there is too much damage
            if (damage >= 20) {
                removeAllRocks();
                Mouse.show();
                gotoAndStop("game over");
            }

        // harmlessly passed
        } else {
            _root[rocks[i].clip].removeMovieClip();
        }

        // either way, remove from array
        rocks.splice(i,1);

    // reposition rock
    } else {
        rocks[i].x = (1.0-rocks[i].dist)*rocks[i].startx +
        ➥rocks[i].dist*rocks[i].destx;
        rocks[i].y = (1.0-rocks[i].dist)*rocks[i].starty +
        ➥rocks[i].dist*rocks[i].desty;
        _root[rocks[i].clip]._x = rocks[i].x;
        _root[rocks[i].clip]._y = rocks[i].y;

        // resize rock to appear closer
        _root[rocks[i].clip]._xscale = 100*rocks[i].dist;
        _root[rocks[i].clip]._yscale = 100*rocks[i].dist;
    }

    }
}
```

The "checkHit" function is called by each bullet as it reaches its destination. This function loops through each rock and checks to see whether the bullet has hit it. If so, then the rock explodes and is removed from the array. The "hits" variable is increased.

```
function checkForHit(x,y) {

    // loop through all rocks
    for(j=rocks.length-1;j>=0;j--) {

        // see if rock will be hit by bullets at this location
        if (_root[rocks[j].clip].hitTest(x,y)) {

            // if hit, explode red and remove from array
            hits++;
            foreground.displayHits = hits;
```

```
            _root[rocks[j].clip].gotoAndPlay("explode red");
            rocks.splice(j,1);
        }
    }
}
```

At the end of each explosion animation, as seen earlier in Figure 16.2, a short script calls "killRock". This function removes the very movie clip that calls it. By doing this, you can remove each rock from the array at the exact moment when it is destroyed, but keep the movie clip around for a few more frames as it explodes.

```
function killRock(clip) {
    // when rock is done exploding, it calls this to remove itself
    clip.removeMovieClip();
}
```

When the game is over, the "removeAllRocks" function is called so that bullets and aster-oids don't hang around on the "game over" frame.

```
function removeAllRocks() {

    // loop through all rocks and take them out
    for(i=rocks.length-1;i>=0;i--) {
        _root[rocks[i].clip].removeMovieClip();
    }
}
```

Loose Ends

The "foreground" movie clip contains the text areas linked to the "hits" and "damage" variables. Unfortunately, because they are down one level inside this movie clip, they won't react to changes in "hits" and "damage", which reside on the main timeline. So, these text areas need to be set with commands such as "_root.displayDamage = damage;". I have called these text areas "displayDamage" and "displayHits" to avoid any confusion.

Other Possibilities

You might want to play with this movie and create your own variations. One idea would be to always have the bullets fire to the same point on the screen. Then, allow the player to use the arrow keys to steer the ship. For instance, if the player moves left, you can foster that illusion by moving all the rocks to the right a bit.

You can also improve the existing game by creating levels and improving how "damage" is displayed. For instance, you could have a damage meter of some sort. When the player is getting close to the maximum amount of damage, a red alert light could even flash.

Space Rocks

Example file: Spacerocks.fla

Now let's recreate the previous game from a different perspective. This time, the ship is viewed as a small graphic at the center of the screen. The asteroids are "space rocks" moving in various directions. This game is like many classic arcade games of the 70s and 80s. Figure 16.3 shows a screenshot of the example movie, Spacerocks.fla. This sort of game should be familiar to most readers.

Figure 16.3
The Space Rocks game features a small ship and rocks of various sizes.

Project Goal

This game is more involved than most and features game levels and limited player lives. The player can be hit by a rock three times. If the player destroys all the rocks, he moves on to the next level where rocks are faster and more numerous.

The player can spin the ship left or right, fire a thruster that will push the ship in the direction it is facing, and fire bullets. After the thruster has been used, the ship continues to move a little bit each frame. As the player spins the ship and uses the thrusters, the velocity of the ship changes using simple momentum. The player can stop the ship by pressing the down arrow.

The bullets are little movie clips that start at the same location as the ship, and move in the same direction the ship was facing when the bullet was fired. Instead of allowing the player to fire a constant stream of bullets, the player can only fire after a short recharge time.

The rocks start off as movie clips at 100% scale with a random direction and speed. When they are first hit by a bullet, they break into two rocks at 50% scale with a new random direction. These rocks, in turn, can break into two smaller rocks at 25% of the scale of the original rock. Beyond that, the rocks just disintegrate. When all the rocks are gone, the level is complete. However, if a rock collides with the ship, the player loses a life.

Preparing the Movie

The library for this movie isn't complex. There are three types of rocks, called "rock1", "rock2", and "rock3". Each time a rock is created, it is chosen from one of the three movie clips at random to give the game some graphic variety.

The "ship" movie clip has a static first frame, but a short animation that starts on the second frame showing the thruster firing. The first frame of this animation is called "thrust". Instead of using *attachMovie* to put the ship on the Stage, the ship is placed in the middle manually, which saves the trouble of creating the instance and setting the location in the code.

There is also a "bullet" movie clip to be used to create the bullets. An "actions" movie clip and a "button" button are used to hold code for the game. A "Play" button is used as the only real button element on the screen.

The movie will have a "start" frame, "play" frame, "ship hit" frame, "level over" frame, and "game over" frame. Each has the appropriate text. All but the "play" frame have a copy of the "Play" button on the screen, but with different code for each instance. Check out the example movie, Spacerocks.fla, to see where all these elements are and what code is attached to each one.

Writing the Code

Like the Space Combat adventure, there will be an "actions" movie clip and a "button" button just off the Stage that have scripts attached to them. The "actions" movie clip contains calls to one function to start a level, and then several functions that move the elements on the screen a little each frame.

```
onClipEvent(load) {
    // set up everything for game
    _root.startLevel();
}

onClipEvent(enterFrame) {
    // move the ship a step
    _root.shipMove();


    // move all bullets a step
    _root.bulletsMove();

    // move all rocks a step
    _root.rocksMove();

    // see if there are any collisions
    _root.checkHits();
}
```

The "buttons" button has a set of *on* definitions that map different keys on the keyboard to various user actions:

```
on (keyPress "<Space>") {
    // fire one bullet
    shipFire();
}

on (keyPress "<Right>") {
    // turn 30 degrees to right
    shipTurn(30);
}

on (keyPress "<Left>") {
    // turn 30 degrees to left
    shipTurn(-30);
}

on (keyPress "<Up>") {
    // move forward
    shipThrust();
}

on (keyPress "<Down>") {
    // stop ship
    shipBreak();
}
```

On the "start" frame, you can take the opportunity to set a few variables when the player presses the "Play" button to start the game. The score is reset to 0, the game level to 1, and the player gets 3 lives.

```
on (press) {
    gameLevel = 1;
    lives = 3;
    score = 0;
    gotoAndPlay("play");
}
```

The functions are all inside the main timeline script for the "play" frame. The first one deals with setting up the game at the start of a level, or just after a player loses a life.

The "ship" referred to in the code is the movie clip instance on the Stage called "ship". In addition to built-in properties of the movie clip such as _x and _y, you'll make up some new properties. The "dx" and "dy" properties represent the amount that the ship moves horizontally and vertically.

The "startLevel" function also creates the "bullets" and "rocks" arrays to hold lists of move clips that represent these elements.

The "level" variable deals with the movie clip levels used in the *attachMovie* command, not the game level. You'll use "gameLevel" for that.

The next step is to create the large rocks to start the level. Two rocks are created for the first level, three for the second level, and so on.

The "timeOfLastFire" variable is used in the "shipFire" function later to make sure that the player cannot fire too rapidly:

```
function startLevel() {
     // ship stationary
     ship.dx = 0.0;
     ship.dy = 0.0;

     // new arrays
     bullets = new Array();
     rocks = new Array();

     // start using movie clip level 0
     level = 0;

     // add new rocks = number of level + 1
     for(i=0;i<gameLevel+1;i++) {
          newRock(100,0,0);
     }

     // all to fire right away
     timeOfLastFire = 0;
}
```

The next set of functions are reactions to keypresses. They all control the ship in some way. The first one rotates the ship a certain number of degrees. If you look back at the two calls to this handler made by the "button" button, you'll see that it is called with the value of 30 in one case and -30 in the other. Those calls rotate the ship 30° in one direction or another.

```
function shipTurn(amt) {
     // rotate the ship
     ship._rotation += amt;
}
```

The next function activates the thrusters. It uses the *Math.cos* and *Math.sin* to translate the rotation of the ship into a horizontal and vertical component. Unfortunately, the _rotation property of a movie clip is in degrees, but the two math functions require radians. To convert, you need to multiply the degrees by 2 × pi, and divide by 360. In addition, you need to subtract 90° so that 0° points straight up rather than to the right.

```
function shipThrust() {
    // thrust ship in direction it faces
    ship.dx += Math.cos(2.0*Math.PI*(ship._rotation-90)/360.0);
    ship.dy += Math.sin(2.0*Math.PI*(ship._rotation-90)/360.0);

    // show engines firing
    ship.gotoAndPlay("thrust");
}
```

On the other hand, if the player presses the down-arrow key, you can easily stop the ship at its current location by setting the "dx" and "dy" properties of the movie clip to 0.

```
function shipBreak() {
    // stop ship
    ship.dx = 0;
    ship.dy = 0;
}
```

When the player presses the spacebar, the ship should fire a bullet. However, it first checks to see if enough milliseconds have passed since the last bullet was fired.

A bullet is created from the movie clip "bullet" and the "dx" and "dy" properties of this movie clip are created and set just like they are for the ship. In addition, a pointer to the movie clip is added to the "bullets" array so that the bullet can be referenced later.

```
function shipFire() {

    // make sure enough time has passed since last fire
    if (timeOfLastFire+200 < getTimer()) {


        // remember time of this fire
        timeOfLastFire = getTimer();

        // create bullet
        level++;
        attachMovie("bullet","bullet"+level,level);

        // set bullet location and direction
        clip = _root["bullet"+level];
        clip._x = ship._x;
        clip._y = ship._y;
        clip.dx = 10.0*Math.cos(2.0*Math.PI*(ship._rotation-90)/360.0);
        clip.dy = 10.0*Math.sin(2.0*Math.PI*(ship._rotation-90)/360.0);

        // add to bullets array
        bullets.push(clip);
    }
}
```

The ship is moved one step per frame by increasing its _x and _y properties by its "dx" and "dy" properties. If the ship moves too far to the right, beyond the 550-pixel limit of the Stage, then 550 pixels are subtracted to make it wrap around to the other side. The same goes for the left, top, and bottom of the screen.

```
function shipMove() {
    // move ship horizontally and wrap
    ship._x += ship.dx;
    if (ship._x > 550) ship._x -= 550;
    if (ship._x < 0) ship._x += 550;

    // move ship vertically and wrap
    ship._y += ship.dy;
    if (ship._y > 400) ship._y -= 400;
    if (ship._y < 0) ship._y += 400;
}
```

Bullets move like the ship does. However, you need to loop through the "bullets" array to move all the bullets. Also, when the bullets reach the edge of the screen, they are removed rather than allowed to wrap around.

```
function bulletsMove() {
    // loop through all bullets
    for(i=bullets.length-1;i>=0;i--) {

        // move ship horizontally and vertically
        bullets[i]._x += bullets[i].dx;
        bullets[i]._y += bullets[i].dy;

        // see if the ship is off the edge of the screen
        if ((bullets[i]._x > 550) or (bullets[i]._x < 0) or (bullets[i]._y > 400) or
        ➥(bullets[i]._y < 0)) {

            // remove clip and array item
            bullets[i].removeMovieClip();
            bullets.splice(i,1);
        }

    }
}
```

Rocks are added to the game through calls to the "newRock" function. Like the "fire" function, this adds a movie clip to the game. However, the function chooses from one of three movie clips named "rock1", "rock2", and "rock3".

The rock is created at a location passed into the function as a parameter, and is also assigned a scale by another parameter. The direction of the rock is decided by random numbers, with the possibility for faster and faster rocks as the game level increases.

The rocks also spin a random amount, either positive or negative.

Pointers to all rocks are added to the "rocks" array so they can be referenced later:

```
function newRock(size,x,y) {
    // create rock clip
    level++;
    rockNum = int(Math.random()*3+1);
    attachMovie("rock"+rockNum,"rock"+level,level);

    // set rock location and size
    clip = _root["rock"+level];
    clip._x = x;
    clip._y = y;
    clip._xscale = size;
    clip._yscale = size;

    // set rock speed and direction
    speed = gameLevel*2;
    clip.dx = Math.Random()*speed+2;
    if (Math.random() < .5) clip.dx *= -1;

    clip.dy = Math.Random()*speed+2;
    if (Math.random() < .5) clip.dy *= -1;

    // set rock spin
    clip.spin = Math.random()*6-3;

    // add rock to rocks array
    rocks.push(clip);
}
```

To make the rocks move, you use similar code to how the ship and bullets move. The rocks wrap around on the screen just like the ship does. In addition, remember to rotate the rocks each step according to their "spin" property that you created.

```
function rocksMove() {

    // loop through all rocks
    for(i=rocks.length-1;i>=0;i--) {
        clip = rocks[i].clip;

        // move rock horizontally and wrap
        rocks[i]._x += rocks[i].dx;
        if (rocks[i]._x > 550) rocks[i]._x -= 550;
        if (rocks[i]._x < 0) rocks[i]._x += 550;
```

```
// move rock vertically and wrap
rocks[i]._y += rocks[i].dy;
if (rocks[i]._y > 400) rocks[i]._y -= 400;
if (rocks[i]._y < 0) rocks[i]._y += 400;

// spin rock
rocks[i]._rotation += rocks[i].spin;
    }
}
```

To simplify things, all the collision detection code has been placed into one function. This function loops through the rocks and the bullets, and uses *hitTest* to determine whether there are any collisions.

When a bullet hits a rock, the location and scale of the rock are recorded and then the rock is removed. If the scale of the rock was above 25%, then two new rocks are created in the same spot. Each of these rocks is half the size of the previous one. Each rock obtains a new random direction and spin.

The "checkHits" function also determines whether any rock is colliding with the ship. If a rock collides with the ship, the player loses a life and goes to the "ship hit" frame. If there are no more lives left, the player goes to the "game over" frame.

One final check that "checkHits" does is to determine whether the "rocks" array has dwindled down to 0. If so, the player has destroyed all the rocks and the movie advances to the "level over" frame.

```
function checkHits() {

    // loop through all rocks
    for(i=rocks.length-1;i>=0;i--) {

        // loop through all bullets
        for(j=bullets.length-1;j>=0;j--) {

            // see if bullet hit rock
            if (rocks[i].hitTest(bullets[j]._x,bullets[j]._y,true)) {

                // remove bullet
                bullets[j].removeMovieClip();
                bullets.splice(j);

                // get size and location of new rocks
                newsize = rocks[i]._xscale / 2;
                x = rocks[i]._x;
                y = rocks[i]._y;
```

```
                    // remove rock
                    rocks[i].removeMovieClip();
                    rocks.splice(i,1);

                    // create two new rocks in its place
                    if (newsize >= 25)  {
                        newRock(newsize,x,y);
                        newRock(newsize,x,y);
                    }

                    // increase score
                    score++;

                    // no need to keep checking bullets against this rock
                    break;
                }
            }

            // see if rock hits ship
            if (rocks[i].hitTest(ship._x,ship._y,true)) {

                // see if there are not more lives
                if (lives < 1) {
                    removeAll();
                    gotoAndPlay("game over");

                // life left, deduct life
                } else {
                    removeAll();
                    lives--;
                    gotoAndPlay("ship hit");
                }
            }
        }

        // see if there are no more rocks
        if (rocks.length == 0) {
            removeAll();
            gotoAndPlay("level over");
            gameLevel++;
        }
    }
```

The "removeAll" function is used just before the "checkHits" function, which causes the movie to jump to a new frame. It removes all the rocks and bullets from the screen so they don't overlap the text on those frames.

```
function removeAll() {
    // remove all bullets
    for(i=0;i<bullets.length;i++) {
        bullets[i].removeMovieClip();
    }

    // remove all rocks
    for(i=0;i<rocks.length;i++) {
        rocks[i].removeMovieClip();
    }
}
```

Loose Ends

As always, make sure the linkage properties for each movie clip in the library is set so that Flash knows to include it in the final file. All the rocks and the bullets need to be linked like this because they are not on the Stage anywhere before the game starts.

I've also created three text areas to represent the "gameLevel", "lives", and "score" variables. I've placed them in separate corners with addition text as labels above each.

Other Possibilities

There are many other features that games such as Space Rocks sometimes have. Occasionally, little "UFOs" float around, awarding you bonus points if you hit them. Often, the ship is equipped with a shield that can be used to protect it from collisions a limited number of times. A "hyperspace" feature zaps the ship to a random spot on the screen and a "smart bomb" feature destroys any rocks within a certain distance from the ship.

This is definitely an excellent game with which a budding ActionScript expert can stretch her wings by adding more and more features—the more challenging the feature is to implement, the better.

Maze Chase

Example file: Mazechase.fla

This next game is also a common genre of classic arcade games that I call maze chase games. Pac-Man and its sequels are probably the best-known examples of this genre, but there are many others.

In the example game, shown in Figure 16.4, the fox runs around a preset maze trying to eat the berries. An evil bunny is also running around the maze. The fox must avoid the bunny while getting to all the berries.

Figure 16.4
The fox tries to eat the berries while the bunny tries to get the fox.

Project Goal

The example game tries to recreate some of the classic features of the maze-chase genre. The berries on the screen disappear as the fox passes over them. The fox can jump from one side of the screen to the other by passing through the tunnel on either side. If the bunny catches the fox, the player loses a life.

Preparing the Movie

If you look at the Mazechase.fla example movie, you will see only a few library items. The main ones are the background, the fox, the bunny, and the berry.

Creating the background is simple, but must be done carefully. Imagine the screen as a grid of squares 25 pixels wide by 25 pixels high. The berries appear at intersections of this grid—at all intersections, that is, except for ones that occur inside the background.

Check out Figure 16.5. This is the "background" movie clip with Flash's grid turned on and set to 25×25. You can control the grid by choosing View, Grid, Edit Grid.

Figure 16.5
With the Flash grid turned on, you can clearly see the intersections where berries will appear.

The background was built using the rectangle drawing tool. The grid helped to create it quickly. Not only are the areas of the grid filled in to create the background, but a line boarder is present around the filled-in areas. This helps ensure that the background walls overlap the edges of the gridlines a little bit. When the program adds the berries at grid intersections, it doesn't add berries to intersections that are right along the edge of a wall.

The "fox" movie clip has a normal static frame as the first frame, but a short biting animation for the rest. When the fox is supposed to eat a berry, you'll send this movie clip to the second frame. This shows the fox biting down, and then returns the fox to the first, static frame.

The "berry" movie clips have two frames. The first has a berry and the second is blank. You'll move each clip to the second frame as the berries get eaten. This way, the movie clips remain on the Stage at all times to guide the fox and bunny, but they are only visible before the berry is eaten.

The "bunny" movie clip is a constant animation. The bunny always moves, so there is no need for a static frame.

All these movie clips, except "background", won't be present until the movie runs and the code creates them with *attachMovie*.

This movie has pretty much the same set of five frames that the "Space Rocks" movie did: "start", "play", "lose life", "level over", and "game over".

Writing the Code

The first frame contains a copy of the "Play" button that starts a new game. Its script not only goes to the "play" frame, but also initializes a few variables:

```
on(press) {
    lives = 3;
    score = 0;
    gameLevel = 1;
    gotoAndPlay("play");
}
```

There is an "actions" movie clip on the "play" frame that has a script attached to it. This script's job is to initialize everything at the start of the game, after a life is lost, and when a new level should begin. The script also calls the "move" and "moveBunny" functions to keep the game going.

```
onClipEvent(load) {
    // set everything at the beginning
    _root.startLevel();
}

onClipEvent(enterFrame) {
    // move the fox
    _root.move();
```

```
// move the bunny
_root.moveBunny();
}
```

All the functions for this game can be found in the main timeline script for the "play" frame. This starts with the "startLevel" function.

The main job of the "startLevel" function is to create the berries. The function does this by looping through 15 vertical positions and 21 horizontal positions, seeking out points on the grid that do not have the "background" movie clip covering them.

The "berry" movie clip is placed at all the proper locations, and a pointer to each movie clip is placed in the "berries" array.

This function also creates the "fox" and "bunny" movie clip instance. It creates and sets several new properties for each clip, including the "dest" or destination for each clip.

TIP

Notice that the "dest" property of the "fox" and "bunny" is set to a short object, such as {x:275, y:275}. This makes it easy to refer to these values. For instance, you could refer to the horizontal destination as "fox.dest.x".

```
function startLevel() {
    level = 0;

    // create berries
    berries = new Array();

    // loop through grid of locations
    for(y=1;y<16;y++) {
        for(x=1;x<22;x++) {

            // see if the background covers location
            if (!(background.hitTest(x*25,y*25,true))) {

                // create a berry and place it there
                attachMovie("berry","berry"+level,level);
                clip = _root["berry"+level];
                clip._x = x*25;
                clip._y = y*25;

                // add to array of berries
                berries.push(clip);
                level++;

            }

        }
```

```
        }

        // create the fox and set his location
        attachMovie("fox","fox",level++);
        fox._x = 275;
        fox._y = 275;

        // also add movement and destination properties
        fox.move = {x:0, y:0};
        fox.dest = {x:275, y:275};
        fox.nextmove = 0;

        // create the bunny and set his location
        attachMovie("bunny","bunny",level++);
        bunny._x = 275;
        bunny._y = 125;

        // also add movement, destination, and remember previous location
        bunny.move = {x:1, y:0};
        bunny.dest = {x:300, y:125};
        bunny.nextmove = 0;
        bunny.last = {x:275, y:125};


    }
```

The "move" function is called every frame and moves the location of the fox according to the "move" object. It has a special provision in the function to recognize whether the fox is about to move off the left or right side of the screen, and wraps the fox around if it does. This makes it possible for the fox to travel through the tunnel on either side of the screen.

The fox or bunny's destination is always the next berry. Even if there is no longer a visible berry there, the movie clip is always there. When the fox reaches this berry, marked by the "dest" object of the fox, then the "eatBerry" function is called so that the berry can be removed if it is still visible. The "nextMove" function is called to determine the next destination.

Note that the fox moves 5 pixels at a time. This works out well because all the berries are 25 pixels apart. Therefore, it takes exactly five steps to reach the next berry. The speed at which these steps are taken is determined by the amount added to the "nextMove" property. In this case, 50 milliseconds are added, which means there will be at least 50 milliseconds between moves.

```
 function move() {
     // see if it is time for another move
     if (getTimer() > fox.nextmove) {
```

```
        // don't allow another move for 50ms
        fox.nextmove = getTimer() + 50;

        // move fox
        fox._x += fox.move.x*5;
        fox._y += fox.move.y*5;

        // see if the fox went though the tunnel
        if (fox._x > 550) fox._x = 0;
        if (fox._x < 0) fox._x = 550;

        // see if the fox reached his destination
        if ((fox._x == fox.dest.x) and (fox._y == fox.dest.y)) {
            eatBerry();
            nextMove();
        }
    }
}
```

To eat a berry, you loop through all the berries and look for one that matches the location of the fox. That berry is sent to the second frame to make the berry disappear. In addition, the score is increased.

As the array of berries is searched for a matching berry, you'll also note any berries that have not been eaten. As long as one berry is found that has not yet been eaten, the level is not yet over.

```
function eatBerry() {
    // assume all berries are gone
    allGone = true;

    // loop through all berries
    for(i=0;i<berries.length;i++) {

        // see if this berry is where fox is
        if ((berries[i]._currentFrame == 1) and (berries[i]._x == fox._x) and
        ➥(berries[i]._y == fox._y)) {

            // remove berry
            berries[i].gotoAndStop("nothing");

            // open fox mouth
            fox.gotoAndPlay("eat");

            // add to score
            score++;

        // if a berry is found that has not been eaten, then level is not over
        } else if (berries[i]._currentFrame == 1) {
```

```
                allGone = false;
            }
        }


    // if all berries eaten, then end level
    if (allGone) {
        gotoAndPlay("level over");
        gameLevel++
    }
}
```

When the fox reaches a berry, the code needs to determine the next destination, if any. The *Key* object is used to test all four arrow keys. If any are pressed, then the "move" object of the fox is set. However, this does not mean that the move is valid.

For a move to be valid, there needs to be another berry in that direction exactly 25 pixels away. If that is not the case, then the "move" object is set back to zeros.

```
function nextMove() {
    // assume no movement
    fox.move.x = 0;
    fox.move.y = 0;

    // check arrow keys and set potential movement
    // also flip fox left or right if needed
    if (Key.isDown(Key.LEFT)) {
        fox.move.x = -1;
        fox._xscale = Math.abs(fox._xscale);
    } else if (Key.isDown(Key.RIGHT)) {
        fox.move.x = 1;
        fox._xscale = -Math.abs(fox._xscale);
    } else if (Key.isDown(Key.UP)) {
        fox.move.y = -1;
    } else if (Key.isDown(Key.DOWN)) {
        fox.move.y = 1;
    }

    // predict new destination
    newx = fox._x + fox.move.x*25;
    newy = fox._y + fox.move.y*25;
    okToMove = false;

    // loop through berries to see if any match destination
    for(i=0;i<berries.length;i++) {

        // found a match, set new destination
        if ((berries[i]._x == newx) and (berries[i]._y == newy)) {
            fox.dest.x = newx;
```

```
            fox.dest.y = newy;
            okToMove = true;
        }
    }

    // special settings for going through tunnel
    if (newx == 550) {
        okToMove = true;
        fox.dest.x = 25;
    } if (newx == 0) {
        okToMove = true;
        fox.dest.x = 525;
    }

    // if destination doesn't match berry, then don't move
    if (!okToMove) {
        fox.move.x = 0;
        fox.move.y = 0;
    }
}
```

The bunny moves in an unpredictable manner. When it reaches a berry spot, the following code loops through all the berries to find the ones that are adjacent to the current bunny location. Then, one of these possibilities is picked at random to be the next destination for the bunny. The one qualification needed is that the new destination not be the same as the previous location. In other words, the bunny cannot suddenly move back the way it came. This forces the bunny down long corridors without any back-and-forth stuttering. However, if the bunny reaches a corner and has only the option of going back the way it came, it is allowed.

The last thing the "moveBunny" function does is to check to see whether the bunny is close to the fox. If it is, then the bunny caught the fox and the player loses a life.

```
function moveBunny() {

    // see if it is time for next bunny move
    if (getTimer() > bunny.nextmove) {

        // don't allow another bunny move for a while
        bunny.nextmove = getTimer() + 60 - gameLevel*10;

        // move bunny
        bunny._x += bunny.move.x*5;
        bunny._y += bunny.move.y*5;

        // see if bunny reached destination
        if (bunny._x == bunny.dest.x and bunny._y == bunny.dest.y) {
```

```
// create an array of possible next locations
possibilities = new Array;
for(i=0;i<berries.length;i++) {

    // calculate distance from present location to berry
    xdiff = Math.abs(berries[i]._x - bunny._x);
    ydiff = Math.abs(berries[i]._y - bunny._y);

    // see if this is an adjacent berry
    if ((xdiff == 25 and ydiff == 0) or (xdiff == 0 and ydiff == 25)) {

        // then this is a possibility
        possibilities.push(berries[i]);
    }
}

// pick a random possibility
do {
    r = int(Math.random()*possibilities.length);

    // get new destination and movement
    bunny.dest.x = possibilities[r]._x;
    bunny.dest.y = possibilities[r]._y;
    bunny.move.x = (possibilities[r]._x - bunny._x)/25;
    bunny.move.y = (possibilities[r]._y - bunny._y)/25;

// use this possibility only if it is not going back to the last spot
// or if this is the only choice
} while ((bunny.dest.x == lastx and bunny.dest.y == lasty) and
➥(possibilities.length > 1));

    // remember the previous location
    lastx = bunny._x;
    lasty = bunny._y;
    }

}


// see if bunny is close to fox
if (Math.abs(bunny._x - fox._x) <= 10 and Math.abs(bunny._y - fox._y) <= 10) {
    if (lives < 1) {
        gotoAndStop("game over");
    } else {
        lives--;
        gotoAndStop("lost life");
    }
}
}
```

Loose Ends

Remember that the fox, bunny, and berry movie clips need to be linked with the appro-priate name. You'll need *stop()* commands for each frame, as well as some frames of the smaller movie clips.

Other Possibilities

There are plenty of features that you can work to add to this game. You could have more than one bunny, special berries that allow the fox to chase the bunnies for a short time. A center "cage" area where the bunnies come out from one at a time, and bonus points that pop up throughout the maze.

Other ideas include having the bunny be a little smarter and chase the fox, have the bunny compete with the fox by eating the berries, and awarding bonus points at the end of each level based on how fast the level was completed.

Moon Lander

⊕⊳ Example file: Moonlander.fla

This chapter ends with a Flash version of a classic arcade game. Lunar Lander was pos-sibly the second computer game ever created. The first incarnation of this game ran on University mainframe computers and was purely text based. Each second that went by, the computer would spit out a line of text telling you where your lander was, and how fast it was going. You could make adjustments as you came down.

Since then, the game has been created in various graphical formats, most of them featuring the side-view used here. Figure 16.6 shows a game in progress.

Figure 16.6

The moon lander descends, trying to make it to one of the landing pads.

Project Goal

The goal is to create a standard lander-style game. The ship starts at the top of the screen. The player controls a powerful vertical thruster under the ship, as well as weaker thrusters on each side of the ship.

As time goes on, gravity pulls the ship down. The player uses the thrusters for a limited amount of time as fuel is consumed every time they are fired.

The player's goal is to land the ship safely on one of the landing pads. Missing the pads, or touching any part of the surface other than the pads, results in the lander exploding.

This game has multiple levels. In the example movie, there are three levels, all featuring a different surface.

Preparing the Movie

In examining the movie clips needed for this movie, first look at the "ship" movie clip. Figure 16.7 shows the full Flash window with the ship movie clip selected. You can see that there are several labeled frames. The first frame is "normal", followed by "up", "left", "right", and "explode".

Figure 16.7

The "ship" movie clip includes the frames "normal", "up", "left", "right", and "explode".

The first frame represents the ship with no thrusters firing. The second has the main thruster firing, moving the ship up. The third and fourth frames show each of the side thrusters. The bottom portion of Figure 16.7 shows the "left" frame. Note that the word "left" refers to the fact that the ship should be moving to the left. The flame of the thruster is, in fact, shooting to the right.

The "explode" frame is the beginning of a short animation showing the ship being blown to bits. This animation is used if the player misses the landing pad.

In addition to a "background" movie clip that does not interact with the code at all, three other movie clips represent the hillsides of the three levels of the game. These clips are named "Ground - level 1" to "Ground - level 3".

The "pad" movie clip is just a simple yellow rectangle that is used to detect when the lander's two feet make a safe touchdown.

The main timeline for this movie is actually quite complex. Table 16.1 shows each frame and what it contains.

Table 16.1   Frames in the Main Timeline

Frame	Contains
start	Contains an introduction to the movie and a "Play" button to start the game.
start level	Warns the player that the first level is about to begin.
level1	The player plays through the first level on this frame. If he doesn't crash, he continues to the next frame.
level1 done	When the player lands safely on level 1, he gets a congratulatory message and a "Play" button that lets him play the second level.
level2	The player plays through the second level on this frame. If he doesn't crash, he continues to the next frame.
level2 done	When the player lands safely on level 2, he gets a congratulatory message and a "Play" button that lets him play the third level.
level3	The player plays through the third level on this frame. If he doesn't crash, he continues to the next frame.
game over	The player is congratulated for making all three landings successfully. A "Play" button lets the player try again.
lost ship	If the player crashes on any level, he is sent to this frame and the game is over. A "Play" button lets him try again.

You'll also have two very simple movie clips, "fuel gauge" and "fuel meter", that consist of a rectangle outline and a solid rectangle. The "meter" is placed inside the "gauge". You'll use code to shrink the "meter" so that it fills less of the "gauge" rectangle as fuel runs out.

Writing the Code

You'll have "actions" movie clips on the three frames "level1", "level2", and "level3". These movie clips contain the calls to the functions needed for the game. Only one function is called when the level begins, and one function is called continuously as the level progresses.

```
onClipEvent(load) {
    _root.startLevel();
}
```

```
onClipEvent(enterFrame) {
    _root.moveShip();
}
```

Both of these functions can be found in the main timeline on the first frame. This script actually starts with a "startGame" function that is called when the player clicks the "Play" button on the first frame. It sets the variable "gameLevel", which appears as a text area in the upper-right corner of the game. It then calls "startLevel" to begin level 1.

```
function startGame() {
    gameLevel = 1;
    startLevel();
}
```

The "startLevel" function performs a variety of tasks. First, it moves the movie to the correct frame according to the "gameLevel" variable. Then, it sets the ship to the top center of the screen. The speed of the ship, which is stored in "dx" and "dy" properties of the "ship" movie clip instance, are set to 0. The variable "gravity" is used to accelerate the ship downward toward the group.

The "hitPoints" and "footPoints" arrays contain various points relative to the center of the ship. You'll check all the "hitPoints" to determine whether the ship has collided with the group. The two "footPoints" are used to determine whether both feet have been placed on a landing pad.

The "pads" array is used to store the names of the three landing pad movie clips on the screen. One of the levels only has two landing pads, but Flash ActionScript is forgiving about such things.

```
function startLevel() {
    gotoAndStop("level"+gameLevel);

    // start ship still
    ship._x = 275;
    ship._y = 25;

    // start ship still
    ship.dx = 0;
    ship.dy = 0;

    // init gravity
    gravity = .1;

    // init fuel
    fuel = 100;
    showFuel();
```

```
    // set collision points
    hitPoints = new Array();
    hitPoints.push({x:-9,y:13});
    hitPoints.push({x:9,y:13});
    hitPoints.push({x:0,y:-10});
    hitPoints.push({x:-8,y:-7});
    hitPoints.push({x:8,y:-7});

    // set landing points
    footPoints = new Array();
    footPoints.push({x:-9,y:13});
    footPoints.push({x:9,y:13});

    // make array from pad clips
    pads = new Array();
    for(i=0;i<3;i++) {
        pads.push(_root["pad"+i]);
    }
}
```

The function "moveShip" is called *every* frame by the "actions" movie clip. This function is used to call a variety of smaller functions that control the ship. It is usually better to break up a long piece of code into such smaller functions.

```
function moveShip() {
    shipThrusters();
    shipMovement();
    checkForLand();
    checkForCrash();
}
```

The "shipThrusters" function checks to see whether any fuel is left. If not, the "ship" movie clip is sent to the "normal" frame. Otherwise, if the player is holding down either the up-, left-, or right-arrow keys, then one of the thrusters is on. The "ship" is sent to the proper frame, and "dx" or "dy" are changed to reflect the effect of the thruster. Fuel is also deducted.

```
function shipThrusters() {
    // check thrusters and adjust speed
    if (fuel < 0) {
        ship.gotoAndStop("normal");
    } else if (Key.isDown(Key.UP)) {
        ship.dy -= .4;
        ship.gotoAndStop("up");
        fuel -= 2;
        showFuel();
    } else if (Key.isDown(Key.LEFT)) {
```

```
        ship.dx -= .2;
        ship.gotoAndStop("left");
        fuel -= 1;
        showFuel();
    } else if (Key.isDown(Key.RIGHT)) {
        ship.dx += .2;
        ship.gotoAndStop("right");
        fuel -= 1;
        showFuel();
    } else {

        // no thruster at all
        ship.gotoAndStop("normal");
    }
}
```

The next function, "shipMovement" will add the pull of gravity. The position of the ship is then modified by the speed of the ship.

```
function shipMovement() {
    // gravity pulls ship down
    ship.dy += gravity;

    // move ship
    ship._x += ship.dx;
    ship._y += ship.dy;
}
```

The "checkForLand" function loops through the "footPoints" and checks whether either foot is inside a "pad" movie clip. If one or the other is not, then the "landed" variable is set to *false*. This is also the case if the speed of the ship is greater than 3, which is too fast for the ship to be traveling for a landing.

If the "landed" variable remains *true* through these tests, then the ship has touched down. All that is needed is to go to the next frame in the main timeline and increment the "gameLevel" variable.

```
function checkForLand() {
    // check to see if both feet are on a pad
    // loop through both feet
    landed = true;
    for(i=0;i<footPoints.length;i++) {

        // loop through all pads
        footDown = false;
        for(j=0;j<pads.length;j++) {

            // see if foot is on a pad
```

```
                if (pads[j].hitTest(ship._x+footPoints[i].x,ship._y+footPoints[i].y,true)) {
                    footDown = true;
                    break;
                }
            }

            // if a foot in not down, then the ship has not landed
            if (!footDown) {
                landed = false;
                break;
            }
        }


        // see if the ship is going too fast
        if (ship.dy > 3.0) landed = false;

        if (landed) {
            // made it
            gotoAndPlay(_currentFrame+1);
            gameLevel++;
        }
    }
```

On the other hand, you also need to see whether the lander crashed. The "hitPoints" array contains a list of points around the ship, including the two feet, the middle of each side, the top, and the bottom center. Because there is no way to detect whether one full object intersects another, you just test these points and use them to determine whether there is a crash. If any of these points is inside the "activeground" movie clip instance, then the ship has crashed. The "activeground" is the "Ground - levelX" movie clip's instance name on each level.

```
function checkForCrash() {
    // not landed, so check for crash
    if (!landed) {

        // loop through all hit points
        for(i=0;i<hitPoints.length;i++) {

            // check hit point against the ground
            if (activeground.hitTest(ship._x+hitPoints[i].x,
            ➥ship._y+hitPoints[i].y,true)) {
                ship.gotoAndPlay("explode");

                // lost life, or game over
                gotoAndPlay("lost ship");
                break;
```

```
            }
         }
      }
   }
```

One utility function used by this movie is the "showFuel" function, which takes the "meter" movie clip inside the "gauge" movie clip and sets its _xscale_ property to the "fuel" variable. Because the "fuel" variable starts at 100 and goes down to 0, it easily translates to be used in the _xscale_ property. If the fuel range were different, then you would need to massage the numbers a bit to make it fit into a 0 to 100 range before applying it to the _xscale_.

```
function showFuel() {
    gauge.meter._xscale = fuel;
}
```

TIP

Note that to get the "meter" movie clip to shrink from the right to the left, the center of the clip had to be placed so that the rectangle extended from the center to the right. If the center had been left at the center of the graphic, then changing the _xscale_ would have shrunk the graphic into the center, rather than from right to left.

Loose Ends

Each "play" button in this movie has a small, one-line script attached to it. Check each one out to see which frame it takes the movie to or what function it calls.

Note that the same "thrust animation" was used for each of the three types of thrust in the "ship" movie clip. For the left and right thrusters, the clip was rotated 90° and -90°. The animation for the two side thrusters was shrunk because these are not supposed to be as powerful as the main thruster.

Other Possibilities

As this game stands, there is no scoring. You could award points for each successful landing, possibly with more points for tougher-to-reach landing pads. You could also give a speed bonus and an unused-fuel bonus. Expanding the game with move levels is as easy as drawing the hillsides. When you run out of ideas, you could always alter the code so that higher levels use the same graphics, but with less fuel available at the start or higher gravity.

Advanced Techniques

- Performance and Optimization
- Loader Screens
- Copy Protection
- High Score Boards

Although the previous chapters demonstrated hundreds of ActionScript techniques, some useful techniques remain that apply to games that haven't been covered yet. Instead of including these concepts in a particular game, this chapter features these techniques by themselves.

In this chapter, you'll look at such diverse topics as optimization, loading animations, high score boards, and copy protection. At the end, you'll get an idea of what other advanced techniques exist.

Performance and Optimization

When using Flash to create games, the issue of speed comes up constantly. Previous versions of Flash did not have a robust enough scripting language to allow you to create many games and also lacked the speed that Flash 5 has.

Even so, Flash 5 can be very slow. Too slow, in fact, for many fast-paced arcade games. However, optimization techniques can help any game run faster.

Using Alternatives

The basic concept behind optimization is that there is more than one way to accomplish any task in Flash. For the most part, this is true. For instance, if you want to move a graphic from one side of the Stage to the other, you can do it with animation tweening or with ActionScript.

Two ways to think about the alternatives available when you are creating something in Flash. The first type of alternative is when you can find a way to accomplish exactly the same task. For instance, moving a graphic with tweening or with ActionScript could produce exactly the same result.

The other alternative is making a change in the program so that it produces a similar, yet somehow different, result. For instance, if the graphic moves across the screen too slowly, you could shrink the graphic to make it smaller, but theoretically faster.

The key to optimization is realizing when there are alternatives and weighing the advantages versus the disadvantages. To see the advantages of an alternative, you could use a technique called benchmarking.

Benchmarking

If you want to compare two alternatives for speed, you need a way to measure that speed. Sure, you could just go by whether something *looks* faster, but that's not very accurate. Benchmarks allow you to test to determine which alternative is faster and just how much faster it is.

A typical benchmark compares two or more alternatives to performing the same or similar task. In each case, the time is marked just before the task begins, and then again when the task ends. The result is the time it took for the task to complete. With a little math, this can be converted into a measurement such as frames per second (fps).

Take the example of a graphic character running across the Stage. Figure 17.1 shows a full-sized fox in the middle of the screen in the process of running from the right to the left.

Figure 17.1

This test has a large fox racing from right to left in 30 frames.

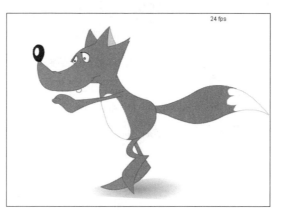

24 fps

In Figure 17.1, you can see that the speed of the movie is 24 fps. The movie is actually set to run at 120 fps. 24 fps is the result of the work that needs to be done by the Flash player to show the animation.

You must use a little bit of code to get the "24 fps" to show up in the upper-right corner. This simple line was placed on the first frame of the movie to remember the time when the animation started:

```
startTime = getTimer();
```

On the last frame of the animation, frame 30, a few more lines of code use the starting time and the current time to calculate how many milliseconds it took for the animation to complete. It then places this in the text area.

```
totalTime = getTimer() - startTime;
totalFrames = 30;
fps = totalFrames/(totalTime/1000);
readout = int(fps) + " fps";
```

You can see all this in the example movie Benchmark1.fla on the Web site in the folder for this chapter. When I run this movie by pressing [Cmd]+Return on my Macintosh PowerBook, I get results ranging from 12 to 15 fps. However, the preview window doesn't show the movie at 100%, but rather scaled up to the size of the preview window. Does this scaling affect performance? Sure does. If I pressed [Cmd]+1 to force the movie to 100% while in the preview window, the frame rate jumps to 15–17 fps.

⊕⊳⊀**Example file: Benchmark1.fla**

> **TIP**
>
> It is important to remember to set your frame rate up to 120 fps, the maximum that Flash 5 will go in cases like this. If you set it to, say, 12 fps, the Flash 5 default, then the animation will never rise above 12 fps. So, even though one technique might be much faster than the other, as long as they both run at 12 fps, you won't see any difference.

So you see that Flash movies play slower in the preview window if you have not set it to 100% scale. What about if you run the final .swf file in the Flash player completely outside of Flash? That's how Figure 17.1 was made, which shows 24 fps. So the Flash player is faster than the Flash application preview window. Flash in the browser (Internet Explorer 5.0) was slower at 8 to 10 fps.

Of course, these numbers only make sense relative to each other. When these tests were run on other computers, some Macs and some Windows, the results were different. Some were slower; some were faster. You can't even be sure that the speed will be the same on another computer of the same make and model. One computer could have different system extensions on it, be involved in more network activity, or have more disk fragmentation. Benchmark tests are only valid when they are performed on the same computer under the same conditions.

Choosing the Best Alternative

Looking further at the previous example, suppose that the resulting 8–24 fps is not good enough for you. For instance, the purpose of the animation could be for the fox to zip quickly from one side of the screen to the other. At 8 fps, or even 15 fps, this doesn't have the effect you wanted.

One alternative might be to shrink the number of frames in the animation from 30 to 15. This should double the speed of the sequence, but lessen the smoothness of the animation. Also, because the fox movie clip controls the speed of the fox's stride, the fox will appear to take half the number of steps to move the same distance.

If that is not an option, then perhaps size is. What if the fox was half the size? One theory could be that because the same amount of vectors are in the fox, no matter what the scale, Flash should take just as long to draw it. Another theory is that because the fox is half the scale, fewer pixels need to be drawn every step, therefore increasing the speed of the fox.

These theories can be tested with the benchmarking script. Using the same movie, but scaling both keyframes of the fox to 50%, you get the same animation but with a smaller fox. The benchmark script will tell you whether the frame rate changed. This movie can be found on the Web site as Benchmark2.fla. You can see the result in Figure 17.2.

Example file: Benchmark2.fla

Figure 17.2

The half-sized fox is much faster than the full-sized one.

The smaller fox is much faster than the full-sized one. In the Flash player on my Power-book, I measured 50–54 fps, more than twice the speed of the previous test. This confirms the theory that smaller graphics will draw faster.

Now, the only question is whether this half-sized fox fulfills your design needs. If it is better to have a fast half-sized fox than a larger, slower fox, then you have your answer.

Benchmarking ActionScript

You can also use benchmark tests to determine whether ActionScript alternatives can make a speed difference. The technique is the same: Measure the time it takes for a task to complete and compare that time against its alternatives.

For instance, suppose you notice that in your code, you use comparisons like this:

```
if (myVariable == true) {
```

You realize that you could have simply stated it this way:

```
if (myVariable) {
```

The first is sometimes easier to read, but you wonder whether the second offers any speed advantage. After all, you could be using hundreds or thousands of such comparisons inside loops and such.

Chances are that either of these comparisons take less than a millisecond to perform. So, comparing one against the other will show too small of a time difference, if any, to measure in milliseconds. So you need to compare thousands of them instead.

The following piece of code is built to compare true/false comparison types. It begins by creating a large array filled with 5,000 true and false values. The creation of this array will not be timed. However, after the array is set, the timing begins. The timed code is a loop that looks at each item in the array and counts the number of items that are *true*.

It determines which are true by comparing them using the == comparison operator. When the code is done, it spits out the total time it took to do the 5,000 comparisons.

```
function benchMark1() {
    // create a new array
    testArray = new Array;

    // fill the array with alternating true and false
    temp = false;
    for(i=0;i<5000;i++) {
        testArray.push(temp);
        if (temp == false) {
            temp = true;
        } else if (temp == true) {
            temp = false;
        }
    }

    // get the start time
    startTime = getTimer();

    // count how many trues there are
    count = 0;
    for(i=0;i<testArray.length;i++) {
        if (testArray[i] == true) {
            count++;
        }
    }

    // get the end time
    totalTime = getTimer() - startTime;

    // show results
    trace("Benchmark Test: using ==")
    trace("Total Time: " + totalTime + "ms");
}
```

By itself, the result of this program means nothing. However, you will also create a "benchmark2" function that replaces the line "if (testArray[i] == true) {" with "if (testArray[i]) {". This is the only difference between the two functions. Therefore, if there is a speed difference between the functions, it must be due to the one line that is different.

The results show that the second option is faster. On my computer, it took 800 milliseconds to complete the timed code in "benchmark1" and only 750 milliseconds to complete the code in "benchmark2". This shows that using the == comparison on a true or false value is slower than just using the value itself. You can try this code in the example movie Benchmark3.fla on the Web site.

⊕▷‹Example movie: Benchmark3.fla

This sort of benchmark test is the type of thing that professional programmers do all the time, regardless of what programming language they are using. If you program in ActionScript a lot, it is useful to develop a constant curiosity about which methods are faster than others. The resulting knowledge from tests like this will allow you to optimize your Flash games.

Loader Screens

Although you should always try to keep the file size of your Flash movies as small as possible, it is inevitable that you will have movies that take longer than a few seconds for modem users to download. As a matter of fact, it might take several minutes for some users to download a game that is several hundred kilobytes in size.

It has become customary for Flash and Shockwave developers to create "loader screens" for these large movies. The load screen is usually the first frame or scene of a movie and is thus streamed to the user's browser first. It then presents a message such as "Loading Game…" to users so they know what is going on.

You can provide even more information to the user while the movie is loading. By using ActionScript, you can show the user just how much of the movie has been downloaded so far, or how much there is to go.

Building a Loader

⊕▷‹Example file: Loader.fla

Figure 17.3 shows the first frame of the example movie Loader.fla on the Web site. This frame appears to the user only after a few kilobytes of the movie have been downloaded. It then keeps the user informed of the status of the download, complete with a moving progress bar in the middle of the screen.

Figure 17.3
Both a progress bar and a text area keep the user informed as the movie loads.

NOW LOADING.

63%

The code to do this is actually quite simple. By using the ActionScript functions *getBytesTotal()*, you can determine how many kilobytes any movie clip contains. If you use _root with *getBytesTotal()*, you can find out how many kilobytes are in the entire movie. Similarly, you can use *getBytesLoaded()* to determine how much of the movie has been loaded so far.

In Loader.fla, there is a movie clip instance of a simple rectangle called "Progress Bar Fill" on the Stage. It was created so that the center of the movie clip is at the upper-left corner of the rectangle. This is exactly how the fuel gauge in the "Moon Lander" game in Chapter 16, "Arcade Games," was created. Because the center of the movie clip is at the left side of the rectangle, you can set _xscale to any number from 0 to 100 and the width of the movie clip will change to fill an area to the right of its center.

You attach a short scrip to this movie clip instance that will read the *getBytesLoaded()* of the main timeline and set the rectangle accordingly. In addition, it passes on some text to the "loadingMessage" text area in the main timeline. When the entire movie has been loaded, it forces the main timeline to move to the "complete" frame. You can see this frame in Figure 17.4. It announces that the loading is complete, and then waits for the player to press a button to continue. This is a good practice because the user might have taken her eyes off the screen during a long download, and you wouldn't want her to miss the beginning of any animation you might have.

Figure 17.4
The "complete" frame waits for the player before continuing to the content in the movie.

```
LOADING COMPLETE.


PLAY
```

```
onClipEvent(load) {
    // get complete file size
    totalFileSize = _root.getBytesTotal();

    // hide progress bar
    this._xscale = 0;
}

onClipEvent(enterFrame) {
```

```
// see how much has been loaded so far
bytesLoaded = _root.getBytesLoaded();

// convert to a value from 0 to 1
amountLoaded = bytesLoaded/totalFileSize;

// convert to a value from 0 to 100
percentLoaded = int(100*amountLoaded);

// set the scale of the progress bar
this._xscale = percentLoaded;

// set the text area in the main timeline
_root.loadingMessage = percentLoaded + "%";

// see if that is everything
if (amountLoaded >= 1.0) {
    _root.gotoAndStop("complete");
}
}
```

Check out Loader1.fla on the Web site to see how it all fits together. The loader is actually scene 1, whereas the rest of the content is in scene 2. A *play()* command is used to continue the movie from the "complete" frame when the user hits the "Play" button.

Example file: Loader1.fla

Note that you won't see much if you try to run the ".swf" file from the Web site or if you try to preview it in Flash. This is because the movie loads quickly from your local hard drive, too fast to see any loading. You'll have to upload the file to your Web site and then try it out in your browser to see the movie in action.

A More Advanced Loader
Example file: Loader2.fla

In the earlier Figure 17.3, you can see that the text area reads "63%". Instead of this type of measurement, you can also provide the user with the amount of bytes loaded and the total amount of bytes. You can do this by changing the "loadingmessage" assignment line in the code to this:

```
_root.loadingMessage = int(bytesLoaded/1000) + "kb/" + int(totalFileSize/1000) + "kb";
```

Then, instead of "63%", you would see "90kb/143kb", which I like much better.

You can also tell the user how fast the download is proceeding by doing a little math. You can set variables to remember the time when the code starts tracking the load, and the amount loaded at that first measurement. Then, you can determine how fast the load is occurring by taking how many bytes have been loaded so far divided by how much time it took. Using this number, you can predict how long it will take for the load to complete as well.

The following code can be found in the Loader2.fla movie on the Web site. This is similar to the previous loader code, but includes all the extra text readouts, such as speed and time left.

```
onClipEvent(load) {
    // get starting information
    totalFileSize = _root.getBytesTotal();
    startTime = getTimer();
    startBytes = _root.getBytesLoaded();

    // hide progress bar
    this._xscale = 0;
}

onClipEvent(enterFrame) {

    // see how much has been loaded so far
    bytesLoaded = _root.getBytesLoaded();

    // convert to a value from 0 to 1
    amountLoaded = bytesLoaded/totalFileSize;

    // convert to a value from 0 to 100
    percentLoaded = int(100*amountLoaded);

    // set the scale of the progress bar
    this._xscale = percentLoaded;

    // get the speed
    timeSoFar = getTimer() - startTime;
    speed = bytesLoaded/timeSoFar;

    // get the time left
    bytesLeft = totalFileSize - bytesLoaded;
    timeLeft = (bytesLeft/1000)*(speed/1000);

    // convert to a number with one decimal place
    speed = int(10*speed)/10;

    // set the text areas
    _root.bytesMessage = int(bytesLoaded/1000) + "kb/" + int(totalFileSize/1000) +
    ➥"kb";
    _root.speedMessage = speed + "k/sec";
    _root.timeMessage = int(timeLeft) + " seconds remaining";
```

```
    // see if that is everything
    if (amountLoaded >= 1.0) {
        _root.gotoAndStop("complete");
    }
 }
```

Other Types of Loaders

Although the previous two loaders are standard, there are many other possibilities. On the simpler side, you could just have a static frame that reads "Loading, Please Wait…" and goes to the next frame when loading is done.

You can make that a bit more complex by placing a movie clip or graphic with a looping animation on that frame.

Still more complex would be a whole scene where each frame represented a different stage of the loading procedure. For instance, each frame could show a character building something. The structure becomes more and more complete as the rest of the movie loads.

To do these types of loaders, it might not be necessary to use *getBytesTotal()* and *getBytesLoaded()* at all. You could instead use *ifFrameLoaded()* to determine whether all the graphics for a specific frame in the movie have been loaded. This could be useful if you want the player to start playing some aspect of your game, but don't want them to continue beyond a certain point until the proper frames are ready.

My favorite suggestion for a loader, however, is to make the time spent for the player more useful. Place the instructions for the game on the loading frame. That gives them something to do rather than just sit and watch the progress bar grow.

Copy Protection

So you've read this book and you decide to make your own game. You spend months on it. When you're done, you have the ultimate Flash game. It's great and you're convinced that it will become super-popular and make you famous.

You post the game on the Web and sit and wait. After a few weeks, you find that hundreds of people have played the game. You also find that another Web site, the home page of some kid from Nebraska, has a similar game on it.

Wait a minute! That's your game! It's on this kid's home page and he claims that he made it! What's worse is that he is getting millions of hits on his homepage. He's taking credit for the game you made.

There are several ways to prevent this. First, let's look at how this happens.

How and Why Games Are Stolen

I've been making Web-based games in Shockwave and Flash for more than five years now. I've found my creations used without permission on various Web sites, from personal home pages to legitimate business pages.

The first thing to realize is that in 90% of these cases, the thief meant no harm. To many people, the Internet has become a huge, free playground. They get tons of content free and never have to think about who owns that content, the cost to create it, copyright issues, or intellectual property issues. It doesn't matter because most of the content is free.

Then, when someone starts to create his own Web site, whether it's just a home page or the start of an online business, he doesn't think about these issues. Instead, he figures that if he can view something free, he can use it on his Web site free. If he sees a cool layout on a Web page, he views the source and copies the HTML. If he sees a neat animated GIF on another site, he right-clicks and saves it to his computer to use on his site. Then, when he sees your game, he takes that too, and places it on his site.

Then there are the people who know it's wrong, but don't understand the harm it does. They feel it is no worse than driving 56 mph in a 55 mph zone. To them, the Internet is one large multi-billion dollar corporation, and they couldn't possibly be doing any harm by putting one little game up on their sites.

I've heard it all, over the years: people who claim I gave them permission to place the games on their sites even though I never spoke to them before; people who claim that because they bought one of my books, anything on my Web site could be placed on theirs; people who claim that "content must be free" and that they are allowed to steal the games.

The methods that people use to get to your Flash content are surprisingly simple. One way is for the thief to view the HTML source of the page where your movie resides, get the name and path of the movie from the "src" parameter in the OBJECT or EMBED tag, and then point her browser directly at the .swf file. After the .swf is the top-level content in the browser, she can choose File, Save As, to save the .swf to her local hard drive.

Even if you come up with some clever way to hide the HTML source for the user, he can always look into his browser's cache files and pick out the .swf of the appropriate time stamp and size.

Preventing Your Game from Running Elsewhere

Example file: Copyprotection1.fla

So how do you prevent someone from stealing your game? You can't. But you can prevent them from running your game on another Web site, thus making the stolen game useless.

The key is the _url property. This property returns a string with the full path of your .swf file. For instance, if the movie is at "http://www.garyrosenzweig.com/flash5book/copyprotection1.swf", that string is what _url will return.

After you have this string, you can break it down to discover the root domain name at its heart. For instance, the above address has the root domain "garyrosenzweig.com". Here is some code from the example movie Copyprotection1.fla on the Web site:

```
// show the full path
urlText = "This game is being loaded from: " + _url;

// get everything between the "://" and the next "/"
c1 = _url.indexOf("://")+3;
c2 = _url.indexOf("/", c1);
domain = _url.substring(c1,c2);

// throw away any prefixes before the second to last "."
c3 = domain.lastIndexOf(".")-1;
c4 = domain.lastIndexOf(".",c3)+1;
domain = domain.substring(c4,domain.length);

// show the root domain
domainText = "The root domain is: " + domain;
```

The usefulness of having the root domain is that you can check it against what the domain of your site should return. The root domain is used because the path to your game might look different to different people. For instance, "http://garyrosenzweig.com" and "http://www.garyrosenzweig.com" take you to the same place, but return different _url results. Also, some sites have more than just a "www." before their domains, such as "www.games.garyrosenzweig.com".

If the root domain is not what the program expects, then the game has been stolen. Instead of the movie then continuing on to play the game, it can go to another frame entirely, preferably with a nasty message.

TIP

You might not want to make the message too nasty. There have been plenty of times where I have given a client a licensed copy of one of my games to be placed on her site and forgotten to adjust the code to allow the game to run on her site. In that case, she'll see your "nasty" message and might have a different opinion of you if it is over the top.

Example file: Copyprotection2.fla

Here is some code that will check the _url against the domain the game is supposed to be at. You can find this code in Copyprotection2.fla.

```
// get everything between the "://" and the next "/"
c1 = _url.indexOf("://")+3;
c2 = _url.indexOf("/", c1);
domain = _url.substring(c1,c2);

// throw away any prefixes before the second to last "."
c3 = domain.lastIndexOf(".")-1;
c4 = domain.lastIndexOf(".",c3)+1;
domain = domain.substring(c4,domain.length);

// go to the proper page
if (domain != "garyrosenzweig.com") {
    gotoAndPlay("stolen");
} else {
    gotoAndPlay("start");
}
```

Instead of having the movie go to a different frame, you could have it call *getURL()* with the address of an HTML page that will have a message on it. This way, you don't have to place that message frame into each movie you make.

How to Get Around Copy Protection

This plan for copy protection is not flawless. There is one simple way for a thief to get around it. He could leave the game on your server, and create his own HTML page where the "src" parameter of the OBJECT and EMBED tags point to the .swf file on your site. He serves the HTML, and you serve the .swf. The _url property correctly reports that the game is on your site, so the copy protection never kicks in.

This is a far better way to have your game stolen, however. For one thing, the .swf is still completely in your control. You could always change its name or move it to another location. If you find that someone has stolen your game this way, you could really play with him by changing the location of the game on your site, updating your own HTML to point to the proper place, and then replacing the old .swf with one that contains a nasty message to the visitors of the thief's site.

More Methods of Protecting Yourself

If you find that someone has stolen your game, either because you left it unprotected, or because the thief found a way around the protection, there are still steps you can take.

The first thing you should do is email the person. After all, most people don't mean any harm and will apologize immediately and take the game down, lesson learned.

If the person doesn't respond, or can't be reached, try emailing his Internet service provider. If his site is something like http://www.biginternethomepagecompany.com /~ joethief/ then you can pretty easily find the http://www.biginternethomepagecompany. com and find an address there. If he has his own domain, go to Network Solutions page (http://www.networksolutions.com), and use its "Who Is" service to find out more about the owner. Network Solutions usually also lists the network service provider for the site, whom you can email after you find his main page.

Although Joe Thief might not email you back or might refuse to take down the game, his ISP is sure to want to take action to avoid a potential lawsuit.

High Score Boards

Most Flash games are played on the Internet. Although this offers great access to the games, it can also offer a level of connectivity and community. A simple way to take advantage of the connectivity is to include a high score board. People can post scores to the server, and then view the best scores of all the people playing the game.

Adding a high score board to your game is no trivial task, however. It requires more than just Flash skills, because a program must be written for the Internet server to receive, record, and organize the scores.

How High Score Boards Work

High score boards can actually be built many ways. One way is to write a Java-based XML Socket program that your Flash game can communicate with via the XML object. Another way is to have your Flash game send and receive scores through JavaScript on the Web page, which then communicates with the server.

The most straightforward approach is to use a server-side Perl script to handle the scores, which is what you'll do here. Unfortunately, this means you'll have to learn about Perl and CGI scripts.

CGI (Common Gateway Interface) scripts are programs that run on Web servers. Perl is a programming language like ActionScript, but it is made to run on Web servers. A Perl program usually ends with a ".pl" or a ".cgi" extension rather than an ".html" extension used for a standard Web page. When the user browses to a Perl program, rather than the text of the program being served like an ".html" page would, the commands of the program are interpreted by the server as Perl commands. If the Perl program contains any output, that output is returned to the Web browser, or, in this case, to the Flash movie.

TIP

Perl is a subject big enough to deserve its own book. In fact, many books have been published on Perl, far more than have been published on Flash. If you want more information about Perl, go to your local bookstore and pick one out.

This example uses two Perl programs to maintain the high scores. The first is "submitscore.pl" and it takes care of receiving a new score from the Flash movie. The second is Getscores.pl and it returns a list of the top 10 scores to the Flash movie.

Both of these programs need to access a small database of scores. CGI programs usually use a server database, such as SQL, to store data. However, this example uses something a little simpler: a plain text file.

Each line of this text file contains a different submitted score. The three parts to this score are the name of the player, the score, and the time it was submitted. The Flash movie submits the name and score to the Submitscore.pl program, which adds the time stamp to it.

The Getscores.pl program looks at the text file with all the scores and performs two functions. First, it examines each score and rewrites the text file from scratch, excluding any old scores. This keeps the high score list fresh with only recent scores. The other function that Getscores.pl performs is to return the 10 highest scores in order to the Flash movie. This list is displayed for the players to see.

TIP

I like the idea of throwing away scores from the database when they get too old. This prevents one or more extreme scores from dominating the database over the period of years. It also encourages good players to return to the game often to reclaim their bragging rights.

The Perl Programs

The two Perl programs are on the Web site as Submitscore.pl and Getscores.pl. To get these programs working on your server, you'll need to upload the files and set their permissions. If you have never done this before, ask your network administrator or Internet service provider about how to do this. Not all servers are configured to run CGI programs. If you are on a low-end or free Internet service that provides Web space to its users, you can probably assume that it doesn't allow CGI programs.

Although this section isn't a "Beginners Guide to Perl," the complete Perl programs with brief explanations of what each section does are shown here. If you aren't familiar with CGI programs, team up with someone who is.

Comments in Perl start with a # character. The Submitscore.pl program starts with a comment, but one that is actually used by the Web server to determine the path of the program that interprets Perl scripts. The path given here is a common path and might work on your server. If not, contact your Internet service provider.

```
#!/usr/bin/perl
```

The first real line of code starts by sending some output back to the Flash movie. This particular piece of output is the text "Content-type: text/html" followed by two line breaks. The first line of any file sent from a Web server tells the browser, or Flash movie in this case, what type of data is coming. In this case, the answer is plain text data.

```
# create header for text document to return
print "Content-type: text/html\n\n";
```

Next, the data is passed to the script from the Flash movie and temporarily stored in the variable "$get_data":

```
# get data passed in
$get_data = $ENV{'QUERY_STRING'};
```

When data arrives over a Web connection, it's usually encoded so that special characters arrive safely. Letters such as A, B, and C are not encoded, but spaces are encoded as "+", and nonalphanumeric characters are encoded as strings, such as "%0A". To reverse this encoding, you use the next two odd-looking lines of code:

```
# convert escape characters
$get_data =~ s/%([\dA-Fa-f][\dA-Fa-f])/pack ("C",hex($1))/eg;
$get_data =~ tr/\+/ /;
```

Next, you get the current time, in Unix server seconds. You'll use this as the time the score was posted. This is better than using the Flash movie time, because people are in different time zones, and some people don't even have their clocks set right on their computers.

```
# get the server time in seconds
$server_time = time();
```

Next is a loop that takes the "$get_data" string and breaks it into parts. It starts out as something like "name=Gary&score=967". This is broken into two items by dividing it at the "&", and then each item is broken into a key and a value by dividing it at the "=".

```
# take post data and create an array of data
@split_data = split("&",$get_data);
foreach $data_item (@split_data)
  {
  ($key, $value) = split("=",$data_item);
  $info{$key} = $value;
  }
```

The text database for your high scores is Highscore.txt. To start this file, upload a blank text file of that name and set its permissions so it can be written to by the Perl programs. The next lines of code open this file so that text can be appended to it:

```
# set filename for highscore database
$filename = "highscore.txt";

# open the database
open(OUTFILE,">>$filename") || exit;
```

After the file has been opened, the program writes a single line of text to it that contains the score, name, and time, and looks something like "967&Gary&978887513".

```
# append the data to the database
print OUTFILE "$info{'score'}&$info{'name'}&$server_time\n";
```

Finally, the Submitscore.pl program ends by closing the text file and returning some information to Flash. In this case, the "resultText" variable is set to the string "OK".

```
# close the database
close(OUTFILE);

# signify data written ok
print "resultText=OK\n";

# end this script
exit;
```

The Getscores.pl program is slightly more complex than Submitscore.pl. It has the task of reading the database, removing any old scores, and then returning a list of the top 10 scores.

It starts the same way as Submitscore.pl. Then, the file opens the database and reads all the contents in an array variable called "@score_text".

```
#!/usr/bin/perl

# create header for text document to return
print "Content-type: text/html\n\n";

# set filename for highscore database
$filename = "highscore.txt";

# read high score data
open(DATABASE,$filename) || exit;
@score_text = <DATABASE>;
close(DATABASE);
```

Next, the program calculates what time it was, in Unix server seconds, exactly seven days ago.

```
# get the server time
$server_time = time();

# how long to keep the scores
# (7 days * 24 hours * 60 minutes * 60 seconds)
$keep_time = 7*(24*60*60);
```

The database is now opened again, but for writing. This new data overwrites the old file.

```
# open database file for writing
open(DATABASE,">" . $filename) || exit;
```

The following loop examines each score and determines whether it is too old. If it is, then it isn't rewritten to the new file.

```
# loop through each score
foreach $score_line (@score_text) {
  # get score data
  @score_item = split(/&/,$score_line);
  # get score time
  $score_time = $score_item[2];
  # if the score is not old, write it back out again
  if ($score_time > ($server_time-$keep_time)) {
    print DATABASE "$score_line";
  }
}


#close database
close(DATABASE);
```

Next, the Perl program sorts the scores. Because the score is the first thing in each item of the score database, the items are sorted by score, in this case from highest to lowest.

```
# sort scores
@score_text = sort { $b <=> $a } @score_text;
```

The next loop takes the first 10 scores and returns them as output. Each item of each line is specially formatted. A line looks something like " 1. Gary 967". The number of the line is followed by a period. Then, the name is included, padded out to 18 spaces if it is shorter. Then the score is included, padded to the left to 9 spaces in case it is shorter.

```
# determine number of scores to send
$num_scores = 10;
$score_count = 1;


# loop through first scores and send the data
print "highScoresText=";
foreach $score_line (@score_text) {

    # take post data and create an array of data
    @split_data = split("&",$score_line);
    # output the line number plus a period
    printf("%2i. ", $score_count);
    #output the player's name, left justified, padded to 18 spaces
    printf("%-18s ",$split_data[1]);
```

```
   #output the score, right justified, padded to 9 spaces
   printf("%9i\n",$split_data[0]);
   $score_count++;
   if ($score_count > $num_scores) { last; }
}


#exit script
exit;
```

All this Perl programming can be confusing if you have never seen Perl before or if you have only ever programmed in Flash. Take comfort in the fact that this sort of project is usually a team effort between a Flash programmer and a Perl programmer. Seek one out if you can.

Demonstration High Score Movie

Example file: Highscores.fla

There are two programs on the Web site that use the high score scripts. The first is a demonstration movie that shows how a score is written to the database, and how scores are then retrieved from the database.

This movie, Highscores.fla looks like Figure 17.5. The area to the bottom left allows you to submit a new score, and the area to the right allows you to view all high scores.

Figure 17.5

The high score demonstration movie allows you to test your Perl scripts.

All the code in the Highscores.fla movie is located in the two buttons you can see in Figure 17.5. Each of these two boxed sections is its own movie clip.

The "Submit Score" section shows the player's name and score in editable text areas. When you run this program, you can type in a name and a score, and then click the Submit Score button. This is the code attached to that button. There are only three lines of actual code.

```
on (press) {

    // location of the "submitscore.pl" program
    url = "submitscore.pl";

    // send variables
    // "score" = game score
    // "name" = player's name
    loadVariables(url,this,"GET");

    // feedback to know that the button was pressed
    resultText = "Sending...";
}
```

You used the *loadVariables* command in Chapter 12, "Quizzes and Word Puzzles," for the quiz and trivia games. In those cases, you didn't send any variables to the server, you just requested a text file. In this case, you are calling a Perl program, both sending it variables and expecting something back. All you should get back is a "resultsText=OK".

The "GET" at the end of the *loadVariables* command tells Flash that the variables will be sent using the GET protocol. This is one of two choices. The other is the POST protocol. Both of these correspond to the two ways that HTML pages can send data to the server with forms.

Unfortunately, you don't have any control over which variables are sent. They all are sent. At least, all the variables that are inside the current movie clip. This is why you should place the submit button in a movie clip rather than in the main timeline. Some games, such as a trivia game for example, might have some very large variables that don't need to get sent back to the server.

In this case, the "score" and "name" variables are sent. These are defined by the text areas inside the movie clip. If you look at the "Text Options" panel for these two areas, you can see that they are mapped to "score" and "name".

The "Get Scores" button has a similar piece of code attached to it, but it doesn't need to send any variables:

```
on (press) {

    // location of the "getscores.pl" program
    url = "getscores.pl";

    // request data
    loadVariables (url,this);

    // feedback to know that the button was pressed
     highScoresText = "Getting High Scores...";
}
```

The text returned by the Getscores.pl program starts with a "highScoresText=". This places the remaining text into the variable of that name, which is also mapped to the text area under the "Get Scores" button. As soon as the text arrives, it is shown there.

Implementing High Scores in a Game

Example file: Whackafoxwithscores.fla

A second high scores example file on the Web site is called Whackafoxwithscores.fla. This is the same "Whack-A-Fox" game from Chapter 8, "Hunt and Click Games," but with a high score board added.

This is an easy movie to add high scores to because it was broken into three scenes. The "Start" scene has been changed to show the high score board when the game loads. In addition to the plain *stop()* command at the start of the first frame in this scene, you'll add the code needed to get the high scores:

```
// location of the "getscores.pl" program
url = "getscores.pl";

// request data
loadVariables (url,this);

// feedback to know that the button was pressed
highScoresText = "Getting High Scores...";

stop();
```

A text area named "highScoresText" has also been added to the middle of the screen. It looks like Figure 17.6.

Figure 17.6

The Whack-A-Fox game now displays high scores when it starts.

```
WHACK-A-FOX
Hit as many foxes as you can

 1. Gary          84
 2. Gary          81
 3. Gary          73
 4. Debby         71
 5. Gary          67
 6. Gary          66
 7. Gary          63
 8. Gary          52
 9. Gary          46
10. Gary          45




        PLAY
```

At the end of the game, in the "End" scene, there is a movie clip with some text areas and a "Submit Score" button. The score of the game must be set inside this movie clip.

The game itself is run by an "actions" movie clip in the "Play" scene. Therefore, the "score" variable is a property of that movie clip, not the main timeline. By adding the line "_root.score = score;" to the script, the main timeline now also have a variable called "score" with the score in it.

When the "End" scene starts, the first frame places this score into the "sendscores" movie clip. It also resets the "name" variable in that movie clip to a blank string.

```
sendscores.name = "";
sendscores.score = score;
stop();
```

Figure 17.7 shows this "End" frame. You can see that the "sendscores" movie clip contains the player's score, a text input area for the player to enter his name, and the "Submit Score" button.

Figure 17.7

The last frame of the new Whack-A-Fox game allows the player to submit his score.

The player types his name into the first text area, but the text area containing the score is not available to him. After the player is satisfied with his name, he can press "Submit Score", which runs this script:

```
on (press) {

    // location of the "submitscore.pl" program
    url = "submitscore.pl";

    // send variables
    // "score" = game score
    // "name" = player's name
    loadVariables(url,this,"GET");

    // go to another frame so that submit cannot be pressed twice
    play();
}
```

The score is sent to the server in the same way that it is done in the Highscores.fla demonstration movie. However, the *play()* command at the end sends the "sendscores" movie clip to its second frame. This second frame is the same as the first, except that it doesn't contain the Submit Score button. This prevents the player from pressing the button more than once and entering several scores.

High Score Board Issues

High score boards seem an obvious improvement to any game. But they bring about some more complex issues that you might not have considered.

By letting players type in anything they want as their names, you are essentially letting them publish something on your Web site. Sure, most players will just type a name or alias, but some will decide that profanity is what goes in the "name" box.

So why not check for curse words in the Flash game or the Perl script? You can do that, but there are many ways to get around it. People will use alternative spellings of words, or put spaces or dashes in between them. Others will use perfectly normal words to say something inappropriate. There's no way to prevent it completely.

Large professional sites usually require that players register before posting scores. But a registration scoring system is far more complex than what is in this chapter. To do this requires a complete database system with security measures to boot.

Another issue is cheating. After a high score board is in place, players will find ways to cheat. It is actually quite easy to do. Methods range from finding ways to pause the Flash game at critical points so the player can catch her breath, to using cheater programs that peek and poke at the memory in the player's computer. This can easily turn 42 points into 42 million points.

You can also use other programming languages to create high score boards. PHP is a Perl-like language that is very popular. Older languages such as C and C++ can be used to make CGI programs as well.

Internet Resources for the Flash Developer

- Flash Resource Sites
- Flash Development Tools
- Flash Screensavers

So you've read this whole book, taken every game and built your own from it, and you're still hungry for more information about Flash? Well, there's plenty to be had. The Web is full of sites for Flash developers, by Flash developers.

Flash Resource Sites

All these sites are independent of Macromedia and contain a wealth of information. You'll find that most have similar content: articles, tutorials, open-source files, and message boards. The quality of the site largely depends on its contributors, especially when it comes to message boards. Every serious Flash developer should find a site or three from the following list that fits his or her style and become a part of that community.

Action-Script.com—http://www.action-script.com/ (German)

Actionscripts.org—http://www.actionscripts.org/

All Flash Tutorials—http://www.tutorialindex.com/Flash/

Art's Flash Class—http://www.artswebsite.com/coolstuff/flash.htm

Asmussen Interactive—http://www.turtleshell.com/guide/

Batch Labs—http://www.batchlabs.com/flash.asp

Canfield Studios—http://www.canfieldstudios.com/flash4/

Chan Design—http://www.chandesign.net/

Cool Resources—http://www.coolresources.com/tutorials/flash.htm

Diamon's Pit—http://www.diamante.cjb.net/

Do Re Media—http://www.doremedia.com/resources.html

Extreme Flash—http://www.extremeflash.com

The Fast Files—http://www.geocities.com/thefastfiles/

Fay Studios—http://www.webpagetogo.com/FS/WD/flashtutorials.html

Find Tutorials—http://www.findtutorials.com/list.asp?category=143

Flahoo—http://www.flahoo.com/

Flash 4 All—http://www.flash4all.de/ (German and English)

The Flash Academy—http://www.enetserve.com/tutorials/

Flashcom Community—http://www.ryanosure.com/flashcom/

Flash Filez—http://www.w3source.net/contentsheets/flash.html

Flash Geek—http://www.flashgeek.com/

Flash Heaven—http://www.flashheaven.de/ (German and English)

Flash Kit—http://www.flashkit.com/ (Recommended)

Flashlite—http://www.flashlite.net/

FlashMaestro—http://www.flashmaestro.fm/ (Spanish)

Flash Magazine—http://www.flashmagazine.com/

Flash Master—http://www.flashmaster.nu/

Flash Move—http://www.flashmove.com/ (Recommended)

Flash Planet—http://www.flashplanet.com/ (Recommended)

Flashplein—http://www.flashplein.nl/ (Dutch)

Flash Portal Europe—http://flash.pagetostart.be/

Flash Pro—http://www.flashpro.nl/

Flash Resource—http://www.flashresource.com/

Flash Skills—http://www.flashskills.com/

Flashwave—http://www.flashwave.co.uk/

Flash Zone—http://www.flashzone.com/ (Recommended)

Flazoom—http://www.flazoom.com/

Gizmos Page—http://www.gizmospage.com/

Kirupa—http://www.kirupa.com/developer/

The Linkz—http://thelinkz.com/

Millenium Flashboard—http://www.x-pressive.com/forum/ (German and English)

Mimics Open Source Download Page—http://www.fortunecity.com/rivendell/krondor/531/opensource.html

Colin Moock—http://www.moock.org/webdesign/flash/

Party Logger—http://www.partylogger.de/ (German and English)

Pro Flasher—http://www.proflasher.com/

Serving Up Web-Friendly Animations: In a Flash—http://www.webreference.com/dev/flash/

ShockFusion—http://www.shockfusion.com

Stickman's Tutorials—http://www.the-stickman.com/

Talk Graphics—http://talkgraphics.com

Training Tools—http://www.trainingtools.com/online/flash5/

Tutorials.it—http://www.tutorials.it (Italian)

UBB Developers Network—http://www.ubbdev.com/

Virtual F/X—http://www.virtual-fx.net/

Warp 9—http://www.warp9.it/ (Italian)

We're Here Forums—http://www.were-here.com/ (Recommended)

XrV Power—http://www.xrvpower.net/

Zero Gravity—http://www.zgravity.co.uk

Flash Development Tools

This group of sites contains tools that help you be more productive when working in Flash. Many of them allow you to extend Flash's capability to do things such as making unusually shaped projectors or screensavers. Others allow you to create graphics that can then be used in Flash.

EXE Caliber http://www.e-nvp.com/devzone/execaliber/—A program that makes Windows Flash projectors open to a specific size and position on the screen.

Flash Exchange http://www.macromedia.com/exchange/flash/—This is an official Macromedia subsite that contains the Flash Extensions Manager add-on to Flash 5. When you add this to your copy of Flash 5, you can take advantage of many free Flash extensions that help you author Flash movies.

Flash Jester http://www.flashjester.com/—A variety of tools including a screensaver maker and a program that lets you customize projectors with special features.

FlaxFX http://www.flaxfx.com/—This program allows you to create text animations that can then be opened and used in Flash.

Illustrate http://www.davidgould.com/—This tool allows you to export Flash vector graphics from 3ds max.

Insane Tools http://www.insanetools.com/—This program lets you create Flash animations—without Flash.

KoolMoves http://www.koolmoves.com/—This tool allows you to create Flash animations and animated GIF files.

Swiff Tools http://swifftools.com/stools/—Several tools, including a screensaver maker, an MP3-to-Flash converter, and a tool that lets you make changes to how projectors are shown on the screen.

Swift 3D http://www.swift3d.com/—This program converts 3D files to Flash graphics.

Swish http://swishzone.com/—This is a tool that allows you to build text animations that can then be imported into Flash.

Flash Screensavers

The following companies' Web sites feature programs that will turn your Flash movies into screensavers:

Bitbull—http://www.wanpatan.com/bitbull/

Flash Forge—http://www.goldshell.com/flashforge/

Flash Jester—http://www.flashjester.com/

Flash Master—http://www.shop4softwareonline.com/corporate/software/fmc.html

Flash Wiz—http://www.flashwiz.co.uk/

Flash Savers—http://www.flashsavers.com/

JSK Digital Media—http://www.jskdm.net/screensaver.htm

Living Screen—http://www.livingscreen.com/

Screen Weaver—http://www.screenweaver.com/

The History of Games

Imagine a world without computer games. It's not that hard considering the first computer game, *Space War*, was created in 1962. Then, it wasn't until the 1970s that the general public could play the first video games.

Imagine being the person to create the first computer game. There was little inspiration to draw on. Today, we can look back on countless video games and home computer games. Almost everything we create is a derivative of something out of the past.

That first computer game was totally original. Since then, computers have revolutionized the world of games. Plus, we have a lot of inspiration.

From *Senet* to *Space War*

Games predate written history. It seems that we have always been interested in building little virtual realities where we can compete.

The Evolution of Board Games

The first board games were racing games, much like today's backgammon. One of the oldest game boards in existence is for a game called *Senet*, which was popular in Egypt more than 2,000 years ago.

Figure B.1
Senet was played by the ancient Egyptians.

The game involved two players, each of whom had several pieces. The players threw sticks, because dice had not yet been invented, and moved their pieces along the board. The goal was to get your pieces to the end, which represented heaven.

This same game was adopted by other cultures for more than a thousand years. Each culture changed the playing pieces and what the game's goal represented, but for the most part the game was the same.

NOTE
Senet's goal was actually to get your pieces to the last few spaces, which represented heaven. Many games used this as their goal. Today's game of hopscotch actually has the same goal, even though most people who play it don't know that the last space represents heaven.

In addition to racing games, another early type of game was a variety of *Nine Men's Morris*. This game involved a board with connected points. Each player had nine pieces and could move one piece per move along one connection to another point. If a player got three pieces in a row, they were allowed to remove one of their opponent's pieces.

This type of game evolved into games such as checkers and chess. The goal was to remove your opponent's pieces, while at the same time protecting yours.

Games like this simulated an all too common theme in human history: war. Other cultures developed games like it, such as *Go* in Japan.

The ultimate war game, chess, evolved out of these early simple games. It started in 6th century India, but did not adapt modern features, such as the powerful queen, until the 15th century.

Chess spread throughout the world quickly, and is seen today by many as the ultimate game: easy to learn, but hard to master. In the 20th century, the best chess players in the world are seen as celebrities, and chess tournaments make headlines.

The world of board games changed to what it is today in the late 19th century and early 20th. Companies such as Milton Bradley and Parker Brothers started inventing, mass-producing, and marketing games. New standards such as *Scrabble* and *Monopoly* were born out of old ideas. In addition, older games were codified by people such as Sir Edmund Hoyle, setting their rules in stone.

In America during the 20th century, a closet shelf full of board games became a standard. Games rose and fell in popularity as efforts by game companies to market them succeeded and failed.

War and Role-Playing Games

Board games are a casual experience for the most part. A typical game is easy to learn and can be played in an hour or two. However, some gamers desired a more engaging experience.

War games have existed in some form or another throughout history. However, the first modern war games were played in the 19th century. Military experts used large tables covered with sand and elaborate figures to plan out and test strategies.

The main purpose of the first war games was to plan out real battles. However, they soon came to be used as training tools as well. Military students would reenact battles and make up scenarios. It was, and still is, a valuable tool.

Simplified versions of war games began to be used for recreation. The author H.G. Wells is often cited as the inventor of the first recreational war game. Boards with grids replaced the large tables. Instead of doing complex calculations, simple dice rolls and rules were used to decide the outcome of moves.

In the 1960s and '70s, war games were mass-produced in boxes with booklets that described the rules and large paper grids to play on. Several new games were produced annually, and magazines were even published on the subject.

From the world of war games came the world of role-playing games. The inventors of *Dungeons & Dragons* were out to make an interesting war game scenario that involved soldiers from the middle ages going into an old castle and dungeon. Before they completed the scenario, they ended up with a whole new game complete with a telephone-book–sized set of rules. When they published a simplified version of these rules, they created a gaming phenomenon.

Dungeons & Dragons spawned many competitors and also many other types of role-playing games. Just about every type of adventure could be found in a box at your local hobby store: science fiction, espionage, old west, and even game systems to handle any type of world.

The role-playing games broke down the idea of what a game was and how long of an experience it was. It created a cottage industry of game companies and players that were willing to try new things. This set the stage for the computer age of games.

From *Space War* to *Pong*

The first computer game was created by Steve Russell and other graduate students in 1962 on a PDP-1 mainframe computer at the Massachusetts Institute of Technology. It involved two space ships that floated around in the gravity-free environment of space and shot pixels at each other. The graphics were actually much better than what was to follow. The game even included a mathematically generated star field behind the ships.

This first game was addicting and fun. It was made freely available by the creators, so it soon found itself on just about every PDP-1 computer at every college that had one. However, commercial success was out of the question, as PDP-1 computers were too expensive to make into arcade machines, and no one owned a personal computer yet.

Meanwhile, the computer game evolved. A game called *Lunar Lander* consisted of absolutely no graphics, but could be played on computers that had no screen, only a spool of paper as an output device. A line of text would appear to tell you your position, velocity, and fuel remaining. You made a move, and the new position, velocity, and fuel update were printed. The object was to land before running out of fuel.

Not far behind these games was the classic *Adventure*. This was a precursor to all computer adventure and role playing games. The game was purely text-based. It described your location, and you gave it commands like "go north" or "pick up sword."

The computer game first came into the public eye with early arcade games, such as *Pong*. These games were first placed in shopping malls, right next to pinball machines and other coin-operated devices. But they soon took over the arcades.

From *Pong* to *Pac-Man*

The first coin-operated video game was Nolan Bushnell's *Computer Space*. It was like *Space War*, with the user controlling a ship out to destroy an enemy flying saucer. The machine accepted quarters.

Computer Space was not very successful. It turned out that the concept and controls were too advanced for people who had never seen a computer before.

Bushnell took his modest profits, only $500, and created his own company: Atari.

NOTE
Atari is the warning call that players give each other in the Japanese game of *Go*.

Atari's first creation was *Pong*, a game much simpler than *Computer Space*. The game was a success. Atari distributed the game through the same channels as pinball machines.

The next step for Atari was to sell *Pong* into homes. Atari teamed up with Sears to sell a home version of the game in 1975. Then, in 1976, Atari introduced *Breakout*, the first of the more complex video game classics. Not only was *Breakout* notable because it brought video games to a new level, but also because it was designed by Steven Jobs, who later revolutionized the personal computer industry.

In 1979, a Japanese company, Taito, developed *Space Invaders*, the first genuine video game hit. It began to take over the arcades. Atari fought back with its own hit, *Asteroids*.

Figure B.2
The heyday of video arcade games was in the early 1980s, but the machines still remain popular today.

Also during 1979 and 1980, dozens of other games were invented in which players fought robots and aliens. However, the next big hit came from a simple maze game where the hero was a yellow dot.

Pac-Man was not expected to be a hit. It was seen as too "cute" to be taken seriously. But kids in the arcades loved it. It was also the first arcade game that appealed to girls as well as boys and the first video game to bring in money from merchandizing.

In 1982 there were 1.5 million arcade game machines in America in about 24,000 arcades and many miscellaneous locations. At the same time, 20 million home video games were sold, which cut heavily into the amount of television watched at home. In 1982, the video game industry was bringing in twice as much revenue as the American film industry.

The early 1980s saw a constant stream of new video games by competing companies. The video arcade industry peaked around that time, and then fell back to the more stable level that we have today. This decline was caused by several factors, including the modernization of the mall and the advent of home game systems.

The Video Game Comes Home

In the late 1960s, an electrical engineer named Ralph Baer began creating the first home video game system. His first models didn't even use microchips. However, they did connect directly to a standard television set. This eventually became the Odyssey game system.

The Odyssey included 12 different games printed on circuit cards. In addition, players had to place a transparent screen over their televisions to provide the background. Players also had to keep track of their own scoring by marking little sheets of paper.

The next advancement was provided by the General Instruments Corporation, which developed a microchip that manufacturers could buy for $5 or $6 that allowed more complex home video games to be developed. Coleco used it to develop the Telstar system.

Soon, companies such as Fairchild, RCA, Atari, and Mattel introduced new game systems that could be programmed. This allowed other companies to develop cartridges for them. The Atari Video Computer System eventually dominated the field. It sold more than 12 million units and more than 200 game cartridges were created for it.

Figure B.3

The home video game system became a household item in the 1980s.

The home video game system is still just as popular today, but the players are different. Sony's PlayStation and Nintendo's N64 system are the two most popular. The PlayStation II has recently replaced the original model. Soon, Microsoft will challenge these two companies with its X-Box console.

These modern home systems rival both the personal computer and the coin-operated arcade machine. The processors are fast, and the CD media or cartridges contain quite a bit of data.

Games Invade Computers

At the same time, the introduction of the personal computer meant that more complex games could be played as well. A huge library of games existed for computers such as the Apple II. It was easy for any programmer, with almost no money, to develop games for computers, as opposed to the expensive manufacturing process of the video game console.

In the 1980s, just about every successful video arcade game was translated to a game for the personal computer. Some of these games were legitimate versions made by their original creators, and others were imitations.

In addition, new games sprung up for the personal computer. Because no hardware had to be built to make the games available, it cost less to develop a game for a computer. The only things you needed to actually manufacture were the floppy disks and any printed materials.

This meant that games with a smaller potential audience could be produced. When modems and bulletin board systems became popular in the late 1980s, you could even make a game and distribute it free.

Eventually the CD-ROM drive gave game developers the chance to create games with a multimedia flare. *Myst* set the standard for CD-ROM adventure games that is still followed today. This game has hundreds of detailed still images.

Today's CD-ROM adventure games feature even more detailed images, along with soundtracks and complex interfaces. In the mid-1990s, *Phantasmagoria* used seven CD-ROMs to create an intense environment.

In addition to volume, computers also allowed developers to experiment with new techniques. Games such as *Doom* started the "first-person 3D shooter" genre. By the mid-1990s, just about every action game on the market fit into this category.

Web-Based Computer Games

Macromedia Flash and Shockwave are part of a new chapter in the history of games. The Web gives people easy access to all sorts of content, and at the same time makes it easy for developers to publish their content.

Although floppy disks and CD-ROMs built the computer game industry, they also made sure that games could only be published by those who had enough money to secure shelf space in software stores. With Web-based games, this is not an obstacle.

The result is that more developers can take their games directly to the people who play them. It also means that companies that would not normally be in the games business are making games. For instance, every major portal has a games section featuring its own games.

Web-Based games are made in either Flash, Shockwave, or Java. However, some games are made with single HTML and server-side scripting, and others are made with lesser-known browser plug-ins.

At the start of 2001, Flash 5 shows considerable promise at becoming the most used game development environment on the Web. Whether this trend continues depends on the developers and what Macromedia has in store for future versions of Flash.

Further Reading

If you are interested in the history of games and computer games, here are some books that you might want to check out:

Screen Play: The Story of Video Games
George Sullivan
Copyright 1983
Publisher: Frederick Warne & Co., Inc., New York, NY

Content: History of computer and video games.

Joystick Nation
by J.C. Herz
1997
Published by Little, Brown & Company Limited

Content: History of computer and video games.

The World of Games
Jack Botermans, Tony Burrett, Pieter van Delft, Carla van Splunteren
1987
Published by Facts on File, Inc., New York and Oxford

Content: History of games. A lot of illustrations.

The Greatest Games of All Time
Mathew J. Costello
1991
John Wiley & Sons, Inc.

Content: Interesting stories about old and new games, the game industry, and video games. Highly recommended.

Game Over: Press Start to Continue
David Sheff
1993
Random House

Content: The history of Nintendo. Highly recommended.

Hackers: Heroes of the Computer Revolution
Steven Levy
1984
Anchor Press

Content: A great account of many computer pioneers, including a lot of information about the gaming industry in the early 80s.

According to Hoyle
Richard L. Frey
1956, 1965, 1970
Fawcett Columbine

Content: Game rules.

The Oxford History of Board Games
David Parlett
1999
Oxford University Press

Content: The history of games.

Family Fun & Games
1992
Sterling Publishing Company

Content: Game rules.

A Brief History of Home Video Games
(An Online Book)
Sam Hart
1996–1999
`http://newton.physics.arizona.edu/~hart/vgh`

Content: Essays about different video game machines.

Index